The Adult Learner on Campus

A Guide for Instructors and Administrators

Jerold W. Apps

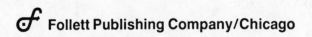 Follett Publishing Company/Chicago

Designed by Sue L. Doman.

Library of Congress Cataloging in Publication Data

Apps, Jerold W   1934–
    The adult learner on campus.

    Bibliography: p.
    Includes index.
    1. Continuing education—United States. 2. Adult education—
United States.   I. Title.
LC5251.A868   374′.973   80-28209
ISBN 0-695-81577-6   AACR1

First Printing

Contents

WITHDRAWN

3

Preface

Colleges and universities in this country are at a major turning point. Thousands of adult learners are returning to school working toward undergraduate and advanced degrees. And these older students are expecting instructors and administrators to make changes for them.

In this book we examine many of these suggested changes. Some of the changes examined and the questions considered are these:

Administrative Procedures and Rules. Is it necessary that many academic programs require full-time study? Is it essential that returning students successfully pass a battery of entrance examinations? Will returning students continue to accept often antiquated registration procedures?

Curriculum. How should the content of the curriculum be changed to embrace the interests and concerns of older students? Should returning students be awarded credit for life experiences? Can course requirements be made flexible enough to recognize the past experiences of students? How can students be involved in the curriculum decision-making process?

Time for Course Offerings. What are the problems in offering courses and other learning experiences at times and places differ-

7

ent from the traditional, such as in weekend formats, in storefront locations, via media, and once a week in the evening?

Instructors and Teaching. What teaching approaches do exemplary instructors of returning students use? How do returning students differ from the younger, more traditional students? Beyond the usual components of the learning environment—the student, the teacher, the content, and the setting—what else must be considered when teaching returning students? How much attention should be given to the learner's family situation, economic conditions, and the knowledge explosion? How do we change the superior-inferior relationship that exists between instructor and student to a sharing relationship?

Support Systems. What specific support systems are necessary for returning students? What are the counseling responsibilities of instructors?

Issues and Controversies. In what way does the large number of returning students challenge colleges and universities to rethink their purposes? How are quality and standards affected by the returning-student phenomenon?

This book is designed for instructors and administrators who work with increasingly larger numbers of returning, often part-time, students. These older students are returning to community college campuses, to vocational-technical school campuses, and to four-year college and university campuses.

Chapter 1 presents an overview of the situation—the numbers of older students on campuses and how the information for the book was gathered.

Chapters 2, 3, and 6 include information about the returning students, how they compare with younger students, some of the problems they face, and how age affects learning.

Chapters 4, 5, 8, and 9 examine the learning environment for returning students and how to improve it.

Chapters 7, 10, and 11 look at exemplary instructors of returning students and the teaching approaches they use, both in class and out of class.

Chapters 12 and 13 consider institutional change and the associated issues and controversies.

And chapter 14 is an annotated listing of resources for those interested in pursuing the various topics further.

Many people helped in the development of *The Adult Learner on Campus*. I particularly want to thank the assistant vice chancellor's office at the University of Wisconsin–Madison for providing travel money for the research.

The eighteen professors I interviewed for the book deserve special mention, for many of the ideas on the pages were their ideas. The professors were Susan Wheelan, Ruth Gillman, Luci Paul, and Robert Schoebel of Temple University; Gayl Ness, Ann Larimore, and Howard McClusky of the University of Michigan; Virginia Griffin of the Ontario Institute for Studies in Education, University of Toronto; David Mustian, Howard Miller, Selz Mayo, Robert Monroe, and William Block of North Carolina State University–Raleigh; Annis Pratt, Judith Hooper, and Burton Krietlow of the University of Wisconsin–Madison; Malcolm Knowles, Educational Consultant; and Ralph Tyler, Educational Consultant.

Returning students I interviewed for this project included Karen Brown, Marsha Baird, Russell Knudson, Val Freysinger, Marge Denis, Marilyn Taylor, Heather Bates, Lee Davies, Marilyn Cooper, Judy Ann Schwenker, Kirsten Alcser, and Suzanne Model. At the time of the interviews they attended the University of Wisconsin–Madison, the University of Toronto, or the University of Michigan.

For reviewing the entire manuscript and offering many suggestions for changes, I want to thank Dr. Donald Campbell, Director of Continuing Education for Health Professionals, University of Illinois, College of Medicine; and Steven Schmidt, a Ph.D. student at the University of Wisconsin–Madison who returned to school after several years away. Others who reviewed specific chapters and offered critical comments included Dr. Joseph Corry, Assistant Vice Chancellor for Academic Services and Continuing Education, and Margaret Geisler, Director of Continuing Education Programs, both of whom are with the University of Wisconsin–Madison; and Dr. Chere Coggins, Academic Planner, University of Wisconsin System.

For support, encouragement, and many useful suggestions I want to thank A. Jean Lesher, my editor.

And a special thank you to Karen Wideen, Carolyn Hackler, and Sally Gurske for the final typing and assuring a deadline was met.

Jerold W. Apps
Madison, Wisconsin

Chapter 1

A Quiet Revolution

A quiet revolution is taking place on college and university campuses across this country. It is a revolution that began several years ago, in the sixties and seventies, and has been building in intensity ever since. It is not a violent revolution. There is no stench of tear gas in the air, no trashed buildings, no jailed demonstrators, no television cameras recording each activity as it unfolds.

Yet this quiet revolution could have an even more profound impact on higher education and on society than did the violent demonstrations of the sixties. (There are many who would argue the student demonstrations of the sixties had little lasting effect on the structure and function of higher education, but that is a theme for another book.)

What I'm referring to is the return of thousands of adults to college campuses, adults who may have attended college for one or more years and then dropped out, adults who may have received a baccalaureate degree but find need for additional education, and adults who may never have attended college.

An assumption made throughout the book is that colleges and universities cannot continue with business-as-usual, given the increasing numbers of these older students returning to work on undergraduate and graduate degrees.

In the middle 1940s, with the return of the World War II veterans, the emphasis was on providing seating space and minimal resource facilities. Today these are not of major concern. With traditional-student numbers declining, facilities and staff will not be a problem.

The problems will be more subtle and more complex. The quiet revolution will come about because older returning students will insist on changes. They will not accept many present-day policies about how registration takes place, when courses are offered, and the times that libraries are open. Increasingly, they will question the quality of teaching and the relationship of faculty to students. They will question the attitude that prevails on many campuses that the faculty is superior and the students are inferior, no matter what their age. It is in these areas that we will see changes occurring on college campuses across this country. Changes in these areas will not come without a struggle, without debate, power plays, and compromise. Revolutions never occur without struggle and conflict, whether they be violent revolutions or quiet, more subtle revolutions of the type I'm describing here. But the conflict can be reduced somewhat, and the time it takes to resolve the conflict shortened, if all concerned are willing to explore the problem in a thoughtful manner.

In chapter 13 I discuss some of the many issues related to the changes that colleges and universities are experiencing or will experience as increasing numbers of older students return to campus. Some of the issues relate to the fundamental purposes of colleges and universities and their relationship to society. For example, many returning students are returning to school to acquire the credentials necessary for employment. To what extent should colleges and universities be a party to the increased emphasis on credentials in our society? To what extent should colleges and universities adapt their curricula to be more in accord with the career aspirations of the returning students? To what extent should colleges and universities modify their administrative procedures, such as entrance requirements and residency requirements, to take into account returning–student needs? To what extent should new approaches to offering courses be considered—weekend, off campus, evenings once a week, over television, and so on—to accommodate students who cannot physically attend traditional classes? To what extent do these modifications lower the standards and thus the quality of the educational programs these institutions provide? These and other issues are examined in chapter 13.

Improvements Needed

This book is written for those in higher education who have responsibility for the teaching and administration of academic degree credit programs.

The major concern of this book is how to improve the learning environment for the adult learner on campus. Several approaches could be followed. A common approach would be to focus on teaching methods that show the most promise for improving adult-student learning. But there is much more to improving the learning environment for returning students than improving teaching methods. Such factors as the adult learners themselves, their motivations, their problems, their developmental progress through the life span, and their adjustment to the aging process are important for instructors and administrators to consider. The curriculum, how it is organized, and the materials that are used by the adult learner must be considered when attempting to improve the learning environment. And finally, the broad area of situational and environmental factors cannot be overlooked. Here are included social, economic, and political forces that influence both the older returning students and the institutions of higher education. Such forces as the women's movement influence the learning environment for returning students in a variety of ways, from the motivations of women to return to school to the nature of the instructional programs these women face once they find themselves in college classrooms.

The general mood of the country toward the place of higher education in society influences the learning environment for returning students as it influences all of higher education. Two diverse moods appear to be operating at the same time. On the one hand are those who argue for a back-to-basics movement throughout education with an emphasis on the development of basic skills at the lower levels of education and job preparation at the upper levels. This view emphasizes education as a servant of industrial society as we now know it. A second view that appears to be gaining some prominence is expressed by such writers as Theodore Roszak, Ivan Illich, and Charles Reich, who talk about a new consciousness that is developing in the country. Roszak emphasizes the right of people to self-discover, to find out what it means to be human.[1] Illich talks about the problems our society's extreme emphasis on schooling and credentials have created. He calls for a deschooling of society.[2] Reich talks about three levels of consciousness.[3] These will be discussed in greater detail in chapter 6.

To improve the educational environment for returning students we must look at all of these factors. We must consider the returning students themselves; this is of vital importance. We must consider the teaching methods being used. The curriculum and the learning materials must be considered, and the many and varied situational and environmental factors that exist must be taken into account.

How Many Adults Are Returning and Why

In the fall of 1979, two- and four-year college and university campuses had an enrollment of 11,500,000 students of all ages. Of that total, approximately 40 percent were part-time students. That compares with only 32 percent of all two- and four-year college students who in 1970 were enrolled part-time. (A large percentage of part-time students are those who are twenty-five years of age or older—those we define as returning students in this book.)

As a case in point, 40,233 students were enrolled at the University of Wisconsin–Madison in the fall of 1979. Of that total, 11,982 were twenty-five or older, or about 30 percent. Higher percentages of older, part-time students are enrolling at two-year colleges than at four-year colleges, but the percentages are increasing in both instances.

Since 1969, the National Center for Education Statistics has conducted surveys every three years to determine participation in adult education. For its surveys, adults are defined as those seventeen and older, and participation in adult education is defined as "organized adult education courses or activities, besides full-time attendance in regular school." "Regular school" includes elementary, junior high, high school, and college degree programs. Part-time attendance in college degree programs is included as adult education, but those adults who attended college full-time are excluded from this survey.

As table 1 indicates, 38 percent of the courses taken by adults for the year ending May 1978 were taken in either a two-year

TABLE 1

Where Adult Education Takes Place

Courses taken by total participants in adult education. Year ending May 1978.

	Number (in thousands)	Percent
Elementary, junior, or high school	2,725	9.4
Two-year college or vocational-technical institute	5,321	18.4
Four-year college or university	5,666	19.6
Vocational, trade, or business school	1,933	6.7
Other school	909	3.1
Tutor or private instructor	1,338	4.6
Business or industry	3,165	11.0
Labor organization or professional association	1,086	3.8
Government agency	2,445	8.5
Private community organization	2,394	8.3
Other	1,268	4.4
Did not know	100	.3
Not reported	544	1.9
Total	28,894	100.0

SOURCE: Adapted from table 2, "Courses Taken by Participants in Adult Education, by Selected Course Characteristics: United States, Years Ending May 1969, May 1972, and May 1978," *Participation in Adult Education, 1978* (Washington, D.C., Department of Health, Education, and Welfare, National Center for Education Statistics, 1980).

college or vocational-technical school, or in a four-year college or university. This amounted to nearly 11 million courses taken by adults in two- and four-year colleges and universities.

Reasons why adults said they participated in adult-education courses clustered around those related to occupations (see table 2). About 53 percent of those who responded to the survey said they participated in adult-education courses for some job-related reasons, either to improve or advance in a current job (38.9 percent), to get a new job (10.5 percent), or for some other job-related reason (3.3 percent). More than 31 percent of those who responded said they participated in adult-education courses for personal or social reasons, while 12.5 percent said they participated for general education.

Past Experiences

Once before in the recent history of higher education we had a situation somewhat similar to today. Immediately following World War II, thousands of returning veterans flooded the campuses to cash in their G.I. Bill of Rights and receive a college education. Higher education wasn't ready for this onslaught of older students. Temporary buildings were thrown up quickly on many campuses, libraries were established in Quonset huts, and the veterans and their families were housed in makeshift structures often some distance from their classes.

There were a few rifts between the traditional, younger students in their late teens and early twenties and the veterans who were mostly in their middle twenties and almost entirely male. In less than ten years the World War II veterans faded from the college campuses, and colleges and universities were mostly back to business-as-usual by the 1950s. Most of the temporary buildings were torn down, and the presence of the older student on campus was only a memory in the heads of the older faculty members.

During the fifties and into the sixties, a few older students returned to campus. Many of them were graduate students who a few years before had earned a baccalaureate degree and then discovered that, to advance in their particular positions, they needed more college-level work. Occasionally an older student who had not completed an undergraduate degree returned to campus to complete a degree program started five or ten years previously. But this person was indeed an oddity.

TABLE 2

Main Reason for Participating

Courses taken by total participants in adult education. Year ending May 1978.

	Number (in thousands)	Percent
To improve or advance in current job	11,228	38.9
To get a new job	3,036	10.5
Other job-related reason	958	3.3
For American citizenship	47	.2
For general education	3,623	12.5
Personal or social reasons	9,019	31.2
For other reasons	784	2.7
Not reported	200	.7
Total	28,894	100.0

SOURCE: Ibid.

Irene Kampen writes about her experiences as a returning student to a major midwestern university in the early 1960s.[4] She recounts in a humorous narrative the many blocks she faced upon re-enrolling in a formal degree program after returning to school. Her problems ranged from the admissions-office people insisting she give them her parents' address to a major professor who couldn't begin to understand why in the world a woman of her age would want to enroll once more in an undergraduate degree program.

In the middle sixties I returned to school to work on a graduate degree, after completing an undergraduate degree some ten years before. I experienced firsthand many of the situations Irene Kampen described in her book. The admissions people insisted I give them my parents' address so they could send my parents my grades. I told them I thought my wife would be more interested in my grades than my parents. I also discovered I needed a loan to complete my graduate work, and the student-loan officer insisted I provide financial information about my parents, who were already retired.

In those days it was not difficult for the adult student to feel out of place, to feel as if the college or university was going beyond its call even to allow you to attend.

But all of this is beginning to change, slowly to be sure, as thousands of older students trek back to the campuses across the country. Many of them are part-time; indeed far more are part-time than full time. The economics of living in this country makes this easy to understand. Many returning students have families who are dependent on them. It is thus impossible for many returning students to attend classes other than part-time.

But the point is that adults are returning to campuses in ever increasing numbers. As we reflect back to the time when the GIs were returning to school by the thousands and compare what happened then with what is happening now, we see some similarities but many differences as well.

Nearly all the veterans enrolling in college after World War II were about the same age—in their late twenties. By about the time the universities had added facilities and instructional staff to handle the bulge of numbers, the veterans were through school and the student body once more returned to the traditional age of eighteen to twenty-two.

Today the returning students range in age from the twenties

on up to the forties and beyond. And the majority of them are women. Facilities will not be the problem either. According to most predictions, the total numbers of students enrolled on college campuses will decrease during the next decade. Projections by the federal government's National Center for Education Statistics indicate a total college and university enrollment of a little over 11 million in 1988 compared to about 11½ million in the fall of 1979.

If past trends are any indication of what we can expect in the future, we could expect the numbers of older students on campuses to at least remain stable, with every indication the numbers will increase.

One reason for suggesting the numbers of adults returning to campus will increase is simply a matter of demography. The median age of the U.S. population is slowly creeping higher. In 1975 it was 28.8. For 1980 it is slightly more than 30 and by 1990 it is predicted to be nearly 33. The reason for the increase in median age is the decline in birthrate in recent years. For instance, in 1975, 93.9 million people were 24 and younger. By 1990 predictions indicate a drop to about 90 million for this age group. On the other hand, those 25–64 in 1975 numbered 97.3 million with a prediction of nearly 124 million in this age group by 1990.

Sources of Information

Several sources of information were used in the development of this book. First, the growing literature of adult education was reviewed for information about adult development, learning, and successful teaching approaches. Chapter 14 includes many of these references.

Second, during the winter and spring of 1979 I visited the University of Toronto, University of Michigan, Temple University, and North Carolina State University, where I interviewed exemplary instructors of adult returning students as well as many students. I also interviewed both faculty and adult returning students on the University of Wisconsin campus in Madison. (For purposes of consistency in information gathering, I defined returning students as those twenty-five and older who had been out of school at least three years.)

To identify the so-called exemplary professors, I contacted the center for returning students at each of the institutions I selected. These centers are variously named. Here at the University of Wisconsin–Madison, the center is called Continuing Education Services.

When no center was present, I contacted the school of education. In each instance, whether contact was made with a center for returning students or a school of education, I asked if they would identify for me up to ten professors, both men and women, whom they believed to be exemplary in their work with adult returning students. I primarily asked for recommendations in the social sciences and in the humanities. The major criterion I suggested the nominators use was that an instructor, from the perspective of the adult returning student, was doing an outstanding job providing learning opportunities for older students.

None of the institutions had any difficulty naming instructors who met the guidelines I set down. Once I had the names, I proceeded to select individual instructors using the criteria of sex and discipline as the primary determinants.

I then phoned the selected professors and asked if I could visit with them in their offices to do about an hour interview that I planned to tape. Of those I selected initially, only one refused and this was because he had a commitment abroad during the time I planned to visit his university.

I conducted organized yet open interviews. I had questions I asked the instructors, but I also probed areas they wanted to talk about. I asked them questions about the number of older returning students with whom they had contact, their perceptions of why older students were returning to school, their perceptions of the problems returning students face, and their ideas of how returning students compared with the more traditional, younger students. I then asked a series of personal questions to determine something of the instructors' leisure-time use, what they enjoyed and disliked about being a college instructor, and what major changes they saw occurring on college and university campuses in the coming decade.

I asked them to describe for me the teaching approaches they used, both inside the classroom and outside the classroom, and the extent to which they used educational technology in their teaching.

Finally, I asked each instructor to describe his or her research and scholarship, in an attempt to determine if being an outstanding teacher detracted from these.

Originally I had planned to interview a sample of students

from each class that each of the exemplary instructors taught. From a practical perspective this became impossible. I did, however, interview thirteen students who had classes with instructors from the University of Michigan, University of Toronto, and University of Wisconsin–Madison. This was not done to check on the information provided by the instructors about teaching approaches used and relationships with older students. Instead, the student interviews provided me information about their backgrounds and reasons for returning to college, as well as some information about the teaching approaches they preferred and the problems they were facing upon returning to school.

All told I interviewed seventeen instructors—seven women and ten men. The departments they represented were as follows: social welfare, psycho-educational processes, psychology (three instructors), history, sociology (two), geography, adult education (three), statistics, political science, English, child and family studies, and sociology and anthropology.

In addition to the seventeen instructors and thirteen students, I interviewed Dr. Ralph Tyler, a national educational consultant. I asked Dr. Tyler questions about the differences between traditional and returning adult students, the changes that universities and colleges will likely need to consider with increasing numbers of older students in the classroom, the reasons why older students were returning to school, the teaching approaches most effective for older students, and any tips he'd like to share with the instructor who, for the first time, faced a class with several older returning students in it.

The third major source of data for this book comes from my own experience, both as a returning student myself at the age of thirty-two and as a professor who has been advising and teaching adult returning students for seventeen years. In my own department at the University of Wisconsin, approximately 95 percent of our graduate students are adult returning students, and an increasing number of undergraduate students are falling into that category as well. In one of my recent undergraduate courses, 50 percent of the students were twenty-five years of age or older, with several in their forties.

Questions Raised

I have attempted to wrestle with a number of questions in this book. Why are large numbers of adults returning to school? How do these older students compare with more traditional, younger students? What factors affect adults as learners? Is the aging process a critical deterrent to learning—and thus are older students less qualified than younger students? What are the components of the learning environment for returning students, both on campus and off campus? What does research tell us about effective teaching-learning strategies that might have application to the college classroom? What are the characteristics of those instructors whom returning students say are exemplary? What teaching approaches do they follow? What problems do these instructors of returning students face? What fundamental changes should colleges and universities consider if they are to be successful in recruiting and educating adult returning students? And finally, what issues and controversies are surfacing concerning returning students?

NOTES

1. Theodore Roszak, *Person/Planet* (New York: Doubleday, 1978).

2. Ivan Illich, *Deschooling Society* (New York: Harper and Row, 1970).

3. Charles A. Reich, *The Greening of America* (New York: Random House, 1970).

4. Irene Kampen, *Due to Lack of Interest Tomorrow Has Been Canceled* (New York: Doubleday, 1969).

Chapter 2

Who Are the Adults Returning to College?

For some years returning students were seen as some sort of oddity. Their numbers were small and instructors and administrators put up with them but usually spent little or no time attempting to find out much about them.

In recent years, with the great increase in the numbers of returning students, several studies have been completed to find out something about returning students. In this chapter, I'll review some of this research as well as share impressions of returning students from the exemplary instructors I interviewed.

The College Board and its Future Directions for a Learning Society project have been interested in returning students and their characteristics. In a study of American adults in transition, they discovered that 36 percent of the population in the country aged sixteen to sixty-five (40 million people) were in some type of career transition in 1978. But what is even more interesting is that, of the 40 million people in transition, 24 million, or 60 percent, said they planned additional education as part of their career change. Other findings include the following:

Those interested in further learning are predominately female, white, and between the ages of twenty and thirty-nine.

There is less interest in learning in rural areas and cities with a population of less than 2,500.

Blacks are considerably less represented than whites.

Hispanics are represented about proportional to their number in the general population.

Those interested in learning are considerably more educated than those who are not. (Adults who have gone beyond high school are twice as likely to indicate interest in more learning as those who have not.)

Those employed are more likely to plan for learning than those who are not.

Those working full time are more apt to plan for more learning than those working part-time or those who are retired.

Adults engaged in professional and technical work are more likely to pursue additional learning than are other occupational groups.

Adults engaged in farm work are least likely to pursue additional learning.

Women with children under eighteen years of age are more likely to seek additional learning than those women with children over eighteen.

Adults living in southeastern states are least likely to pursue additional learning.

Those living in Pacific Coast states are most likely to be interested in more learning.

Divorced adults and single adults who have never married are more likely to plan for more learning than others.

Widowed adults are less likely to participate in additional learning than those who are not.[1]

The College Board Research reported above dealt with all providers, not merely colleges and universities. Of those adults in the survey who said they anticipated further participation in education, 36 percent said they preferred a four-year college or university, and 18 percent said they wanted to attend a two-year college. No attempt in the research was made to sort out any unique characteristics of those adults who said they preferred colleges and universities over other adult-education providers.

But enough about general statistics concerning the characteristics of those who are returning or said they planned to return. Let's turn to several students who have returned and let them tell us in their own words something about themselves and how they came to return to college.

Typical Stories

The first student we'll meet was working on a doctorate at the University of Toronto at the time of my interview with him. He was in his thirties.

"I finished my undergraduate degree in 1959, and I started a master's program in science. I was a physiology student then, and I worked one year toward that degree and decided I didn't want to continue. Then I got a chance to teach in a nursing school. I was to teach anatomy and physiology. I taught at this nursing school for a year and a half and then became registrar of the school. About that time the nursing school was becoming part of a community college, and I was in charge of getting all the nursing school records into the community college's computer. And I taught at the same time.

"I decided to leave that school and went to work for another community college in North Bay, in mid-northern Ontario. There I taught physiology, hematology, and blood banking. You need to know that, before I worked on my undergraduate degree, I had worked as a medical technologist, so I had had some practical experience with those courses. I began to do a lot of work with volunteer agencies at North Bay about that time, and I was also running a training program for telephone distress workers. It was about that time I really got interested in education. I enrolled at the University of Toronto, in the Ontario Institute for Studies in Education, on a part-time basis. They offered some courses at North Bay. I drove to Toronto for some courses, and I enrolled in their summer program. And I finished a master's program.

"After finishing the master's program, I decided I would like to go on in a doctoral program and I asked for a sabbatical leave from the college where I taught. They decided not to give it to me, but they did say I could have a leave of absence. So I took that and went down to Toronto and started a doctoral program. I planned to stay just one year, but I discovered it was kind of catching, and also I wanted to continue working on my research project. So I asked if I could stay away from my college another year. They said no, so I quit. And I took another year of full-time study . . . and that brings me up to the present."

The second returning student I'll introduce is a married woman with children aged eleven and eight at the time of the interview. She was working on a master's degree in education at the University of Wisconsin–Madison.

"I graduated in 1964 from Washington Square College, New York University, with a B.A. in history and twelve credits in education. New York City, at that time, would let you teach without student teaching. So I taught for a year in New York, and then my husband and I were married and we moved to Princeton, New Jersey. I couldn't get a job right away because it was really tough in New Jersey with a history background to find something. So I worked at Gallup and Robinson, which is part of the Gallup organization, in market research from September of 1965 to about November of 1965 doing advertising-type work, and I really didn't like it at all. I missed the classroom. I was testing a dummy magazine; we were constantly testing ads, different varieties of ads. I didn't like the job and when a different job—a teaching job—opened up, I took it. I began teaching seventh- and eighth-grade English in a community near Princeton.

"I really had bad classes the first year. The second year they felt sorry for me, I think, and they gave me some very nice classes. I liked my third year of teaching best. I began to feel like I was really doing something and I enjoyed it. Then we moved to Wisconsin, and I was told Wisconsin wouldn't hire me because I didn't have student teaching. I never followed up on that. After the teaching experience I had in New York City and in New Jersey, with really tough kids, I just didn't want to go back and student teach.

"During those first years in Wisconsin I began teaching part-time at the vocational school. I taught knitting and crocheting, which I had learned on my own. I taught one or two classes a week at night. When my littlest one was in kindergarten half-days, I decided to come back to school. They were five and eight then, so I took only one class a semester for the first year. I started back as a special student and just taking classes. I took some classes in mental retardation and working with special children. Then I decided I just didn't want to work with the retarded. So I switched into a master's program in adult education. I am up to taking two courses a semester now."

The third student I'll introduce was a senior in sociology at the time of the interview. When she graduated from high school, she attended a secretarial school and worked as a secretary until she married and had children. She and her husband moved to upstate New York, where she began working in a school for emotionally disturbed teenagers. She worked at this school from 1966 until 1968. Her husband took a job with Oscar Mayer and they moved to Pennsylvania. In Pennsylvania she began work with the volunteers on a probation program that was just starting there. "I became actively interested in the probation program. . . . I enjoyed it a lot. And I started thinking, 'You know, I really should go to school. I'm doing all these things that you really should have an education to be doing,' " she said.

She said she was also beginning to have problems with her confidence in her job. She often felt she was over her head. They were transferred to Milwaukee and at that time had a new baby. But she said she was still thinking about school. They were transferred back to Pennsylvania and then to Chicago. While in Chicago, she started working as a teacher's aide in the elementary school her children attended. A short time later, a policy was passed requiring teacher's aides to have college credits.

"Here I am," she said. "I have lots of life experience and I have lots of experience working with children, but I don't have any college credits. I decided I would go back to school and went out and registered at a small community college. It was very nice . . . small classes, just a fantastic experience for me. I started out taking two courses and slowly built up to taking twelve credits a term."

She told me she hadn't been a good student in high school, so she really felt good about doing well in the community-college courses. She became a sociology major and accumulated several credits before she and her family moved to Tennessee, where they lived for eleven years. There she enrolled in another community college. "I had a fantastic experience there," she said. "I did really well, enjoyed my classes, and had just about completed a two-year degree. I was maybe short two or three hours when we moved again, this time to Madison, Wisconsin."

After considerable difficulty with transferring credits and becoming established in the Madison community, she began work once more on her sociology degree, which she planned to finish at the end of the semester I interviewed her.

I am not suggesting that these students are representative of all the students returning to school, because they are not. Each student who returns has his or her own story to tell as to why the decision to return to school was made, what combinations of life events influenced the decision, and so on. These students are simply interesting examples of those who are returning.

Reasons Given

Why do people who are past the so-called school-going age decide to begin or to return to college? The last major group of adults returning to college were veterans returning from World War II. But then the reasons were obvious. Thousands of young men had their formal college training interrupted by the war; many more went directly from high school into the military service. And besides, the government, through its veteran benefit program, provided a monetary incentive for these men to return to school.

Whereas in 1945 the vast majority of those adults returning to school were men, today the majority are women, as we noted in the previous chapter. However, today there is no national event that can be credited with influencing people to return to school. When we see thousands of adults returning to school, the majority of them being women, it is easy to say, "It makes no sense. Why should large numbers of women, many of them married and with families, many of them living in comfortable homes and well supported by husbands with well-paying jobs, want to return to school?"

Some research has been completed on reasons why adults, particularly women, are returning to school. Hazel Markus, in a 1976 research project, reported, "It is clear that difficult financial times is a major factor precipitating a return to school (for women). Another important factor that seems to foster a return to education is employment. Nearly half of these women report that their job, in one way or another, caused them to consider a return to school. Many women also report that their decision to continue schooling came during marital conflict or following a separation or divorce. . . . less than 5 percent indicated that the women's movement was important to their decision to return to school."[2]

Markus, who was reporting on women who had participated in the University of Michigan's Center for the Continuing Education of Women, said self-enrichment and personal growth were seldom given as goals for returning to school, unless they were tied to some other goal.

Elizabeth Douvan discovered similar reasons when she analyzed the research about women returning to school. But she goes a bit further and talks about both internal and external factors that affect the decision of women to return to school. She says, "On the one hand when women tell us their reasons, they allude primarily to internal factors: they want to prepare for jobs, enlarge their horizons, refresh their skills or spirits, gain personal independence—positive forces working to attract them to learning. Yet in those studies that include intensive interviews or information about the woman's family and her relationships with important others in her interpersonal network, we discover that there are other forces operating in the decision: the empty nest, problems with her husband or her mother, geographic dislocation. Forces in the social milieu create a tension or irritability which urge her to action, to some movement which will get her out of an uncomfortable situation."[3]

A study conducted by the Future Directions of a Learning Society project of the College Board discovered that 83 percent of adult learners named some change or transition in their lives as the motivation to start learning. About half these adult learners said changes in their jobs and careers—they needed to learn to get a job, to get a better job, to keep the job they had, or to advance in their job—motivated their return to education.[4]

Ralph Gallay and Ronald Hunter, in a study of 100 adult part-time undergraduate students at Rutgers University, University College, found each of the following nine reasons as either a major or a minor reason why these adults returned to school. In this study, 65 of the respondents were men and 35 were women. (Respondents could give more than one reason.)[5]

Reasons for Returning	Percentage of Returning Students
Professional growth, other than increased salary	97%
Self-esteem	96%
Long-range economic security	92%
Increased salary	90%
Social status and prestige	58%
Family expectations	53%
Authoritative figures (teachers, clergy, supervisors)	50%
Peer opinions	47%
College social life	17%

One of the questions I asked the instructors I interviewed involved their perception of the reasons why adults were returning to school. The reasons they gave could be placed in six categories: occupation-related reasons, social acceptability, life enhancement, change in life situation, society's premium on degrees, and university recruiting. Although all of these were perceived as reasons, with the first ones more important than the latter ones listed, it is impossible to consider them apart from each other. In other words, an adult may return to school to find a better job, which in turn is seen as a way to life enhancement. The whole process may have been triggered by some life transition such as divorce. A university's ad in a newspaper may have provided the necessary information about availability of an adult-oriented program, while also demonstrating society's more relaxed attitude toward adults' returning to school.

Occupation-related Reasons

In the opinion of the instructors I interviewed, occupation motivated adults to return to college more than any other reason. As a professor of political science said, "Adults are returning to college because they have been passed over for a promotion and they see a degree as a definite asset in a promotion or for salary increases. Others would like to move up in their jobs. Some persons may be working as specialists and would like to move into administration."

This professor went on to share an example of a young woman he'd had in class: "One of the best students I had in my class in public administration last fall was a young woman about thirty-four who was a housing inspector for the city of Raleigh, North Carolina. She had never been in a college class before she came in my class. She is happily married, has children, and she is very ambitious. She has seen opportunities for women improve in city government, and she has felt that her lack of any kind of degree is a handicap. She has the intelligence to become a very fine analyst in policy areas. And she's an excellent student, spends a lot of time studying, and is very thorough. Yet she's very relaxed about it all."

Career change was reported by several of the exemplary instructors as a reason why adults are returning to school. A professor of psychology shared the example of a woman who finished in his program.

"One of the persons who finished two years ago was a woman in her forties. Her husband is a professor of biology on this campus. She started out in English, has her master's degree in English, and then became interested in psychology. She came to our department and began working on her degree. She was a superior student and worked her way through to the completion of her doctorate in psychology. Now she's teaching at one of the junior colleges in the city and is also doing an internship at a local hospital to round out her qualifications as a psychologist."

A professor of social welfare reported that many older students enroll in her department's program because social welfare, particularly for women, "is a major that leads to a job." She also said her program attracts a fairly high proportion of minority students "because the social work profession can be a job entry for a minority person."

A professor of geography pointed out some economic realities: "The economic condition of the whole country is such that women find themselves obliged to work. And they know that they're going to work at very dull jobs in which they get 60 percent of the salaries of men doing the same jobs, unless they can get out of that trap, and the only way to get out of the trap is by education."

Increasingly, many professional people are forced to return to some kind of formal education because of mandated continuing education plans, either through laws passed by state legislatures or by the requirements for relicensure and recertification by professional organizations.

Louis Phillips, from Furman University in Greenville, South Carolina, has attempted to keep a running account of legislation mandating continuing education in this country. He reports that every state has legislation mandating continuing education for some of its professionals.

Of course, public-school teachers have been mandated to continue their education for many years. This often means they are compelled to work toward graduate degrees to maintain their teaching license, or at least to be eligible for salary increases.

One of the major arguments for mandatory continuing education is technological change and the knowledge explosion. As the argument goes, if the society is to be assured of competent, caring professionals, these professionals must be forced to continue their education. Unfortunately, there is no clear evidence to support the contention that forcing a professional to continue his or her education will ensure that the professional is competent. Nevertheless, mandatory continuing education continues to be one of the occupation-related reasons why many professionals are returning to school.

It's Socially Acceptable

Some people claim the women's movement has made it more socially acceptable for women to return to school, and this in turn has also influenced many men to return. It's slowly becoming acceptable for adults to attend school, even though many of them may be twice the age of their fellow, more traditional students with whom they attend classes.

According to one of the professors I interviewed, a professor of adult education, a major reason why we see so many women returning to school at this time is because a dormant pool has been released. He said, "The whole women's movement is a re-awakening of a relatively dormant pool of scholars that we have in our society. While this re-awakening will bring a surge, indeed has brought a surge over the last five years and will probably continue over the next five years or ten years, it will probably plateau. The relative number of women returning may decrease in ten or fifteen years because of the backlog we are dealing with having been in school."

This professor believes that many middle-aged adults now returning to school were college dropouts. He says that once a person starts college, even if he or she drops out, "there is an inertia that sets in, and these people are going to start again, at some time in their lives."

A professor of English recalled the early beginning of the Radcliffe program for returning students: "In about 1960, when I was in the Boston area, a program was set up at Radcliffe, and the idea began to spread that it was all right for older students to go back to college. Before that the age difference often made people uncomfortable about going back. Many older persons figured college was for young kids and they didn't belong there. That was particularly so with women. After 1960 women began to believe it was all right to go back and finish a degree or go back and get another degree. Going back to school was not going to de-sex them and make them unfeminine."

A professor of psycho-educational processes believes that, increasingly, women are of the attitude that after raising a family it is appropriate to say, "Now it's my turn to do something creative and different." The professor pointed out, "A significant number of our master's and doctoral students are women with kids, ages twelve to fourteen and up to twenty-five or thirty. They are coming back to school with the attitude that 'now it's my turn. Now I'm going to make a name for myself. Now I'm going to be Dr. So-and-So instead of Dr. and Mrs.' "

A professor of geography said it in another way. She talked about the many barriers that have prevented women from continuing their education, barriers that are slowly lifting. She pointed out that the American woman "has been under great social pressure to get married and drop education or to go to work and support the family while the men went on to education. Her brothers got college educations, but she didn't. She was expected to go out and get a job. A young woman quit high school and became a secretary, and that was her life. So these women had barriers put up in front of them, and even today, many of them have not articulated their aspirations for further education."

And finally, a professor of sociology explained how sometimes a crisis point, a major decision, is necessary for adults, particularly women, to be accepted by colleges and universities. He cited one such incident that had a major effect on his campus.

"We had a court case in 1970. A small group of women brought suit against the university for HEW discrimination and the Department of Health, Education, and Welfare put its hand on the water tap and said, 'Change,' and the university started hurrying around to change things. They even put a lot of money and a lot of publicity into this business, and I think that certainly brought a lot of women back to our campus. For one thing it provided a fellowship program which put out information that [in effect] said, 'Now we've got money for nontraditional students, which basically means women over twenty-five who have raised a family and want to come back.' "

Life Enhancement

Some adults are returning to school to improve the quality of their lives. But as I pointed out earlier, many people see their lives enhanced through some occupational change, rather than going back to school with life enhancement as the sole purpose. But there are exceptions.

A political science professor told about people in his classes who he believed were bored with their lives and saw college work as a way out. "I think of a man who recently began our program. He's an oil distributor. He withstood a bout with cancer and said he simply enjoys the courses. He says going back to school is not going to make him any more money; he just likes to be in school. He's done well too. He was around forty years old when he started with us."

A professor of history shared a similar example: "A man and his wife both came back to school in their mid-forties. He had owned his own import-export business and was doing well. But he got tired of simply running his business, even though it involved traveling to Japan several times a year. He said to himself, 'There's really much more to life than this.' And so he decided he wanted to study history and become a professor. His wife's reasons were similar, and I think included wanting to keep up with him and really looking for a new way, a new life-style, basically. One of the ironies is you find in the same classroom people leaving an occupation which other people in the class would give their eyeteeth to get into, breaking their backs to get in the courses, get the degrees, and try to find jobs . . . and in the same class somebody is just fed up with, say, being a librarian, and there are two or three people who would be glad to change places if they could do it."

Change in Life Situation

Though often combined with some other reason for returning to school, some change in life situation is mentioned by many returning students as a major motivator for returning. For example, a professor of child and family studies said, "Of the women who are returning to school especially, perhaps half of them are returning because of some changes in their life situations: divorce, widowhood, or something like that."

A psychology professor agreed. She said, "Life crises, which may mean frequently a marriage broken up—that's a common kind of life crisis. Another kind of life crisis is when the kids move away from home. These women are trying to do something with their lives and often decide there is another life out there, and they want to do something about it, so they return to school."

Societal Premium on Degrees

Though sometimes implied but not mentioned by returning students, the idea that one has to have some kind of credential to land many types of jobs seems a reality of the times. And this attitude toward obtaining credentials seems to be on the increase. Where once certain types of jobs required a bachelor's degree, now many of them are requiring or strongly encouraging master's degrees. Thus certain types of master's degree programs have become very popular in recent years—master's degrees for elementary and secondary teachers, master's degrees for social workers, and master's degrees in business administration for persons going into the various administrative jobs in the business world. As a professor of social welfare explained, "A reason many people are returning to school in my area of study is because many of them have been working in social work as paraprofessionals and want to get a degree because social work is becoming more and more a credentialed profession."

University Recruiting

Many university officials would like to believe that adult students are returning to school by their own motivation. Indeed this is often the case, as we have pointed out above. But many colleges and universities in the past few years have begun to recruit actively adult students for their classes and programs. Many institutions have begun extended timetable programs, an approach that means offering regular college courses late in the afternoon and in the evening. Several institutions have taken regular courses and offered them in a weekend format, again to encourage the attendance of older, returning students. Many colleges and universities have taken courses into communities, often many miles from the main campus, in an attempt to encourage participation by returning students.

Along with these various modifications in presenting programs go considerable recruiting efforts, often referred to as marketing.

At this time, it's impossible to know the extent to which university recruiting of this "new student" audience is a major factor in motivating adults to return to school. It would seem obvious that some combination of the reasons listed above, with university recruitment, would have some effect. An adult who, for a variety of reasons, feels a need for additional learning but doesn't know where the opportunities are available will not return to school. Thus recruitment can play an important role.

As one of the instructors I interviewed said, "Many colleges and universities, for purposes of economic survival, are seeking older students simply because the pool of pink-cheeked teenagers who come to campus full time is drying up. Universities are being much more aggressive in seeking out a new clientele to take the place of the youth."

As we shall discuss later, too many institutions are making only cosmetic changes in an attempt to entice adults to return, not realizing that more profound changes may be necessary if such programs are going to be successful.

Another professor whom I interviewed believed that adults were increasingly coming back to school "because we've gotten across to these people that institutions of higher education exist, and particularly land-grant institutions of higher education exist where the tuition is relatively low, so it's an inexpensive kind of arrangement."

In other words, in his mind, the recruitment effort has been successful—see all the adult students on campus?

Obviously the reasons why adults return to school are not simply explained. It would appear from the evidence available so far that the reasons are many and closely interwoven. A divorce may trigger a woman to return to school because she needs to work and doesn't like the idea of spending the rest of her life as a barmaid or at a grocery checkout. It is likely that thousands of women are returning because they had dropped out of college to get married and now, for the first time in their lives (and likely the first time in history), society doesn't frown as much on women participating in degree programs. And as we just pointed out, the decline in traditional-student numbers, with more decline predicted in the coming years, motivates colleges and universities to recruit adults openly as a way to their survival.

Summary

Adults returning to school may be characterized as follows: they are more often women than men, they are most often between the ages of twenty and thirty-nine, they have a better formal education than those who do not return, and they are likely to be employed and in professional or technical work.

The reasons adults return to school include those related to occupations—either beginning an occupation, changing occupations, or improving in one's occupation; social acceptability for adults to attend college; life enhancement; change in life situation; society's premium on degrees; and university and college recruiting programs for older students. Seldom, however, is there just a single reason why adults return.

NOTES

1. See Solomon Arbeiter et al., *40 Million Americans in Career Transition,* Future Directions for a Learning Society, The College Entrance Examination Board (New York: 1978). Also see George W. Bonham, "Inching Toward the Learning Society," *Change,* July–August 1979, for an interesting summary of the College Board research.

2. Hazel Markus, "The Return to School," *Educational Horizons,* Summer 1976, pp. 173–174.

3. Elizabeth Douvan, "Summary and Conclusions," *Newsletter of the Center for Continuing Education of Women, The University of Michigan,* vol. 10, no. 1, Summer 1977.

4. From oral report given by Carol Aslanian of the College Board at the 1979 National Adult Education Conference in Boston.

5. From Ralph Gallay and Ronald V. Hunter, "Why Adults Are Pursuing a Part-Time Education," *Collegiate News and Views,* vol. 32, no. 2, Winter 1978–79, p. 14.

Chapter 3

Comparing Adult Learners with Traditional Students

There are obvious dangers when attempting to make generalized comparisons between returning students (those twenty-five or older and out of school for some years) and traditional students (those eighteen to twenty-two who have gone to college directly after high school graduation). Many differences exist within each of these groups. Nevertheless, it is also possible to point out some rather important differences between the two groups. This is done with full knowledge that there are exceptions, as there usually are when we try to generalize.

In addition to differences, there are areas where the two groups are similar, even where many people might expect differences. For example, intellectual ability. Many people believe that, as we grow older, our intellectual powers decrease. As I will point out more specifically later, this is simply not the case. We do not lose intellectual ability as we grow older. Sometimes it may appear as if older persons have less intellectual ability when they are compared to younger learners. This is especially evident when a group of older learners and a group of younger learners are subjected to the same timed examination. Two factors operate that make it appear older adults are less able intellectually. For one reason or another, younger learners place a good deal of value on doing things quickly. In fact, much of the formal educational establishment these days still places considerable emphasis on speed of performance and recall of factual information. Unfortunately, accuracy is often compromised for speed. Because many, if not all, returning students come to school from some type of work setting, the attitude of speed over accuracy is often inappropriate. In most work situations, a fairly high degree of accuracy is emphasized. To be sure, many work situations also emphasize speed. But first accuracy, then speed, not the other way around. So the adult learner wants to take more time on examinations to make certain the responses are correct before answering.

Also, as I will discuss later, because the amount of life experience is considerably greater for older students, many examination questions present paradoxes for them. They want to offer many alternative responses, not a simple response recalled from some lecture.

And finally, as we grow older, our reaction time slows. Most of us simply cannot react to timed situations as efficiently as we could when we were younger.

Unfortunately, many people conclude for the reasons mentioned above that, because it takes older students longer to complete timed examinations, they are, therefore, intellectually deficient when compared to younger students. This conclusion couldn't be further from the truth.

We are beginning to see empirical research projects that look at differences between older and younger students. I'll mention one such study here. At Stanford University first-year doctoral students were compared. Two groups were defined. One group, called continuous students, had an average age of 22 years. The second group, called discontinuous students, had an average age of 27.7 years. The continuous students were those who had not been out of school for more than a summer's vacation. Discontinuous students had left school for at least two years between the time they finished undergraduate studies and the time they began the doctoral program. Data from twenty-five pairs of continuous and discontinuous students were analyzed.

In addition to exploring intellectual ability, researchers looked for two things: satisfaction with the program and commitment to complete the program. All the students involved in the research took the Graduate Record Examination, and no differences were noted between the two groups. And interestingly enough, there were no differences between the two groups of students in terms of their satisfaction with the program and their commitment to complete the program.

Of course it could be argued that the number of students was small, and even the discontinuous students were still relatively young.

We can observe several rather obvious differences between traditional and returning students. Where traditional students are primarily students, returning students are not. The returning student is first and foremost a business person, a homemaker, a parent of children, a community volunteer, a professional person, and a host of other roles that are a part of the lives of adults in our society. The role of student has to take its place among all the other roles.

Ralph Tyler also points out an important difference between traditional and returning students: "The returning students are not distracted by a variety of problems that concern growing up. Young people growing up question whether they will be able to get a job, will they be able to marry and make that kind of adjustment, will they really be able to take adult responsibilities. These returning students have already demonstrated that they can take adult responsibilities. They have some ideas of the sorts of jobs they want, although they are less certain of their ability to prepare for them because of having been out for a time. The older students worry often whether they can really get back into the harness and learn again, but they're much more straightforward in their goals and less ambivalent about what it is they want to accomplish while they're in college."

In addition to that mentioned above, we can look at the broad range of differences between traditional and returning students in four major areas: (1) life experience, (2) motivation, (3) academic behavior, and (4) problems faced.

Life Experience

Anyone who has worked with returning students is immediately aware of the great wealth of experience these adult learners bring to the classroom. As we will see later, this can be both an asset and a problem to instructors of returning students.

As a professor I interviewed said, "I teach a course in local government. Many of the undergraduate, traditional students don't give a darn about local government. Why? Their only association with local government may have been getting a traffic ticket from a police officer. Occasionally they may be aware of their parents' having had property annexed, and they're paying more city taxes, and they're getting their garbage picked up by a city truck instead of by a man who owns his own . . . but they don't find much to relate to.

"But for the returning student, things are different. Most of the people who were in my class last fall were either in a public agency or a semipublic agency. Most of them have from two to fifteen years' experience, and they've begun to raise questions. They raise questions about the future, where they are, where they're going, what's going to happen, and what they need to do. The returning students' environment is a work environment and a social environment. There is little I need to do to get returning students interested in the topics I teach."

Another professor I interviewed used a personal example of when he, as a returning student, was in graduate school and compared this experience with the traditional graduate students he works with now: "I recall when I started graduate school I was one of those who had taken time out from undergraduate and graduate school. Those of us who did that, most of us anyway, were involved in some kind of political or dissent movement, or some kind of civil rights activity. Some of us were involved in radical politics, some in the peace movement of the late 1940s and early 50s. When we came back to graduate school, we were a rather organized, sometimes quite politically motivated group of students. We had seen a lot of things outside of the classroom.

"About the time I was leaving graduate school, all of that changed. We began to see a group of young kids, and they were really young—twenty-one, twenty-two, twenty-three. They were very energetic but stupid, narrow, and with no sense of what life was about. They knew how to take examinations and that was it. The returning students bring with them a much broader sense of what life's all about. The traditional students are more oriented toward taking tests. They're wordsmiths who snow professors."

Of course all the many and varied experiences brought to the classroom by returning students also make the class extremely varied. As another instructor pointed out to me, these returning students are "much richer in terms of their personalities. They're more diverse in terms of class, social background, culture, and occupational experience." The traditional students, she said, "have led cookie-cutter lives, and as students they are not as intrinsically interesting."

Another longtime professor said it this way: "Working with the undergraduate who has had little experience is like dropping a pebble down a very deep well and waiting for it to hit, but it never hits. With an older student it hits mighty fast. Older students get the point quickly."

Motivation

Nearly every instructor I interviewed for this project commented about the motivation of the returning student. As one professor said, "Motivation to learn is high; it is the force that drove them back to college."

In comparing the returning student to the traditional student, another said, "They're much more purposeful. They know what they want, and therefore, they're much more highly motivated. They are willing to give an extra effort because they have a goal."

Several instructors said the difference in motivation between the traditional and the returning student often related to the reason for being in school. Many traditional students are in school because their families expect them to be there, they haven't thought of any alternative to being in school, their friends are all in college, and so on. Many of them do not have a clear goal as to why they are there. For the returning student, the goal for being in school is usually much more clear, and thus the motivation is much more goal specific.

One instructor mentioned a side benefit of the high motivation that returning students have. In his opinion, the highly motivated returning students could compete very well with the traditional students, even when there was a difference in intellectual ability. He said, "The highly motivated returning student can outperform the less motivated traditional student, who is sometimes brighter. Motivation makes the difference."

Academic Behavior

Several differences are apparent when we compare traditional and returning students in terms of academic behavior. As we might expect, the traditional student's learning approach is highly influenced by formal education. The returning student's learning approach is more often influenced by informal education. This is only logical. Traditional students are continuing students. They have spent many years in the formal classroom by the time they arrive in college. In one sense, they know no alternative to formal learning, even though their lives may include many opportunities for informal education.

Returning students have spent many years learning since they left a formal school situation. They have been participants in community meetings of various types, such as parent-teacher organizations. They learn from the radio, TV, newspapers, and magazines they read. They learn from church and volunteer work in which they have participated. They learn from the social activities of which they have been a part. This learning is clearly informal, often unstructured, and often not even called learning by those who participate in it.

Traditional students, because they have spent the majority of their lives in a classroom, are less sure of themselves in informal learning situations; in fact they often doubt the value of informal learning. Many are of the opinion that unless a teacher is involved, and unless it happens in a classroom, somehow it is not education. Any learning that may result is of less quality than that learning which results from classroom experiences.

It is clearly understandable why this should be. When people have spent their lives in the classroom, where diplomas and degrees and grades are given high value by our society, it is little wonder that some persons might question the value of informal education and the learning that results.

Another difference between the returning student and the traditional student relates to educational routine. Traditional students are well acquainted with academic rules, regulations, and campus routine. They know how to work the system; they know how to get the courses they want during registration. They know how to use the library and find books that seem not to be available. They have contacts with examination files and students who have taken courses before them. They are aware of which instructors to avoid if possible, and which to attempt to get. They know how to arrange their schedules so they can have maximum free time for study. They are professional students.

Returning students, on the other hand, have likely forgotten the various shortcuts they used before when they were in college, if they had even been in college. If they haven't forgotten, they soon discover that it's not the same on campus today compared to when they attended. They are often overwhelmed with the red tape associated with course selection and registration. They are put off by the admission procedure with its concern for past transcripts and batteries of placement tests. So the entire process of returning to the campus can be, and usually is, a bewildering experience for returning students.

Related to the differences in ability to know and use the system to their benefit are the differences in study skills of traditional students compared to returning students.

Initially upon returning to school, older students often have problems with concentration, reading, writing, numbers, and finding resources, compared to younger, traditional students.

Lack of concentration is the first problem that needs to be overcome. Most returning students come from work situations, whether it be the home, a business, or a factory, where interruption is usual and often. It is rare for most of these people to have an hour or two of uninterrupted time in their lives. The phone is ringing, children are crying for attention, a peer wants to talk, and so on. Being able to organize time for study and then being able to concentrate and not waste the time are problems for many returning students. One student said, "I worked so hard to free an hour of time in my schedule to read an assignment, and then I found myself daydreaming, or my mind flitting back to the supper meal or a child that is not doing well in school—a thousand interruptions crying for my thinking attention."

Then there is the problem of reading. Most adults (children too, for that matter) have not learned how to read. That's not to say that they can't understand the words they see on the printed page. But the tendency is to expect to read everything in the same way. In many college courses, particularly in the social sciences and the humanities, the reading lists are long and often include entire books to be read. The student who believes that he or she must read all these materials in the same way is soon far behind in course work and feeling quite insecure about being a student. (For those interested in exploring alternative approaches to reading, I would refer them to *Study Skills: For Those Adults Returning to School.*[1] This book also has information about schedule planning, writing, vocabulary building, taking notes, using resources effectively, and taking examinations.) Learning how to read intelligently is one of the first skills returning students must master, for they usually have limited reading time.

For many returning students, writing is also a problem. One of the instructors interviewed for this project said, "Many of the returning students have been in jobs or in work where written communication was not important. They could read the instructions, or what have you, but beyond that they have problems. One returning student came to my office to talk about a paper he had written and said, 'Professor, I tell you, I've always had trouble makin' them verbs and nouns match up.' "

On the positive side, though many of the returning students lack or are rusty with their basic writing skills, they are much more likely to reflect their own thinking in what they write than to rely totally on reference material. As a professor said, "They're much more likely to say, 'I think . . .' and not reference every other line. Kids coming right out of undergraduate school believe that when you write a term paper you reference, and you should not have your own thoughts expressed. These older students— they have their own thoughts, and they are very likely to commit them to paper."

Skill in the use of numbers is a problem for many returning students. As several of the instructors I interviewed pointed out, use of numbers is a particular problem for the older women who are returning to school. One professor said, "In my last statistics class I did more tutoring with older women than anybody else in the class." Those interested in following up the problem that is commonly referred to as "math anxiety" should refer to Sheila Tobias's work about this problem and how to overcome it.[2]

A related problem many returning students have with numbers is knowing how to do various procedures without an understanding of the meaning of the procedure. "I had a woman in class some years ago who could do mathematical procedures faster than anyone I've ever seen," one of the professors said. "She happened to be a chemist. She could do it quickly, but she didn't have the foggiest notion of what was implied by the correct answer. She said she'd gone through a parochial school where she learned algebra. The teacher had a little wand. Every time she made a mistake the teacher whacked her across the fingers. She had learned how to do algebra, but she never understood what it meant."

Closed-mindedness and open-mindedness were mentioned by some of the instructors interviewed. One professor said, when describing the returning students he knew, "Many of them come with a set of values of right and wrong and there's no in-between. Consequently, for some students, it takes a while before we can get a clean enough slate to begin the learning process."

But this position was refuted by other instructors. As a professor who worked with many women returning students said, "Returning students are not as likely as the traditional student to think there is Truth out there somewhere that they can find. I think they are far more comfortable with the sort of ambiguity we find in the social sciences. They don't seem to have the need to put everything into little boxes the way the younger, more traditional student does. And I think this makes it both more difficult and more exciting for the instructor."

Although most returning students have some problems with study skills upon returning to school, the vast majority are able to overcome them in a relatively short period of time. For those coming back to full-time study, six weeks to two months seems to be the minimum time for adults to become students again, with sharpened study skills. Some will take most of a semester. Those coming back part-time may take a year, even more, to become comfortable once more with reading, writing, using the library, and the other skills necessary to be an effective student.

Returning students are serious students. "They've allocated time and money to getting a degree or at least improving their marketability as a professional. They're not likely to mess around very much; they want to get on with it," pointed out one of the professors I talked with. Another professor said, "Returning students are more serious in a positive sort of way; they take things more seriously; in fact, they take things too seriously sometimes. I find them to be extremely responsible and reliable in terms of having worked on or fulfilling assignments." And still another said, "I think it's true that older students don't want to fool around. They want to get down to business . . . and they want their money's worth. They're not interested in a lot of talk; they want the real stuff."

This professor went on to give an example of a situation that often disturbs the older returning student: "I'm told by students that in many classes it takes fifteen minutes for the class to get started—administrative stuff . . . and the teacher often spends a lot of time telling stories, throwing his or her ego around . . . the usual kind of thing. The older students don't have time for that."

A sociology professor offered still another example of the seriousness of returning students: "Students who are the traditional types, who have come through undergraduate school into graduate school here, know very well that when you have a reading list from a professor with twenty books on it, if you read one and a couple of book reviews you can get by. Getting by and getting a good grade are important to these more traditional students. On the other hand, the older, returning student takes more seriously the suggested readings, those required readings, and wants to do it all, wants to learn something about these things. They don't want to read just enough to pass an exam. I've seen much more anxiety among the returning students over whether there's time enough to do all the reading."

The relationship to instructors is also different when we compare traditional with returning students. As a professor said, "Returning students are argumentative. They are more inclined to question material that is presented. They are more inclined to sort or filter material that is presented through their own life experience and reject some and accept some on the basis of that kind of criterion."

Another instructor pointed out very succinctly, "The returning student is ready to work. They want the class to work, and they want the instructor to work."

The literature of adult education talks about the self-directed nature of the adult learner. Although many adult learners do enjoy and even expect to have the opportunity to be self-directed in their learning, at least initially upon returning to school they expect, and often need, some structure.

One professor noted, "It's assumed that older students are ready to take responsibility for their own learning. Yes and no. They chafe under authority at some points. They often question the teacher who attempts to be profound in wisdom and knowledge and is telling them what to do. But at the same time they have a need for structure."

I'll say more about the power relationship between the instructor and the student later. But let it suffice to say that, particularly for the new returning student, there is sometimes a perceived tension between the instructor as authority figure (in a structured learning situation), and the instructor as resource person and learning facilitator (in a relatively unstructured learning situation).

Because learning is change and not simply the accumulation or the adding of something, there is constant reorganization and restructuring. For many returning students this involves unlearning, for some a most difficult task. For many returning students the difficulty is not in dealing with what is new but in relating what is new to what has previously been learned. As William S. More points out, "We have to undertake this process of unlearning frequently in our lives, particularly when we become adult students. And it is the experience of most adult students that this is very often not an easy task. It is not an easy task because it is tied up with the whole problem of attitude change. All of our behavior is an expression of what we are and what life has made us, and this includes the attitudes which we have developed. Everything we do reflects what we think and feel about people, events, objects and phenomena."[3]

Problems Faced

As I pointed out above, many returning students have problems adjusting to school—problems with concentration and time use, problems with study skills, problems relating to instructors and class situations, and problems with unlearning. In addition to these academically related problems, returning students have other problems that set them apart from the younger, more traditional students. Four major categories of problems can be identified: (1) unrealistic goals, (2) poor self-image, (3) social-familial problems, and (4) a sometimes excessive practical orientation. Let's look at each of these.

As Ralph Tyler pointed out, "Some of the returning students have unrealistic goals, especially persons who have been out of school for quite a while. Take the woman who has spent considerable time in the home raising a family. Conditions have changed for what is required in an occupation. When she returns to school and begins to discover that it's going to take her much more time than she first anticipated, she's likely to modify her program because time is more important to her than it is to a younger person."

An implication of this is, of course, having counseling available for returning students so they know what is required before they launch into a program of study.

Negative self-image is a problem for many returning students. Malcolm Knowles, one of the instructors I interviewed and a national figure in adult education, said, "There's kind of a negative self-image that's been developed from years out of academia, and now, as they come back into academia, they're wondering, 'Will I look dumb? Will I look silly? Will I fail?' And so a good deal of attention has to be paid to helping them build a positive self-image, and particularly by giving them some success experience early in their tenure as returning students."

Annis Pratt, an English professor I interviewed, talked about a thirty-five-year-old woman who had returned to school. "She had a writing block and this is often typical of an older student. She thought she had a congenital inability to write. Well, many of my traditional undergraduate students have writing blocks. But it's easier to talk them out of it than it is to talk an older student out of it. The older student has been running around for ten years thinking she can't write. The older students tend to be more frightened and have more writing blocks.

"This woman I mentioned produced three brilliant papers, but each one caused an agony. . . . the older student coming back to school and into an English writing course goes into shock."

Probably the most common nonacademic problem faced by returning students, particularly those married and with families, has to do with changing life-styles and problems related to spouse and children.

As David Mustian, a sociology professor I interviewed, pointed out, "Most of the returning students have been established for some period, carrying on careers and having a means of livelihood. Then they come back to school and try to be, as one older student said, a 'real student' again. They encounter a number of stresses in home life. Whether the spouse is supportive or not to what they are doing is often a problem. Most of these students have taken a tremendous change in monetary support. They're living on shoestring budgets. A number of them say they don't spend the time they want with their children. So their children are paying a price for them being in school, in their minds."

Gayle Ness, another sociology professor, observed that returning students have "the immediate and understandable problems of having a wider variety of constraints than traditional students . . . demands on them, family and children, and so on. It is often difficult for them to manage, so they cannot spend hours a day shooting the bull with other students and going to classes. They have other claims on their time and they move back and forth between these. And that produces a considerable tension. We see some divorces, particularly women who are coming back and then they begin to split apart from their husbands and marriages fall apart."

As we have pointed out earlier, returning students are serious and highly motivated. They also tend to be highly practical. They want to see a direct relationship of what they are studying to a possible career or job opportunity. They expect to see how all the pieces of a college curriculum fit together. All of these can be and often are positive attributes—though they may be challenging to professors and administrators who have not had these questions raised before.

But on the other hand, an extreme emphasis on the practical can be a negative characteristic as well and can be viewed as a problem for the returning student. Some returning students are in search of easy answers, answers that appear to be practical and allow them to move forward with their studies.

In describing a situation where a student was looking for an easy answer, a professor of sociology and anthropology pointed out, "I talk about a theoretical framework, and I have students write a paper outlining a research project. Some of them come into my office and start looking around as if to say, 'Now I know you got some of those little rascals around here someplace. Why can't you pull one out and let me have it?' " They assumed the research proposal was an exercise, rather than an activity for each student to develop individually.

Summary

Although returning students are similar to traditional students in some respects, the two groups also differ in several important ways. The major areas of difference are (1) life experience—the returning students bring a wealth of experience to the classroom; (2) motivation—the returning students are highly motivated, with this motivation often related to a specific goal for attending college; (3) academic behavior—returning students often have problems adjusting to university life, including learning academic procedures, rusty study skills, inability to concentrate, and adjusting to problems associated with unlearning; and (4) other problems—unrealistic goals, poor self-image, social-familial problems, and sometimes an excessive practical orientation.

NOTES

1. Jerold W. Apps, *Study Skills: For Those Adults Returning to School,* 2nd ed. (New York: McGraw-Hill, 1981).

2. Sheila Tobias, *Overcoming Math Anxiety* (New York: W. W. Norton, 1978).

3. William S. More, *Emotions and Adult Learning* (Lexington, Mass.: D. C. Heath and Co., 1974), p. 19.

Chapter 4

The Learning Environment: Societal Influences

We now shift to an examination of the returning student's learning environment. In this chapter I will concentrate on the societal influences on the learning environment for returning students. In the following chapter I will examine the traditional influences. But to understand learning environment, we first must look at learning itself, and how I am using the term.

Learning Defined

Educators, particularly those who research and write about education, have difficulty agreeing on what the term *learning* means. For some, learning is defined as a change in behavior—the behaviorists take this position. For others, learning is personal development; for still others, it is developing the mind. Many talk about learning as the accumulation of knowledge, and still others talk about learning as a problem-solving activity.[1] A common element in all the various definitions of learning is change. A person who has learned is somehow different than he or she was before the learning took place. The change may be a new idea the learner has acquired or even a new way of understanding an old idea. The person who has learned may now have a new skill he or she can perform or a new insight gained from solving a problem.

As we mentioned earlier (in chapter 3), adult learning often involves unlearning as well.

Another dilemma in understanding learning is the difference between "random learning" and "planned learning." Random learning is what we learn through the process of living. It is ongoing and occurs almost all the time. When we take a walk and observe something along the way we haven't seen before, we are experiencing random learning. When we read a novel and discover an insight into an interpersonal relationship that applies to our lives, we have experienced random learning. It is that learning for which we have not planned. We have not planned it for ourselves, and no one else has planned it for us. It is also possible to experience random learning in a planned learning situation. For instance, returning students attending a class on American history may learn a great deal about their skills as writers from the instructor who reads portions of their written assignments to the entire class. Yet assessing writing ability is not mentioned as one of the objectives of the course.

Planned learning is deliberate. It is either learning we have designed for ourselves or learning that others have designed for us. When we participate in a class, as students, we are participating in planned learning. When we organize a self-directed project (perhaps we want to learn how to make wine and we select some books from the library and talk with a friend who makes wine), we are participating in planned learning.

Education is thus planned learning. Or to be more formal, education is an organized and planned activity with the intent that learning will result. So what we are talking about in this chapter and the one following are the influences on the total learning environment, as it specifically applies to the returning student. We are concerned about both planned learning and random learning, but our emphasis will be on planned learning.

A Holistic View

Several obvious elements make up a learning environment where the emphasis is on planned learning. These include the learner, what is to be learned, the teacher (who in self-directed learning situations is also the learner), and the physical setting in which the teaching and learning occur.

Many educators would have you believe that once the educator is aware of each of these factors he or she knows what is necessary to be an effective teacher. In fact some educators take an even narrower view. As one educator wrote: "The key . . . for optimizing the learning process is to divide the course into a number of learning units, define all the skills, attributes, and competencies that your course is to require of the student. Then, using the basic principles of learning, choose the instructional format and learning activities that will create the most efficient learning outcomes for the student in achieving the objectives that you have set for him to accomplish. It is a systematic design procedure which can't help but be successful for the student and provide hero medals for the instructor."[2]

The approach so clearly and precisely outlined above will work in many situations. But in many situations it will not "create the most efficient learning outcomes," particularly when working with older returning students. Why not? Because several influences on the learning environment are not included in this rather simplistic recipe.

Learning environments for returning students must be thought of holistically; that is, all that affects the lives of the returning students also affects them as learners. We cannot look at returning students in isolation from the rest of their lives.

The holistic view of the learning environment is even more dynamic than simply assessing a series of influences that affect the learner. The various influences on the learning environment often affect each other. For instance, one of the societal influences on the learning environment is the knowledge explosion we are experiencing. The knowledge explosion often affects instructors who are impressed with the vast increases in information in their fields of inquiry and feel compelled to include increasingly more information in their courses.

What I have not done is to indicate which of the many influences on the learning environment are more important. The learning environment for the returning student is extremely complex. It compels both instructors and administrators of programs for returning students first to be aware of the influences and, second, to work toward changing those influences that can be changed in a way that will enhance the learning environment.

Below I discuss several societal influences on the returning student's learning environment. The influences mentioned are not of the same order. Some are specific and relate solely to the learner Others are much more inclusive and in one way or another affect several aspects of the returning student's life.

The Learner's Family

If a spouse is not supportive of a learner's return to school, if the learner's children succeed in making the returning student feel guilty, the returning student can be greatly affected. Sometimes a family situation is such that a divorce is triggered by a spouse returning to school, or the returning student is forced to drop out of school to maintain a marriage. See chapter 6 for more about guilt, particularly as it affects women returning to school.

Economic Situation

There is little the economic situation of the country does not affect in one way or another. And thus it must be considered as an important dimension of the learning environment for the returning student.

The inflation rate in the United States (at this writing) has a profound effect on the lives of everyone. Many women have found it necessary to return to the work force for families to maintain a level of income to which they have been accustomed. For many of these women, particularly those who aspire to a level of work that pays more and has greater challenge, returning to a college or a university for additional training is the first step before seeking employment. Many of these women are already employed in the lower-paying jobs and will continue to be so as they pursue a college education on a part-time basis.

Of course the soaring inflation rate in the country has a great effect on the educational institutions themselves. Many of the innovations that may be necessary to make learning opportunities for returning students more positive simply can't be afforded. At least that is the view taken by many colleges and universities. I am talking about such innovations as revised curricula to take into account the specific needs of the older returning student. I am talking about keeping the library open during unusual hours to accommodate part-time students. I mean offering classes on weekends and in the evenings. I mean providing some of the course materials in audiovisual, self-study packages. In one way or another each of these changes, some merely structural in nature, costs the institution additional dollars that they do not have.

Some institutions respond to tax cuts and limited or dwindling support by cutting back to what the institutions consider the basics. They retrench themselves much as a turtle does when it perceives adversity in its path. Unfortunately, with its head pulled into its shell, not much of anything happens. And these institutions become prime candidates for closing their doors.

At the same time that inflation is having an adverse effect on the operating costs of colleges and universities, those that are tax supported also face limited increases in tax dollar resources and even, in many instances, actual decreases. Translated into operating decisions, many colleges and universities are faced with cutting programs. And sometimes the cuts are most easily made with those programs that are new and not yet completely accepted—programs for returning students, for instance. Another response to tax cuts is for institutions to raise their tuition costs to cover the less than adequate tax support. This has the effect of keeping away from the institutions many returning students who simply can't afford the higher tuition rates.

Another related aspect of the economic situation in this country is career changing. Many adults, both men and women, change jobs three or four times, sometimes more, during their working years. And as I pointed out earlier, many people interested in career change see formal education as a way to accomplish the change.

So the current economic situation in this country has and will likely continue to have a great effect on the learning environment for the returning student. In terms of the classroom, the instructor, and the curriculum, one impact of the economic situation is the return of students to school with a single-minded interest in vocationalism and career development.

Knowledge Explosion

The so-called knowledge explosion we have experienced in the world during the last century, and that we continue to experience today with ever increasing intensity, has a profound effect on the learning environment of returning students.

In a high-technology society thousands of new ideas, many of which result from highly sophisticated scientific research, are available every year. These ideas change the nature of work in many businesses and industries, and workers are forced to learn in order to keep their jobs. Some of these workers, particularly those in the professions, return to colleges and universities to maintain their job skills. Many professionals are forced to return to school by federal or state laws designed to make certain that designated professionals are keeping up to date with the new knowledge. Also, professional organizations, such as organizations of attorneys (state bars), require their members to participate in continuing education activities to keep their licenses to practice.

The results of mandatory continuing education have a profound effect, not only on the professionals who may participate only because they are forced to, but also on the learning environment generally. One of the hallmarks of adult education has been its voluntary nature. Adults usually participate because they want to, not because they are forced to. Mandatory continuing education is on the increase across the country. But the effects on the overall learning environment of increasing numbers of adults who are forced to attend classes is not yet known. What is known are the problems associated with forced attendance at the elementary and secondary levels of education. Ivan Illich, John Holt, and others have written extensively about these problems.

Many people, both inside and outside education, view educational institutions and teaching as following a market model. A supply of information is accumulated in warehouses called educational institutions. These institutions organize advertising campaigns to stir up interest in their information products so consumers (students) will buy them. Educators and media serve as the transporters of this information from the institutional warehouses to the people who buy it.

With an increasing supply of information (the knowledge explosion), educational institutions are constantly searching for more efficient delivery systems so that more information can be moved from warehouse to consumer in less time and for less cost. Little is done, unfortunately, to decide which of the truckloads of information is worth moving out of the warehouse. And there is usually no concern about the meaning of this information to the student purchaser. The assumption is that the information will have an equal meaning to everyone, or that it is someone else's responsibility to worry about meaning and not the educational institution's.

This attitude toward the educational process appears to be on the increase and affects the learning environment of returning students, particularly those students who attend institutions where this attitude is prevalent.

A Search for Meaning

At the same time that large numbers of adults are returning to school with career and occupational interests, a sizable number of adults are returning to add another dimension to their lives, to add a sense of meaning. These adults are employed, usually in well-paying jobs. They have already acquired considerable formal education; many of them have at least one college degree. But now they are returning to school because either they felt their previous formal schooling was too vocationally oriented and they want to explore new, broader areas of inquiry, or they were introduced to a liberal arts education and now, when they are older, more experienced, and more mature, want to pursue these ideas further. More than twenty colleges and universities around the country have established or are establishing special degree programs for returning students with an emphasis on arts, humanities, and sciences.

Moorhead State University in Moorhead, Minnesota, represents one of the newcomers with its Master of Liberal Arts program designed specifically for the returning student. Johns Hopkins University has an older, more established program in this area.

So the returning student with an interest in a broader, more liberal-arts-type education and with little or no direct vocational interest in the curriculum is another influence on the learning environment that in some ways runs at cross purposes to the returning student with a vocational interest.

Population Shift

As we pointed out in chapter 1, the median age of the population of the United States is increasing. This trend means decreasing numbers of traditional-age college students. Predictions vary as to the extent traditional-student numbers will decline, but there is general agreement there will be a decline.

How convenient for educational institutions that adults are returning to school in increasingly larger numbers to fill the chairs vacated by the traditional-age students. At least so it would seem. But as George Bonham, editor of *Change* magazine, points out, "Even when the potential learners are out there, the ability of traditional campuses to accommodate them must still be seriously questioned. Serving sizable numbers of adults in transition with major success may also require a fundamental transformation of the entire college community."[3]

Thus how colleges and universities respond to declining enrollments of traditional students will affect the learning environment of returning students, either positively or negatively, depending on the response. (See chapter 12 for a more in-depth discussion of college and university changes suggested by increasing numbers of returning students.)

Negative Image of Adult Education

One of the major reasons why many colleges and universities will not and are not moving quickly to accommodate large numbers of returning students is the negative image adult education has in many higher-education institutions. For many people adult education is viewed as something men and women do to keep themselves occupied—learning to knit, learning the latest in French cookery, studying carpentry, learning to belly dance. Many educators view adult education as superficial, unimportant, and sometimes simply silly.

As Fred Harvey Harrington, a former president of the University of Wisconsin system, points out, "Despite the gains, adult education is not yet recognized as a full partner in most colleges and universities. Attitudes include indifference, skepticism (especially as to quality), and even open opposition, most noticeable in the colleges of liberal arts."[4]

Harrington quotes a 1968 poll reported in the *Chronicle of Higher Education* that a cross section of faculty members put adult education thirty-seventh in importance among forty-seven college and university functions. These faculty members put adult education far behind faculty rights, research, and undergraduate teaching.

There has no doubt been some improvement in the attitude of faculty toward adult education in the years since 1968, especially with the reality of declining enrollments haunting the professional positions of many faculty members. But one needs only talk with faculty members long identified with traditional-age college students to learn that much negativism about adult education remains.

To further make the point, Harrington quotes a response he received when he asked a faculty member about adult education. "Adult education," this faculty person snorted. "That means second-rate courses taught by second-rate teachers to second-rate students."[5]

A view that somehow the education of adults is an inferior activity when compared to the education of youth has and will continue to have a profound effect on the returning students' learning opportunities. Because the education of adults is assumed by some instructors to be superficial and without standards, they will proceed to make it so. Because the education of adults is second-rate, why expend any resources on the activity? These are some of the obvious effects of adult education's image on the learning environment.

Lack of Understanding of Adult Education

Directly related to the poor image of adult education is the rather poor understanding of it. Those who do not understand adult education include prospective students, traditional faculty members, administrators, and even many who call themselves adult educators. What people have experienced in adult education is usually the extent of their knowledge of it. If a person has taken a course in financial management taught by an ad hoc instructor, this is his or her image of adult education. If another person was part of a community development group led by an extension agent, this is adult education for that person.

Few have an understanding of the breadth of adult-education offerings, both those that are degree and credit related as well as those that are not.

Lack of understanding can have a great effect on the learning opportunities for returning students, particularly if the instructors and the administrators involved do not have an image of adult education in the college classroom.

Business-Industrial Model

In our highly competitive, high-technology society, business and industry have become increasingly concerned with speed, efficiency, and cost effectiveness. Considerable emphasis is placed on measuring outputs based on inputs. And in recent years management by objectives (MBO) has become quite popular in many business firms.

Many business leaders also hold positions of importance in higher education, serving on boards of regents, boards of trustees, alumni associations, and the like. And likewise, many college and university officials also serve on the boards of directors of businesses. From this close association of business and industry with colleges and universities, it is probably inevitable that leaders in these two endeavors would borrow ideas from each other. Thus many colleges and universities have borrowed heavily from the management ideas that serve business and industry, resulting in some problems for colleges and universities and having no small effect on learning opportunities for returning students.

Although I won't dwell on the matter here, critics of our present business-industrial society quickly point out that the system followed by business and industry doesn't work well there either. As Erich Fromm points out, "Man, as a cog in the production machine, becomes a thing, and ceases to be human. He spends his time doing things in which he is not interested, with people in whom he is not interested, producing things in which he is not interested; and when he is not producing, he is consuming."[6]

Aside from the problems associated with how business and industry operate, the assumption that educational institutions can follow the same procedures is ludicrous. Learning is not a commodity that can be compared to profits. We cannot assume that, given so many inputs of instructor lectures, or library books, or student loans, we can expect a predictable output of learning.

Following the business-industrial model of education, we find educators designing educational programs based entirely on behavioral objectives, written in such a way that learning outcomes can be measured. The procedure has considerable appeal to taxpayers and decision makers who have to defend college and university budgets. Unfortunately the approach of tightly defined, measurable behavioral objectives provides a narrow, incomplete educational experience at best. Worse, it may sour learners toward further education or condition them to seeing education and learning as mechanical and preplanned.

The effects of the business-industrial approach on the returning student's learning opportunities are many. Rather than opening up the returning student to a new adventure in learning, with perhaps an emphasis on occupational preparation, and also preparing the learner for a life of learning, a strict adherence to the business model as I have described it cripples learners. The returning student should have the opportunity to explore, to examine ideas that go beyond those described in the course syllabus, and to have the opportunity to bring into the learning situation past experiences that relate to what is being discussed. Not only should the returning student have an opportunity to gain new knowledge, but there should be ample opportunity for the returning student to be able to discover the personal meaning of the new knowledge. Otherwise the learning is shallow and incomplete, though it may be sufficient to pass a test and convince a writer of behavioral objectives that the objectives of the learning experience have indeed been met.

A related dimension of the learning environment is an extreme emphasis on accountability. Again, a narrow interpretation of learning leads to easy measurement and a satisfaction of those who insist (for good reason, I might add) that educational institutions be accountable for the tax dollars spent.

Though not discussed here, there are ways and means for education to be accountable for its efforts without adopting an evaluation procedure designed for business and industry, where profits can be measured against dollars expended.[7]

Summary

The learning environment for the returning student includes much more than student, teacher, classroom, and textbook. In this chapter I introduced the idea of the learning environment as including everything that affects the life of the returning student and the institution where he or she wishes to pursue further education. I explored several influences on the learning environment, including (1) the learner's family, (2) the economic situation, (3) the knowledge explosion, (4) a search for meaning, (5) the population shift, (6) the negative image of adult education, (7) the lack of understanding of adult education, and (8) the business-industrial model.

NOTES

1. See Jerold W. Apps, *Problems in Continuing Education* (New York: McGraw-Hill, 1979), pp. 150–161, for a further discussion of various approaches to defining learning.

2. Lee Harrisberger, "So I Want to Change, What Do I Do Now?" *American Society for Engineering Education*, Proceed-

ings of the 1977 College Industry Education Conference.

3. George W. Bonham, "Inching Toward the Learning Society," *Change,* July–August 1979.

4. Fred Harvey Harrington, *The Future of Adult Education* (San Francisco: Jossey-Bass, 1977), p. 5.

5. *Ibid.,* p. 7.

6. Erich Fromm, *The Revolution of Hope* (New York: Bantam, 1968), p. 40.

7. See the following as examples of approaches to accountability that go beyond a simple input-output approach: Arthur W. Combs et al., *The Professional Education of Teachers: A Humanistic Approach to Teacher Preparation* (Boston: Allyn and Bacon, 1974), chap. 10; and Don E. Gardner, "Five Evaluation Frameworks: Implications for Decision-Making in Higher Education," *Journal of Higher Education,* vol. 48, no. 5, September–October 1977, pp. 571–93.

Chapter 5

The Learning Environment: Traditional Influences

Traditional influences on the learning environment for returning students include the students, the instructor, what is to be learned, and the setting for learning.

The Returning Student

Each returning student brings much to the learning setting that affects the learning environment, both positively and negatively. What returning students bring not only influences their own learning opportunities but also often affects other learners.

Some of these influences I have already mentioned, such as the reasons for returning to school, the varied life experiences returning students bring to the learning setting, the level of motivation for learning, how these students relate to academic rules and regulations, and the problems many have with study skills and adjustment to academic life during the first few months they are back in school.

In the next chapter I'll discuss many characteristics of the adult that affect his or her learning progress, such as change in abilities to function with age, the ability to learn, intelligence, memory, generational differences, psychological barriers, and adult life cycles.

The Instructor

In any planned learning situation the instructor is a critical element, unless of course we're talking about self-directed learning, where learners plan their own learning. Here, though, our focus is on the learning setting where there is an instructor.

For returning students, the instructor is often the key to their success, sometimes the key to their even continuing in school. The early experience returning students have with their instructors upon returning to school often has a considerable effect on their future success as students.

Two characteristics of the instructor are essential to the success of returning students: the instructor's skills as a teacher and the instructor's working philosophy.

Instructor's Skills

Although some progress has been made to elevate the prestige of college teaching, teaching as a function still drags far behind the prestige of research and scholarly writing. True, many colleges and universities now provide teaching awards of one kind or another and give some publicity to outstanding teaching. Nevertheless, it is the outstanding researcher that is given the greater acclaim.

Aside from the recognition that universities, and society in general, give to outstanding researchers, there are other reasons why colleges and universities have an abundance of average and below-average teachers.

Christopher Jencks and David Riesman maintain college teaching is not a profession in the same way research is. They write, "There is no guild within which successful teaching leads to greater prestige and influences mediocre teaching, nor any professional training program that develops pedagogic skills in a systematic way. . . . Under these circumstances it is hardly surprising that a great deal of teaching at both the graduate and undergraduate level is dull and ineffective. No form of success that depends on luck and individual initiative is ever widespread."[1]

Few graduate programs that prepare college teachers give any attention to the teaching process itself. Graduate students working to become college professors spend many hours attending research methodology classes and statistics courses. They work in the laboratory or in the field collecting data. They work with a computer to analyze the data collected and then devote hours to writing and revising and, finally, defending a piece of research. Prospective college professors spend half their graduate training, and sometimes even more than half, learning to be researchers and scholarly reporters. The rest of the time is spent attending subject-matter courses where the student's field is studied in considerable depth.

These college teachers in training will often take not even one course, workshop, or seminar related to college teaching. To be sure, many graduate students work as teaching assistants, supervised by experienced professors who guide them in sharpening their teaching skills. But the experienced teachers are often themselves poor teachers, for they have come through the same system that the graduate students they supervise are experiencing. If by luck of the draw the graduate student happens to work with an outstanding teacher, and there are some of these around in spite of the system, then he or she may receive better than average preparation for the profession of college teaching. But this happens by accident, not by design—and it happens quite infrequently.

Two reasons often given for poor college teaching are large college classes and the demand that teachers must publish as well as teach. Both these reasons have some merit, but they are more excuses than reasons. Not only is there poor teaching in large classes, but there is also poor teaching in small classes. And, as I shall point out in greater detail later, publishing and teaching can often complement each other.

Steven Cahn says the reasons for low-level competence among college teachers is the inability of higher education "to recognize the crucial principle that intellectual competence and pedagogic competence are two very different qualities. One cannot be an outstanding teacher without knowledge of subject matter, but to possess that knowledge does not guarantee the ability to communicate it to a student. And this ability is by no means easy to acquire. The number of great teachers is as small as the number of great artists or scientists. And just as an artist needs to master necessary skills, so a teacher must do the same."[2]

Cahn suggests that college teachers teach fifth graders for a time. Fifth graders will not put up with poor teaching. They throw paper airplanes, make faces at their neighbors, and otherwise show their disapproval of poor teaching. Traditional college-age students fall asleep and the college instructor, who lacks teaching skills, has no positive feedback about his inadequacy. Returning older students are more like fifth graders; they will not put up with poor teaching.

Several issues relate to college teaching and the returning student. What should be the amount of involvement for the instructor of adults in the teaching situation? Some argue that instructors who take an indirect role, who encourage students to share experiences and who emphasize the group process for learning, are really not performing their roles as teachers but are encouraging the pooling of ignorance.

On the other side, instructors who take a more direct leadership role in the classroom are accused of fostering a dependency relationship that has been so much a part of formal education. Adult education claims to be developing autonomous learners who are able to sever dependency relationships with instructors, yet the instructor who takes an in-charge leadership role encourages rather than severs dependency relationships.

Another issue is the heavy emphasis on presenting content for its own sake, with little attention to the learning of skills, values, the meaning of the content to the student, and the feelings expressed by the student toward what is learned and how it is learned.

An old issue is whether one particular teaching approach, say group discussion, is better than another, say lecturing. We'll say more about this issue in chapter 8.

It should be obvious that the instructor's skills have a considerable influence on the learning environment for the returning student. But perhaps even more important than the instructor's skills is the instructor's working philosophy. It is the instructor's philosophy that provides a foundation for the approaches the instructor uses inside and outside the classroom as he or she works with returning students.

Instructor's Working Philosophy

Whether aware of it or not, all instructors have some semblance of a philosophy or belief system that guides their behavior. For instance, we all have beliefs about the nature of humans. We may never have written down these beliefs, but we nevertheless have them. And what we believe about the nature of humans provides a foundation for how we relate to other people, and particularly how we see our role as instructors of returning students. That is not to say that how we behave as instructors and our beliefs do not come into conflict and are not at times contradictory with each other. But this conflict is more apt to occur when instructors have not examined their beliefs.[3]

The instructor belief areas that appear to have the greatest relevance for the learning environment of returning students include (1) beliefs about humans, (2) beliefs about returning students, (3) beliefs about teaching and learning as applied to adults, (4) beliefs about knowledge, (5) beliefs about other instructors, and (6) beliefs about the purpose of an educational program for returning students.

Beliefs About Humans

Fundamental to any philosophy for instructors of returning students are their beliefs about the nature of humans. Today's educational literature often includes three views of the nature of human beings: (1) the Freudian view, (2) the behaviorist view, and (3) the humanistic view. Each of these views is prominent today and influences how people see the development of human beings. Educators tend, either explicitly or implicitly, to subscribe to one of these views.

Freudian View   Sigmund Freud (1856–1939) believed that a human's behavior was determined by biological drives and the way each person was able to cope with these drives. Freud believed the human psyche was divided into three sections: the id, the ego, and the superego. The id consisted of the unconscious instincts and urges that come from the adult human's animal origins. Freud believed these unconscious instincts were powerful, antisocial, and irrational. Freud saw the ego as the sum of a person's conscious awareness. The superego was the censor or the sense of conscience a person has derived from society. According to Freud, the id and the superego were in constant conflict. A person's behavior at any given time was the product of a specific inner drive or conflict and the resulting balance that developed among the forces of the id, the superego, and the ego.

The superego was not something each person was born with; it developed as the person learned the customs and morals of society. According to Freud much of the basic direction of a person's life was established in early childhood, often by the age of five. The way Freud saw this basic direction altered was through psychoanalysis. Many of Freud's views were wrapped up with problems each person had with sexual attraction toward the opposite parent. And according to Freud, much of human behavior could be explained by the effects of sexual libido.

Freud also believed that human beings had selfish, aggressive views toward their fellow human beings as a part of their instinctual makeup. Cooperation was possible only when these primary urges were repressed by pressure from society. But when this happened, the individual's true makeup was distorted.

Some of the life-span development research is built on a Freudian base, emphasizing instincts and drives that are a part of each person and thus can be predicted to occur in various modes of behavior during the life span.

Behaviorist View   The behaviorist approach to viewing human beings grows out of the work of such researchers as John B. Watson (1878–1958) and B. F. Skinner of Harvard University.

Floyd Matson sees the behaviorist view of humans as similar to viewing people as machines.[4] Matson argues that the idea of person as machine comes from our society's emphasis on the importance of machines. Because our economy is so dependent on the industrial model, which is in turn dependent on machines, it seems only logical that people in our society begin to see everything in the world in terms of machines, including people.

Matson sees many people working in industry, as well as in many other places in our society, including those areas we call the human services, acting like machines. They go through the motions of some routine activity without any conscious thought of what they are doing, the importance of what they are doing, whether there are better ways of doing what they are doing, and so on. They simply do, as a machine would, without ever questioning. The emphasis is on efficiency and productivity. Questions of purpose, direction, quality, and value get in the way of the twin idols, efficiency and productivity.

The behaviorist approach assumes human behavior is dependent on external, environmental influences. The behaviorists put much emphasis on the idea of stimulus-response as the reason for changes in people's behavior. Their thinking traces back to the work of the Russian psychologist Ivan Pavlov, who demonstrated he could make dogs salivate when he struck a tuning fork, even though he gave them no meat.

Another characteristic of the behaviorists is a close association with the scientific method. The behaviorists are interested in measuring the various stimuli that persons face and measuring the behavioral outcomes that people display.

There are obvious differences between the Freudian view and the behaviorist view of human beings. The Freudians believe that human action is motivated by inner drives and instincts. The behaviorists believe human behavior is caused by external, environmental forces.

Both approaches view the human as an animal, albeit an extremely well developed and complicated animal. Both believe that much human behavior can be predicted.

Humanistic View Beginning in the early 1940s, a new view of humans developed. A new psychology of human behavior appeared that was deeply concerned with people as human beings, and as something more than animals.

Where the Freudians purported that human behavior was influenced by internal drives and instincts, and the behaviorist view proclaimed human behavior as a function of external, environmental influences, this new humanistic view made the radical statement that human beings were free agents, that they were creators of their own future. As Floyd Matson points out, "The central point of the humanistic model is that man is free, in a sense and to a degree unknown to animal, vegetable, or mineral. . . . the claim is that human existence is open ended rather than predetermined, that it is characterized primarily by choice and contingency and chance rather than by compulsion."[5]

Gordon Allport, a psychologist, says the humanistic view of humans "maintains that the person is not a collection of acts, nor simply the locus of acts; the person is the source of acts. And activity itself is not conceived as agitation resulting from pushes by internal or external stimulation. It is purpose. To understand what a person is, it is necessary always to refer to what he may be in the future for every state of the person is pointed in the direction of future possibilities."[6]

Some key words used by humanists to describe the nature of human beings are *active nature, individuality, freedom, dynamic internal world, search for meaning,* and *social dimension.*

Active nature refers to the human's propensity to act on the sensory data he or she receives. Humans do not wait to be acted upon; they have the potential for acting, for creating, for doing. They are not globs of malleable clay to be worked on by outside influences, as the behaviorists suggest. Nor are humans caught up in their animalistic instincts and drives that determine their behavior for the rest of their lives.

Although the humanists would agree that humans share many biological characteristics with one another, each person is nevertheless profoundly unique and different from every other. This individuality contributes to an excitement of being a part of the human race, for every human is an unexpected collection of characteristics and traits.

Freedom is a characteristic the behaviorists claim does not exist in human beings. Every act, they claim, is externally determined. The human organism has no ability to act differently from the way the stimuli presuppose the organism will act. The humanists, on the other hand, claim the human is free to make decisions about life and living. The human is neither determined by internal instincts (Freudian view) nor controlled by environmental stimuli (behaviorist view). Many humanists agree, though, that some human acts are internally influenced and, likewise, some acts are influenced by environmental stimuli.

Mumford writes about the dynamic internal world of the human: "The existence in man of a dynamic internal world, whose essential nature cannot be probed by an instrument, and can be known when it finds expression in gestures and symbols and constructive activities, is a mystery as profound as the focus that binds together the components of the atom and accounts for the character and behavior of the elements. . . . In man that mystery can be experienced, but not described, still less explained: for the mind cannot mirror itself from within. Only by getting outside itself does it become conscious of its inwardness."[7]

Human beings have much more than the potential for survival, claim the humanists. Victor E. Frankl,[8] Joseph R. Royce,[9] and others claim the human being's search for meaning is one of the profound characteristics that set human life apart from other life. A search for meaning, these writers claim, is a lifelong quest of human beings, starting in childhood and continuing on until death. It is an elusive concept that is seldom caught, but constantly sought. When the human person believes he or she has meaning in life, then a new meaning is looked for, in a never-ending search.

Many humanists also see the importance of each human as

part of a larger social order. Paulo Freire is one who says to be a human "is to engage in relationships with others and with the world, it is to experience that world as an objective reality, independent of oneself, capable of being known."[10]

This view suggests humans are, at the same time, influenced by the world and influencers of the world, in a dynamic interaction. Erich Fromm is another psychologist who says humans define their humanity in terms of the society of which they are a part.[11]

Today we see evidence of educators following one of these views of human beings in their day-to-day planning and teaching. Many are not aware that they are following a particular philosophical view because they have never examined what they believe about humans. They have followed the pattern set down in their department, or they have followed a pattern they experienced as students.

Which view of human beings—the Freudian, the behaviorist, or the humanistic—is most consistent with providing a beneficial learning environment for the returning adult student? Any one of the three positions could be argued as appropriate. But from the research I have done to date on the returning student, the evidence leans toward the humanistic view as providing the foundation most consistent with what returning students expect in a learning environment and with what the exemplary instructors I interviewed indicate they are doing.

Beliefs About Returning Students

How should I view the returning student? is a question some instructors who have not before worked with older returning students ask. The exemplary instructors I interviewed answered this way: accept returning students as adults, as people who have had a variety of experiences, as people who have held jobs, raised families, paid taxes, served on community boards, and worked with volunteer organizations. It's not at all uncommon for many returning students to be older than the instructor. And this can pose some problems, particularly for the instructors who insist on being aloof and distant from their students.

Sometimes titles get in the way. As one of the instructors said, "I found a lot of people who didn't want to call me Doctor. They felt more comfortable calling me David." For some instructors it takes an effort to climb down from the professorial pedestal and treat the returning student as a peer. That is not to say that the professor denies his training and expertise in the subject being considered. Not at all. What the exemplary instructors told me is the importance of the instructor's recognizing the vast knowledge represented by the older students in a class and then developing a learning climate so all can share—the instructor and the students—in advancing the learning situation.

There can be some important fringe benefits from treating the returning students as peers. As an exemplary instructor pointed out, "When I'm operating interdependently with students, I'm learning about the content they are learning. I'm not just learning more about these particular students, I'm learning more about the content we're dealing with. That's when it gets exciting, and that's when it feels like a mutual investigation, mutual exploration, mutual creation . . . that's exciting."

Of course the fundamental beliefs that adults are able to learn, that they have come back to school for important reasons, and that they are excited about the prospects of gaining more formal education must not be overlooked. Holding these beliefs is essential to a satisfactory relationship with returning students.

Beliefs About Teaching and Learning

There are a variety of views about the nature of learning and the relationship of teaching to learning. Several of the exemplary instructors mentioned the importance of focusing attention on the students and their learning, rather than on the teachers and their teaching. As one said, "The faculty member has no meaning as a teacher unless he's there to facilitate learning. So the instructor should ask, 'What are the problems of the student in learning?' and 'What are the various stages in learning?' and then the instructor should modify his behavior accordingly, rather than saying, 'Which of these things will I present at a lecture?' 'Where will I have discussions?' and so on."

Another of the exemplary instructors said, "I prefer to think about teaching not in the sense of what I should do as a teacher, and what I do as a teacher, but from the sense of what's going on in the learners. I don't know how to describe the difference this orientation makes, and how it affects the classroom environment, but I'm convinced the orientation does have an effect. So I've been giving a lot of energy to trying to figure out what does go on inside learners, where they are, what are the processes they experience. Then I try to communicate this back to learners, so they can begin to become aware of what they are experiencing and can become more effective at being a learner."

To help people become aware of their particular learning style is one way to help them learn more easily. However, many instructors, unfortunately, work on the assumption that all people learn in the same way, and thus one teaching approach will fit all learners.

Instructors of returning students have the responsibility of being content experts in the traditional sense of what it means to be a professor—having something to profess. But as several of the exemplary instructors pointed out, the professor makes the content available to the student in terms that are relevant to the learner. This means that the instructor must, at the same time, be concerned about facilitating the learning situation and being a content resource for the students.

One problem with this view about the nature of the teaching-learning situation—a focus on learners and facilitating learning—is its acceptance by some of the returning students. Many of them have come from learning situations where they did not learn how to learn but instead came to depend on instructors to provide them with answers. Until they have had the opportunity to experience the joy and satisfaction of being self-directed learners, they often expect the teaching approach that they experienced and remember, even though for many of them it may not have been a pleasant experience.

As an instructor I interviewed explained, "I would like to see the teaching-learning situation we have in the university based on an interdependent relationship; not independent, but interdependent. We have trained people to be dependent learners in most instances, and it's difficult for them to make the transition to become interdependent. Interdependence transcends both dependence and independence. If you are interdependent you can choose to make some circumstances, where it's appropriate for you, be dependent. You can in some circumstances be independent; you can go out and work on your own. And that's okay if it's appropriate to you. The interdependent thing means a mutuality, a sharing among people, a sharing of students with each other, a sharing of students with professors."

In summary, the exemplary instructors that I interviewed have beliefs about the nature of teaching and learning that are at variance with those of instructors who see teaching as presenting information to students, who soak it up like so many sponges stuffed into lecture-hall seats. The exemplary instructors are more concerned about learning and its facilitation, more concerned about learners and their learning, than they are concerned about the various teaching approaches they might choose.

Beliefs About Knowledge

The question of what is knowledge is easily answered by many instructors. They will say knowledge is what is in books, in films, in research reports, and in the heads of professors. But to many instructors working with returning students, knowledge is more.

One of the instructors I talked with described what she called internal and external knowledge. According to this professor, many students come back to the university with the notion that knowledge is all out there, in books, in the heads of professors, and so on. Then these students begin to discover that they have a lot of knowledge inside them, based on the many experiences they have had in their lives. Some students go through the stage of rejecting all external knowledge, all the knowledge that is stored in the libraries and in the computer banks, all the knowledge that the professor has. They reach the conclusion that the only "true" knowledge is what they have experienced.

After a while, according to this professor, these students begin to realize that the so-called external knowledge can be combined with their own personal, internal knowledge. This is a way of dealing with knowledge that makes sense to many returning students, for it allows them to recognize and affirm the value of their life experiences.

Internal knowledge, or latent content, is a special aspect of adult education. As Paul Bergevin, John McKinley, and Robert Smith point out, "Latent content in adult education is unique content, distinct from the content of youth education. Latent content does exist for youth, but the latent content of youth arises out of experience obtained in childhood roles and environment. Adults, however, bring to an educational situation experience that is organized differently from that of youth. This qualitative difference arises from the fact that much of the latent content for adults results from their experience in functional adult roles. . . . In addition, a learner's residual feelings and ideas arising from experience in his pre-adult past must be considered as latent content if they are activated in the adult educational activity."[12]

Unfortunately, many instructors fail to acknowledge the legitimacy of the student's experience as knowledge.

Beliefs About Other Instructors

The exemplary instructors I interviewed had some rather strong beliefs about their peers' effectiveness in working with returning students. One point they emphasized was the importance of the instructors' being able to relate theory to practice. And in order to keep up with the practice in their fields, several exemplary professors said it was necessary for the instructors to spend some time in the field. As one of the exemplary instructors said, "I'll tell you it's difficult to get many of these instructors out of the building, except to go home. Trying to get a classroom instructor to walk downstairs, get into an automobile, and drive forty miles to spend a day in a public school system, or a community college system, is almost impossible."

Another of the exemplary instructors suggested that all instructors who work with returning students spend time on their sabbaticals working in life-work situations other than teaching to acquire some feel for the practice of their fields.

As an exemplary instructor pointed out, "The professor who has been teaching traditional students is often not teaching human beings. He's dealing with automatons who have been so socialized in the elementary and secondary schools that they move right in and accept blindly a situation that the returning students are not going to accept. If the instructor is not willing to change, they will back up and they will do what they have to do and probably smile in the classroom—but eventually, if there are enough of them, they will start raising hell on campus. They won't go out trashing or anything like that. But they will go to the deans and the administrators and will insist that changes be made."

Beliefs About Purpose

Instructors, as well as others, need to wrestle with the question, What is the purpose of higher education as it relates to the returning student?

A few years ago I wrote that the purposes of adult education generally are these:

1. To help people acquire the tools for physical, psychological, and social survival. This includes job skills, skills for interpersonal relationships, and skills for coping with day-to-day living.

2. To help people discover a sense of meaning in their lives. Here I talked about helping people discover and achieve personal

creativity, helping them learn to appreciate the satisfaction that goes with excellence, and presenting to people alternatives that allow them to benefit from emotional and intellectual discovery.

3. To help people learn how to learn. The emphasis here is on developing in people the confidence to organize learning projects on their own, so they are not always and entirely dependent on a person or an institution for their learning.

4. To help communities (and in general, society) provide a more humane social, psychological, and physical environment for their (its) members.[13]

What Is to Be Learned

When we discussed knowledge from the perspective of the instructor's working philosophy, we mentioned two basic types—internal and external. (As noted before, some writers refer to internal knowledge as "latent content.")

Internal knowledge is that which comes from the returning student's life experiences. External knowledge is that found in books, professors' heads, and other resources.

In every learning situation there is the potential for a balance between the internal knowledge the returning students bring with them and the external content that is embodied in the course syllabus. The balance between the two types of content will have a considerable influence on the learning environment, particularly on what the instructor does and what the students do in the learning situation.

If what is to be learned is primarily external content that is foreign to the returning student, say a course in computer science in which none of the students have had any experience, the instructor will use a teaching approach that is considerably different from the one used if he or she were teaching a course, say on family relationships, where the returning students have had considerable experience.

When the likelihood is that learners will have considerable internal knowledge, it behooves the instructor not only to help bring this knowledge into the learning situation, but also to provide ways for the returning students to find some meaning in their knowledge. And beyond helping returning students find meaning in their experiences, their internal knowledge, the instructor must also help them relate their internal knowledge to external knowledge.

The Setting for Learning

At least three dimensions of setting are important to the learning environment for returning students: the actual facilities, administrative support, and resources. Facilities refer to adequate classrooms, student meeting places, audiovisual aids, and the like. In terms of classroom facilities, a minimum requirement is having movable chairs. For no matter how large the class group, there will be times when the larger group can be, and should be, broken into smaller groups for purposes of discussion. Yet it is not uncommon to find lecture halls on every university and college campus across the country with their chairs bolted to the floor, neatly lined up in straight rows from front to back. A criterion to use in assessing facilities for returning students is, Do the facilities get in the way of learning? In my judgment immovable chairs often do.

Earlier, when we discussed the economic situation as an external dimension of the learning environment, we mentioned how it has an effect on the administration of colleges and universities and their choices of where they will spend their limited resources. As we have mentioned several times, some changes will be necessary on college and university campuses with increased numbers of returning students. (In chapter 12 we will say something about what these changes might be.) The point is, the extent of (or lack of) administrative support for returning students will have a considerable effect on the learning environment for these students. For instance, registration procedures designed for traditional full-time students often need modification for returning part-time students. Times when classes are held often need to be adjusted to accommodate the returning student.

The setting for learning also includes the availability of resources. Because most of the returning students are part-time students and full-time employees, they have limited time to search for library books, consult with professors, and the like. Sometimes the limited-time constraint of the returning student is interpreted to mean lack of interest in doing library work or out-of-class activities. In most instances the returning student is as interested as or more interested than the traditional student in out-of-class work. But because of various restrictive rules, daytime library hours, and limited office hours for instructors, the returning student cannot get to these resources. Such limitations on access to resources can have an extremely negative effect on the total learning environment for the returning student.

Summary

The traditional learning environment for returning students consists of these dimensions: the student, the instructor, what is to be learned, and the setting for learning. All of these have great impact, particularly the student and the instructor (when we are considering formal learning situations). In chapters that follow we will look at the returning student as learner in some depth. In this chapter we explored two essential characteristics of instructors that we believe make a difference when teaching returning students—the instructor's skills and the instructor's working philosophy of education. The components of a working philosophy that we examined included beliefs about (1) humans, (2) returning students, (3) teaching and learning, (4) knowledge, (5) other instructors, and (6) the purpose of higher education as it relates to returning students.

NOTES

1. Christopher Jencks and David Riesman, "The Art of teaching," *The Professors,* ed. Charles H. Anderson and John D. Murray (Cambridge, Mass.: Schenkman Publishing Company, Inc., 1971), p. 61.

2. Steven M. Cahn, ed., *Scholars Who Teach* (Chicago: Nelson-Hall, 1978), p. ix.

3. Refer to Jerold W. Apps, "A Foundation for Action," *Materials and Methods in Continuing Education,* ed. Chester Klevins (New York: Klevens Publications, Inc., 1976); and Jerold W. Apps, *Toward a Working Philosophy of Adult Education* (Syracuse: Syracuse University, 1973) for more detailed information about an approach to use in examining beliefs in adult education.

4. Floyd W. Matson, *The Idea of Man* (New York: Dell Publishing Co., 1976).

5. Ibid., p. xi.

6. Gordon W. Allport, *Becoming: Basic Considerations for a Psychology of Personality* (New Haven: Yale University Press, 1955), p. 12.

7. Lewis Mumford, *The Myth of the Machine: The Pentagon of Power* (New York: Harcourt Brace Jovanovich, 1964, 1970), p. 418.

8. Victor E. Frankl, *Man's Search for Meaning* (New York: Beacon, 1963).

9. Joseph R. Royce, *The Encapsulated Man* (Princeton: Van Nostrand Reinhold, 1964).

10. Paulo Freire, *Education for Critical Consciousness* (New York: Seabury, 1973), p. 3.

11. Erich Fromm, *The Revolution of Hope* (New York: Harper and Row, 1968).

12. Paul Bergevin, John McKinley, and Robert M. Smith, "The Adult Education Activity: Content, Processes, and Procedures," *Adult Education: Outlines of an Emerging Field of University Study*, ed. Gale Jensen et al. (Washington, D.C.: Adult Education Association of the U.S.A., 1964), p. 272.

13. Jerold W. Apps, *Problems in Continuing Education* (New York: McGraw-Hill, 1979), pp. 89–101.

Chapter 6

How Age Affects Learning

As I travel around the country, talking with instructors and administrators who work with returning students, and as I talk with returning students themselves, I hear several different perspectives about the nature of the returning student as a learner.

I've run into a few instructors and administrators who believe returning students shouldn't be on college campuses. These persons argue that the returning student missed a chance at education when it was available, when the student graduated from high school, and it is too late to do anything about it now, at least in a formal way. According to this small group of instructors and administrators, these older students ought to enroll in vocational courses if they need job skills. They should enroll in noncredit courses offered by various institutions and agencies if they need something to take up their time now that the children have grown and left home. These instructors and administrators generally agree a college degree program is a mistake for the adult. Returning students shouldn't take up valuable space in our colleges and universities, and particularly they should not affect the nature of instruction and the content and organization of the curriculum because of their presence on campuses.

One of the reasons for this attitude relates to the perceived purpose of colleges and universities. Many say the role of a college or university is to prepare young men and women for a place in society, to add to the knowledge in the various disciplines, and to be of service to the community in which the institution is located; for example, faculty members serve as consultants, the institution provides cultural opportunities for the community, and the like. Those persons who argue that universities and colleges are to prepare young people for a place in society are highly suspicious of the older returning student. They question whether the returning student is able to do college-level work; they surmise that one of the major reasons the person either dropped out of college or never started was poor academic performance. The returning student is viewed as indecisive in terms of career goals and is thus seen as "unsettled" and likely unsuited for formal college work.

A second large group of instructors and administrators, much larger than the first group, are those who see no differences between the traditional students and the returning students. They, of course, recognize returning students as older and having been out of school for several years. And there is usually some acceptance of the fact that these students are probably working and raising a family. But these instructors and administrators argue that presently many traditional students are also working and raising families.

This attitude toward the returning student is usually not expressed in words. It is expressed in actions. The curriculum shows no modification even when up to 50 percent of the students are twenty-five or older. The way the courses are taught, and when they are taught, is not modified even when more than half the students are returning students. The availability of resources—library, faculty time, counseling service—is not changed just because large numbers of returning students find it difficult to use them.

A third group represents those instructors and administrators who are aware of differences between traditional and returning students and are concerned about what kinds of adjustments their institutions should be considering in light of these differences. They have a positive attitude toward the returning student as a learner but believe the returning student's learning can be enhanced with certain modifications in policies and procedures. In this chapter we will explore the returning student as learner. We will explore some of the changes that we all face as we age and their effects on our ability to learn. We will look at intelligence and memory. We will examine the effect of generational differences in a learning group composed of returning students. Psychological barriers to learning will be explored, and finally, we will examine some of the recent adult-development literature and the clues it provides the instructor who works with returning students.

Changes with Age

Anyone reading this book who is past forty, or even younger, knows full well that ability to function does change with age. The aging process has an effect on our visual acuity, our hearing ability, and our reaction time. And, of course, all three of these functions are related to the teaching-learning process.

The old saw "You can't teach an old dog new tricks" likely comes from the conclusion that, as certain functions change with age, our ability to learn also changes. This conclusion is, of course, totally false. But nevertheless certain changes do occur as we age.

Vision

Our ability to see increases rapidly during childhood, peaking at about age eighteen. From eighteen until about forty there is a gradual decline. For many people, there is a sharp decline from about forty to fifty-five, and the decline continues, but less rapidly, throughout life. After age eighteen, there is a slow decline in our ability to adapt to the dark (night driving can become an increasing problem), and field of vision also narrows somewhat. These figures are based on averages computed from large numbers of people. Many persons at age forty-five do not wear corrective lenses, but many more do than don't. Defective eyesight that is not corrected can be a deterrent to learning, but for most people near-normal vision is available with corrective lenses.

It behooves the instructor of adults to recognize the possible visual problems some adult students experience, to provide large, clearly produced visual material, to make certain light conditions are proper in classrooms, and to combine audio and visual formats when presenting material.

Hearing

By the time we are adolescents our ability to hear the very low sounds and a few high sounds starts to decline. The peak hearing performance appears around age fifteen and rather steadily declines throughout the rest of life. For persons under the age of twenty-five, the incidence of any hearing loss is about 1 percent. The rate of decline begins to increase around age forty-five. For those between the ages of sixty-five and seventy-four, the rate of hearing loss is about 10 percent, on the average. Most of the hearing loss is at the high sound frequencies.

In addition to a decline in the ability to hear sounds, one also hears more slowly with age. This means that it takes us longer to translate the meaning of sounds and respond to them as we grow older.

There are obvious measures an instructor of older students can take to assure that those who may have some hearing loss can have a useful learning experience. Talk slowly and deliberately and with sufficient volume that everyone can hear comfortably. Provide sound amplification if the room is large. Face the group so people can get clues from nonverbal expressions.

Reaction Time

Reaction time is the time it takes for a person to respond in some way when he or she sees, hears, feels, tastes, or smells something. For instance, as we get older, it takes us longer to move our foot from the accelerator to the brake when we are driving.

In a learning setting it takes us longer, as we get older, to respond to multiple-choice questions on a timed test. And thus the timed test may more accurately be measuring our reaction time than our knowledge of the questions.

Somewhere in young adulthood our reaction time peaks. It slowly declines during middle and old age. Peak reaction time is about age twenty. At fifty most people have about the same reaction time they had at about fifteen.

Physiologically, reaction time involves a sensation of some stimulus by a sense organ, a transmission of this information to the brain, perception, and then a selection of some response to the stimulus. Research suggests that reaction time involving visual sensation is somewhat slower than reaction time involving auditory sensation.

A compensation for decreasing reaction time expressed by many adults is increased attention to accuracy and care in responding to situations. In fact, in some instances, an increasing concern for accuracy may appear to be a slowdown in reaction time.

For the instructor, a major consideration is to avoid situations for adults that are timed or high pressure. Research evidence suggests the adult student will be frustrated in tightly timed situations and will often perform poorly. However, given enough time to perform the task, whatever it is, the older student will often perform at a higher level of accuracy than will the younger student.

For those instructors who hold efficiency in learning as a major guide for their activities, rethinking is necessary. Efficiency, meaning in this instance the speed at which learning can take place, is a problem for the adult learner. As we shall see later in this chapter, adults can learn almost everything and with little difficulty, but it often takes them more time than it does for younger students.

Ability to Learn

Can adults learn as well as children? Can older returning students learn as well as traditional-age students? These are questions that have been with us for a long time. And there are many answers, some of them couched in myth and superstition.

Many in this country still believe that learning is something we do in the early years of our life, and to even talk about adult learning is inappropriate. Of course this attitude is rapidly disappearing as thousands of adults across the country participate in one learning activity or another.

Depending on how learning activity is defined, some research suggests that nearly everyone, sometime during every year of his or her life, takes part in some kind of learning activity.[1] This may vary from a carefully planned family trip, with information collected from a variety of sources, to taking a formal course for credit at a university or college.

From all this learning activity it's quite obvious that adults can learn, even though some people continue to believe they can't. Let's look at some of the specifics.

Intelligence

When people talk about learning ability for adults, they almost immediately bring up the topic of intelligence. The assumption is that intelligence is closely related to learning ability. And the question is, Does intelligence decline with age?

The assumption is essentially correct, but the answer to the question is fairly complex. One of the problems faced in attempting to answer the question is to define the term *intelligence*. Many define it as how one performs on a test. But there are others who believe that the definition is far too narrow and that intelligence is considerably more than what can be tested in measurable terms. These persons say that certain dimensions of adult intelligence may be measured with tests, but other dimensions, perhaps as important or even more important to adult performance and learning, cannot be measured.

Ledford J. Bischof is one of those who question a unitary view of intelligence. He says we have several intelligences and that intelligence is a human behavior. Bischof defines intelligence as "the variable capacity to solve problems of all kinds that the human is likely to encounter in life."[2]

The most widely used test for adult intelligence is the Wechsler Adult Intelligence Scale.[3] Some research has been done to equate scores on the Wechsler test with learning effectiveness.

The Wechsler test provides scores that indicate ceiling performance of adults on mental tasks. What the Wechsler test apparently provides is some guess about the ability of adults to perform verbal learning in educational settings. Alan Knox maintains that the test provides "a general estimate of ceiling performance on mental tasks. Adults who score high on the WAIS typically learn more effectively when they make a maximum effort than do adults who score low on the WAIS and make a maximum effort."[4]

Knox also says that few people operate at ceiling performance, which implies that, even though persons may score somewhat lower on the WAIS, they may do better than their peers who scored higher, providing their motivation is higher and they perform nearer their ceiling capacity. And, as Knox argues, even if it is true that certain indices of learning ability do decline with age, "if the person functions throughout adulthood at no more than two thirds of young adult capacity, a decline in ceiling capacity of less than one third by old age would have no practical effect on performance."[5]

But what happens with age? Do adults tend to lose intelligence as the years progress?

Unfortunately, most of the research done on this question is based on intelligence test scores such as the WAIS. So the results have to be viewed somewhat cautiously, recognizing the limited view of these tests. Two types of research have been conducted, longitudinal studies and cross-sectional studies. Longitudinal studies are conducted by testing the same group of adults periodically. Cross-sectional studies are accomplished by testing, at the same time, a group of persons representing different ages to note differences.

The longitudinal studies show a high degree of stability of intelligence between ages twenty and fifty, and often beyond. Knox, in his summary of these studies, points out that many of them were done with people who had college experience. He also concludes that "there was evidence of a somewhat greater increase or stability in learning ability for the more able adults, in contrast with the general adult population, although increases and decreases with age occurred at all ability levels."[6]

Cross-sectional studies, on the other hand, tend to report declines in intelligence-test performance with age. But there are some interesting variations. As Knox points out, "It appears that the most intellectually able people increase their learning ability more rapidly during childhood and adolescence, reach a higher plateau later in young adulthood, and then either continue to increase gradually or maintain learning ability during adulthood. By contrast the least intellectually able people increase learning ability more slowly, reach a lower plateau earlier, and decline more rapidly."[7]

P. B. Baltes and K. W. Schaie studied 500 adults whose ages ranged from twenty-one to seventy.[8] Over a period of seven years they followed this group of adults using Thurstone and Thurstone's Primary Mental Abilities Test and Schaie's Test of Behavioral Rigidity. Their research with the two tests resulted in the identification of four dimensions of intelligence: crystallized intelligence, cognitive flexibility, visualization, and visuo-motor flexibility.

Crystallized intelligence reflects the skills we acquire from formal education and from living. It includes skills with numbers, language, and inductive reasoning. Cognitive flexibility is the ability a person has to shift thinking from one approach to another, such as work with antonyms and synonyms. Visualization is the ability to organize and process visual materials. And visuo-motor flexibility is the coordination of visual and motor tasks.

Baltes and Schaie found that crystallized and visualization scores increased dramatically with age, even for those persons older than seventy. According to their research, cognitive flexibility remained about the same through the aging process. Of the four, visuo-motor scores were the only ones that declined.

Baltes and Schaie also found that the years persons were born made a difference in their ability to perform on the tests. They found that those persons born in 1906 performed less well than those born in 1913. We'll say more about generational differences later in this chapter.

Cattell studied the theory of fluid and crystallized intelligence.[9] Fluid intelligence includes a person's ability to do abstract reasoning, to perceive complex relationships, to form concepts, and to engage in short-term memory. Fluid intelligence is independent of experience and education. Testing procedures used to measure fluid intelligence include rote memory, word analogies, and verbal reasoning with common materials.

Crystallized intelligence is one's ability to perceive relationships and to do formalized reasoning—a definition similar to the one used by Baltes and Schaie above. The subtests used to measure crystallized intelligence include tests of general information, vocabulary tests, and arithmetic reasoning. In contrast with fluid intelligence, crystallized intelligence is dependent on both formal education and experience.

What is interesting about this theory is that a combination of crystallized and fluid intelligence covers most of the learning tasks an adult will face in a formal educational setting. And the two approaches complement each other. Some learning settings require more crystallized intelligence, others require more fluid intelligence.

Now to the changes with age. Both crystallized and fluid intelligence increase during childhood and into adolescence. Fluid intelligence tends to peak during adolescence and decline somewhat during adulthood. On the other hand, crystallized intelligence continues to increase throughout adulthood. In a review of several research projects, Knox concluded, "Beyond age sixty, as well as before, continued growth of crystallized intelligence depends on the continuing acculturation through information seeking and educative activity."[10]

We could conclude that, as persons grow older and decline somewhat in fluid intelligence and, at the same time, increase in crystallized intelligence, their overall ability to learn can remain relatively stable. Decline in fluid intelligence is compensated by the increase in crystallized intelligence. People are able to substitute experience for so-called native ability and come out ahead in many learning situations.

What can we say then, in summary? Insofar as intelligence is concerned, we need not worry about the ability of returning students to learn. They can learn most things as well as younger, more traditional students. Because of their vast experience, they may be able to learn some things better. It is erroneous for instructors and administrators to say that returning students have declining intelligence and therefore do not have the potential for undergraduate or graduate education as adults.

Other factors, beyond intelligence, also affect the adult student's learning.

Memory

Most people, when they talk about learning, bring up the topic of memory. This attention to memory is, of course, based on the assumption that much of learning is the accumulation of knowledge, facts, and information, whatever we want to call it, for later recall and use.

All learning, in one way or another, and to a greater or lesser extent, involves memory. The question is, then, To what extent does our memory decline with age? Many older people, beginning in the middle years, complain that their memory is not "as good as it once was." Is their statement accurate, or does it merely represent a cultural influence that has been passed from generation to generation—as we get older it is expected that memory will decline?

Memory includes three phases, which are commonly referred to as (1) registration, (2) retention, and (3) recall. Registration is the exposure to stimuli through the senses, which is then encoded into the brain. Or to say it even more simply, registration is becoming aware of something through seeing, hearing, smelling, feeling, or tasting, and then storing it for future reference. Retention is the persistence of the material that has been encoded. And finally, recall, or remembering, is the process by which a search and retrieval takes place for the information that has been stored.

Research suggests some differences between that which is stored for immediate and short-term memory and that stored for intermediate and long-term memory. However, most memory testing for adults has been with immediate and short-term memory. The results of this research suggest that the ability to retain information in the immediate and the short-term memory declines very little throughout most of adulthood—if the material that has been encoded is meaningful, if it has been accurately encoded, and if the amount is not unreasonably large. Another conclusion of this research is that remembering information is easiest when the recall situation is similar to the situation where the registration of the material occurred.[11]

Knox describes a particular kind of memory problem faced by older adults. He says that older adults may experience problems with memory when they try to respond to and store new information at the same time they are trying to recall stored information. "This occurs, for example, when someone's comment triggers a flood of older memories and the next few sentences are missed. Over the years, as adults acquire more information related to a topic, they can make more cross references and potential connections between new and stored information. As a result, older adults tend to expand the scope of search when trying to recall information, which takes more time and may result in greater interference with the new material to be learned."[12]

In general, as adults grow older, the ability to recall or remember information declines somewhat. Part of this decline is related to memory decay, but a larger part of the decline is related to interference from other stored information.

Research also indicates that the better adults can cluster and organize information for storage, the greater their ability to recall the information. That is, those persons who have developed the ability to organize information into related clusters will tend to have better recall than those who do not have that ability.

Research in this area also shows that persons with high verbal ability show little or no differences in recall ability throughout the aging process. For those persons with lower verbal ability there is significant decline in recall ability from young adulthood on to old age.

There is some decline in registration ability with age, but most memory decline is in the ability to remember information. And this is directly related to how well the information is organized at the time of registration. The more highly organized the information is for a person, the more likely he or she is able to remember it at a later time.

Forgetting is related to how strongly the information was originally registered, whether or not the material has been used, and interference from other information. Material poorly registered (poorly learned) that is seldom used and is competing with newer, opposing information stands a high possibility of being forgotten.

Knox suggests several approaches educators can follow to help adults overcome problems with inadequate memory.[13] A general summary of his suggestions follows:

1. Present new information with aids that will help the learner organize it. Suggest ways in which the material may be organized. Give examples of how others have organized material like this. For instance, an instructor might show how the material may be organized to illustrate the relation of major to minor points.

2. Pace each learning situation so that the learner is allowed time to master the material. In a class situation an instructor could present several new ideas, then have the group discuss them before going on to more new information.

3. If the learning situation includes a series of sessions, include a review of previous important material at the beginning of each new session. Cover the main points again, summarize the examples, and perhaps even add a few new examples about the points covered at the previous session before going on.

4. Combine visual with verbal means in expressing ideas. For some persons a visual representation is more clear than one expressed only verbally. Sometimes the simple writing of a word on a chalkboard or on a flipchart will help make an idea clear.

5. Provide opportunities for practice and application of material. This can be through discussion, through the actual application of the material in a real-life situation, and through the redoing of material in a different form. For example, in a class I teach on various educational philosophies, I first discuss with the group something about each of the philosophies, their assumptions about the nature of learners, and the like. Students during this time read about these philosophies in out-of-class situations. I then set up a practical situation, where I divide the group into subgroups, each subgroup with the responsibility of translating a particular educational philosophy into a series of practical guidelines. Students, in carrying out this assignment, not only need to become thoroughly familiar with the philosophies but also must be able to translate the meaning of the philosophies into a practical situation.

6. Provide some type of feedback to learners so they have some sense of whether or not their understanding of something is essentially correct. Of course this will vary with what is being

learned. But if an adult is learning to swim, having feedback from an instructor as to how well the person is progressing helps the remembering process. Discussing abstract concepts in a small group of peers often serves as a feedback to learners who wonder if they are afield in their understanding.

Generational Differences

The instructor working with traditional-age college students of approximately eighteen to twenty-two years finds many similarities among them. They were all born at about the same time and they have essentially experienced the same social and economic forces as they grew up. Exceptions are noted, of course, for those who represent low income or minority groups.

The instructor who faces a group of returning students may note an age range from twenty-five to the fifties and beyond. Such a group is far more diverse than it is similar, if for no other reason than the differences represented by the different generations involved. Some in the group will have lived during the depression of the 1930s and will remember vividly the hard economic times they and their parents experienced. This experience, whether these people realize it or not, has had and continues to have a profound influence on their values and attitudes. Some in the group will have served in the various wars we have experienced during the last quarter century, a few in World War II, some in the Korean conflict, some in Vietnam. And this experience will have had an effect on these persons as learners. Some in the group may have been student activists during the turmoil of the 1960s, and this has had an influence on their lives.

The point is that, in any group of adults, there are vast value and attitudinal differences as well as obvious differences in age, experience, prior education, and the like. And these value and attitudinal differences have a considerable effect on the learning process. We have in this country adults holding to various clusters of values, and some say that the country is going through a type of value transformation.

Charles Reich, in 1970, wrote about three levels of consciousness.[14] Consciousness I individuals hold to such values as self-interest, competitiveness, suspicion of others, emphasis on the individual's winning by himself or herself, and a general assumption that the nature of humans is essentially bad (in other words, do it to others before they do it to you). Society was viewed as a competitive arena, with people winning and losing and a very definite pecking order.

Reich defined Consciousness II persons as holding such values as the importance of technological development and big government. Persons must value something bigger than themselves, such as a conglomerate business of which they may be a part and a big government to which they pay taxes and show allegiance. Persons view their own lives in light of how well they are doing within some organization. Many of the values of a highly industrialized society are the Consciousness II values that Reich talks about. The prime values are science, technology, organization, and planning.

Consciousness III represents a quite different set of values, and according to Reich is a part of much of the youth culture of the late sixties. The person is once more emphasized, not the organization of which the person is a part. Consciousness III values strongly question so-called linear and analytic thought, the mainstay of the Consciousness II people. The values of Consciousness III begin with the self but do not begin with selfishness. One does not defer life's meaning to the future but sees value in the present. One looks at society first from the perspective of the humans and natural life that make it up, not from the perspective of the organizations and institutions that are seen as artificial products of the society.

Values in Consciousness III include the importance of the individuality of each human being, not to be determined by a comparison with other human beings. One strives to be honest at all times with others and rejects the idea of manipulation of others for personal or organizational gain.

Although there are obviously many exceptions, the point of Reich's work is that older generations tend to espouse the values inherent in Consciousness I and II, and the younger generation, which came of age in the 1960s, is more apt to espouse the values of what he calls Consciousness III.

With the advantage of witnessing the passing of the seventies and the beginning of the eighties, it's obvious that not all young people have accepted the values of Consciousness III. Many of the values expressed by those who were young people in the late sixties and seventies are consistent with competition, technology, and the development of highly technological big business. So, at least on an observational basis, we cannot completely tie values to different eras of time. Yet it's important for the instructor of returning students to recognize that, within any class of, say, thirty returning students, a variety of values will be represented. These values will, in turn, have a considerable influence on expectations of the students in terms of what they are studying, the kinds of instructional approaches they desire, their relationships with their instructors, and so on.

A classroom made up of returning students is at the same time more challenging for the instructor as it is more exciting because of the diversity of values represented in the group.

Psychological Barriers

Many returning students face a variety of psychological barriers that often get in the way of learning and make the return to school less than a pleasant experience. Three common psychological barriers are (1) lack of confidence as a student, (2) recall of previous formal learning, and (3) guilt feelings.

Almost every adult who returns to a college or a university after some years away from formal education has some doubts about ability to study: Will I be able to keep up with the reading assignments? Will I be able to write acceptable papers? Will I be able to pass the examinations? Will I be able to keep my mind on my academic work when the responsibilities of my life tug and pull me in many directions at the same time?

And at another level, the adult returning student, having heard about the myths of declining memory and intelligence, wonders if the capacity to learn is still there. Of course declines in hearing and vision, if present, only add to the lack of confidence felt by the returning student.

Many of the feelings about confidence as a student are related to the person's sense of self or identity. Those persons who have more fragile self-concepts are usually the persons who have the strongest negative feelings about their roles as students.

Some researchers of self-concept theory go so far as to say how one perceives and what one perceives is influenced by one's concept of self. LaBenne and Greene claim that "a person with a weak self-concept and who is unsure of himself is more likely to have a narrowed perceptual field."[15]

By this they mean that the more unsure persons are, the more likely they are to perceive situations in a way that is less than the reality of the situations. According to LaBenne and Greene, a person behaves as the result of how he or she perceives a situation at the time of the action. Thus a person, to follow their argument, who has a poor self-concept perceives situations in a more limited way and may then behave in a manner that is inappropriate to the situation.

To translate this into learning situations, the person with a poor self-concept may perceive the learning situation in a limited way and indeed miss the point of the learning situation entirely because of the limited perception.

Recalling previous formal learning experiences is a psychological barrier for many returning students. The tendency is to recall unpleasant learning experiences that may go back as far as high school. Or, for some persons, the memories include a very unpleasant one or two years of college when grades earned may have been poor, when the instruction was remembered as boring and unrelated to anything in the person's life, and when the person may have been dropped or encouraged to drop out.

These unpleasant memories can come flooding back to many returning students, giving them pause and causing them considerable anxiety as to whether they made the right decision in returning and whether college or university life, five or ten years later, will be any better than before.

There is no denying these persons may have had unpleasant learning experiences, for a variety of reasons—some student related, some institution related, and some simply a factor of the societal mood at the time the student may have attended school. But what many returning students with this concern fail to realize is that they've had successes in *informal* learning situations since they left school.

These successes have come from participation in courses such as how to fill out your income tax return, gourmet cooking, and how to care for a preschool child. People tend to overlook the pleasant associations that often come from many of these learning situations.

People also overlook all the learning they have done simply to survive as mature adults in our society—learning a new job, keeping up to date with changes on the job, learning how to manage a household, learning how to manage time to take into account the hundreds of demands put on today's adults.

This type of learning is often not considered learning. People simply recognize the need to do it and they do it. In fact, if one were to ask these people what they had learned in the past six months, they'd often reply, "Nothing." They fail to account for this unstructured, unorganized learning. And if, after some probing and their recognition of learning, we asked them if the learning was unpleasant or pleasant, they'd often reply either that it was pleasant or that they hadn't thought about how they liked what they were doing.

Nevertheless, there are many people who equate learning in the college or university setting with their previous formal learning experiences. They fail to recognize that, even though an early learning experience may have been quite unpleasant, they have had many pleasant learning experiences since. Thus there is no logical reason why a return to the college and university classroom should be an unpleasant experience.

Guilt feelings are psychological barriers for many returning students, particularly the returning woman student with a family. Judith Hooper, in research with returning women students and their families, reported that these women suffer considerable guilt about the possible effect of their student role and its impact on the family, particularly the children.[16]

Based on responses to a research instrument, Hooper was able to place the twenty-four families she researched into three groups. One group of families she called sex-agreement, one sex-disagreement, and one egalitarian. In the sex-agreement group, the woman in the family performed the traditional woman-mother roles of caring for the family, even though she was also a student. In the sex-disagreement group, the woman performed these traditional roles but believed they were wrong and wanted to see them changed. In the egalitarian group, father, mother, and children had worked out means of sharing many of the household tasks to give mother more time to pursue her studies.

In terms of guilt, mothers in the agreement and disagreement groups had a lot of it. Mothers in the egalitarian group had less, but it was still present.

Interestingly, mothers in the agreement group—where the mother performed regular household tasks and agreed this is the way it should be—cared for their families as they had before they went back to school. College attendance was a load placed on top of the family responsibilities.

The disagreement-group mothers were interesting too. They were expected by the family to perform the traditional household tasks, but they believed this was inappropriate for them. They saw going back to school as a lever to force change in their families—to cause their families to share in the household work load. Hooper concluded that these women were likely precipitating crisis situations in their families.

Men going back to school also experience guilt feelings in many cases. As a condition for returning to school, they often find it necessary to leave full-time employment for a part-time job, often at a lower pay rate. And they believe their families are deprived of many of the things they were able to have when they were working full time. The mother, if she had not been working, may be forced to return to work in order for the family to have sufficient income during the time the husband is in school. For some men, this produces considerable guilt.

And lastly, the father with school-age children often feels considerable guilt because his work and his schooling leave little time for the children. When they want to do things with him, he either finds it necessary to study or is too exhausted to participate with them. All these feelings can, of course, serve to get in the way of academic study.

Though not really classed as guilt, another feeling that many adults have upon returning to school is an uncomfortable feeling about being in school at age thirty-five or forty or whatever the person's age might be. Though considerably diffused today, the attitude that school is for kids and young adults is a latent feeling in our society. This feeling sometimes troubles the returning student and contributes to a host of other potential barriers to effective participation and learning.

Adult Life Cycles

For many years ongoing research examined the various stages children go through as they grow from birth to adulthood. But only quite recently has there been a concerted effort to examine the life stages of adults. Today several schemes are available that attempt to explain how adults grow, develop, and change as they proceed from early adulthood to death.

Bromley, in 1966, classified all of human life into sixteen stages, from conception to senescence.[17] For adult years, Bromley applied the following stages:

Period	Approximate Age
Early adulthood	21–25
Middle adulthood	25–40
Late adulthood	40–60
Preretirement	60–65
Retirement	65 years and older
Old age	70 years and older
Senescence	Terminal illness and death

Robert Havighurst divided the life span into six age periods.[18] In his classification system, there are three adult periods: early adulthood (18–35), middle age (35–60), and later maturity (60 and over). Havighurst went further than to merely associate ages with various periods of one's life. He, through his research, attempted to associate what he called developmental tasks with each life period. Havighurst concluded that, if a person failed to complete a developmental task in a given period, the person could expect developmental problems in ensuing periods.

Following are examples of the developmental tasks he associated with the adult life stages:

Developmental Tasks of Early Adulthood

Selecting a mate
Learning to live with a marriage partner
Managing a home
Getting started in an occupation
Finding a congenial social group

Developmental Tasks of Middle Age

Achieving adult civic and social responsibility
Establishing and maintaining an economic standard of living
Developing adult leisure-time activities
Relating to one's spouse as a person
Assisting teenage children to become responsible and happy
  adults
Adjusting to aging parents

Developmental Tasks of Later Maturity

Adjusting to decreasing physical strength and health
Adjusting to retirement and reduced income
Adjusting to death of spouse
Establishing satisfactory physical living arrangements

Carl Jung (1875–1961) is considered by some to be the father of the modern-day study of adult development. During his early years he was a disciple of Sigmund Freud but split with Freud in 1913 to form his own school, which he called Analytical Psychology. Jung attempted to understand human development as a product of external cultural forces as well as internal psychological processes. Where Freud tended to be more interested in child development, Jung focused his attention on adult development.

According to Jung, the young adult, hard pressed with the responsibilities of a young family, work, and community, and often still dealing with the conflicts of childhood, cannot reach full development. At about age forty, the age Jung referred to as "the noon of life," a person has the opportunity for a fundamental change. For Jung this transition time was the most crucial in a person's life. Jung also considered this time a period with high hazard potential, for if anything went wrong with the transition the person's personality might be permanently crippled.

During this transition time of the late thirties and early forties, adults put aside their youthful interests and develop new interests that, according to Jung, are less biological and more cultural. The person who reaches this period of life and who handles the transition is transformed into a spiritual man.[19]

Jung identified what he called "individuation," a term meaning the time when an adult becomes uniquely individual. It is a time when a person is able to utilize inner resources and to begin to pursue his or her own aims. Persons begin to generate new levels of awareness, understand more fully, and develop new meanings of experience.

Jung thus divided adult life into two segments, early adulthood and late adulthood, with the approximate age of forty as the transition time. He stressed that an adult really does not become complete until the second half of adulthood, when the problems and challenges of early adulthood are put aside and a person can become a complete functioning human being.[20]

Erik Erikson proposes eight ages of a person's ego development.[21] Erikson's stages (I will use this term here, though he prefers to call them ages) are expressed in terms of a dichotomy. He suggests that one can be successful or unsuccessful during each stage of one's life, and he further offers examples of what success and failure bring within each age category. Erikson's approach includes three stages for adults: early adulthood, middle adulthood, and late adulthood. During early adulthood, he says, a person wrestles with intimacy and isolation. Intimacy means a capacity to commit self to others. Isolation means avoidance of intimacy, with resultant character problems. Within middle adulthood, one is faced with the tension between generativity and stagnation. Generativity means being productive and creative for self and others, with concern for guiding the next generation. Stagnation means being egocentric, nonproductive, and excessively self-living. During late adulthood, the person is faced with resolving the tension between integrity and despair. Integrity refers to an acceptance of one's life, a sense of completion, a sense of being undivided and unbroken, and an acceptance of death as the final condition for life. Despair refers to a realization of the failure of one's life, a loss of faith in self and others, and a sense that time is too short to start another life with different approaches.

More recently, Gail Sheehy developed what she called "passages" faced by adults as they move through life.[22] What is interesting about Sheehy and Levinson, whose work will be described later, is that both of them do not describe life stages for children and youth but immediately commence discussing life stages from an adult perspective. Sheehy describes six passages, which come from her own research and are based on the work of other researchers such as Erikson, Gould, and Neugarten.

1. Pulling Up Roots. Sheehy says this occurs about age eighteen and is evidenced by a strong desire of a young adult to sever relations with parents and look for beliefs that are consistent with one's age rather than with one's parents'.

2. The Trying Twenties. Whereas Pulling Up Roots was concerned with internal struggles such as attempting to answer the questions, Who am I? and What is Truth? this passage, according to Sheehy, is concerned with externals. Questions include, How do I get started in a job? Who has done or is doing what I want to do? and Will they help me? The concern here is doing what we *should* do, with the *should* often coming from the person's family, the cultural situation, and the person's peers.

3. Catch-30. This is the time for an evaluation by persons who are approaching thirty. Is life going for them as they intended? Is their marriage satisfactory? Is their job satisfying? For many people it means a new start, in a new job, with a new spouse. What was worked out in the twenties in terms of personal relationships and occupational direction is often abandoned with the hope of working toward more realistic goals.

4. Rooting and Extending. A settling down begins to take place during this passage, which occurs during the early thirties. People in this passage are buying homes, working hard at careers, and attempting to be successful.

5. The Deadline Decade. According to Sheehy, people around the age of thirty-five begin to experience a crossroads in their lives. Once again they begin to examine their lives very critically.

People begin to ask such questions as, Why am I doing this? and Do I really believe in what I am doing? For many people this is the time when they begin to discover their true selves, not selves that have been totally influenced by the culture. For women, age thirty-five is often seen as a last chance—a last chance to bear children, a last chance to return to school and begin a new career.

For men the Deadline Decade is the time when the push for success in careers is great. Men see this as the last chance they have to show their superiors that they are different from others and thus should be in line for promotion to top positions. For many men, it is during this time that they seek a second career, an opportunity to pursue work that is more consistent with the self that has begun to emerge during this time. For career women, the same phenomenon occurs.

Passage through the Deadline Decade may continue for as many as ten years, from age thirty-five to forty-five. But during the mid-forties, a sense of stability is once more achieved.

6. Renewal or Resignation. Sometime during the mid-forties, there is a lessening of the turmoil that was characteristic of the previous passage. Persons achieve a new stability. This can take two forms. Those who muddled through the previous passage without really making a careful assessment of their lives may now become resigned to their lives as they are. They accept unhappy marriages and jobs that are dead-ended and boring. For those who confronted the Deadline Decade and found a sense of renewal, these may be some of the best years of their lives. Friends once more become very important. Life is seen as enjoyable and meaningful.

Finally, we'll include a brief summary of Daniel J. Levinson's work on the adult life cycle. Levinson takes into account biological, psychological, and social dimensions in his description of four broad stages of the life cycle: childhood and adolescence (age 0–22), early adulthood (17–45), middle adulthood (40–65), and late adulthood (60 and over).[23]

Each era in a person's life, according to Levinson, is more than simply a developmental stage or a period. Levinson says the eras he defines in the life cycle are analogous to the acts of a play or the major segments of a novel.

Levinson's research was based on data from forty men who were between the ages of thirty-five and forty-five and were equally divided among four occupations. One group of ten comprised factory hourly workers, another group of ten was made up of company executives, a third group of ten included academic biologists, and a fourth group of ten was made up of novelists.

Levinson says there is an overlap between the eras; one is just beginning as the previous one is terminating. This transition between eras takes as many as four or five years. In his research he found the transition seldom taking less than three years and rarely more than six years. The various eras are quite different from one another and require a person to make a rather dramatic shift. For example, according to Levinson, the preadulthood era ends at twenty-two, but early adulthood may begin at about seventeen. The transition from early adulthood usually extends from forty to forty-five.

The early adulthood period begins at about seventeen or eighteen and ends at about forty-five. A person's biological functioning is at its peak during the years from twenty to forty. During the early years of the era, a person peaks in such abilities as learning specific skills and in such physical activity as competitive sports.

But this is also a period of considerable stress and contradiction. Instinctual drives are at their height, particularly in the early years of this era, yet the residues of childhood conflict often prevent gratification of these drives. The era is characterized by great energy, capability, and potential, but with considerable pressure from family, peers, and the culture.

Middle adulthood begins with the transition time that lasts from about forty to forty-five. This is the time of the so-called mid-life transition, more popularly referred to as mid-life crisis. According to Levinson, there is no single event or happening that universally signifies the beginning of middle adulthood, as puberty marks the transition from childhood to adolescence. But one does get a picture of the transition if the lived life is studied, rather than searching for a single criterion. Changes occur in biological and psychological functioning, as we have noted earlier in this chapter. Now persons begin to recognize that they are part of a generation for which there is an older generation and a younger generation. According to Levinson, one's age peers, those who are members of one's generation, are those who are not more than six or seven years younger or older. Thus a person's generation covers about twelve to fifteen years. Persons in this middle-adulthood group have the special task of becoming aware of both the child and the elder in them and in others.

In terms of career, the person in the middle-adulthood phase of life asks questions that evaluate past performance, assess present level of accomplishment, and compare what one has done and is doing with the dreams one had for career accomplishment.

By this time in one's life, a person begins to see the importance of being complete and balanced instead of one-sided and unbalanced. Until this time, a person often has valuable aspects of the self that have been neglected or suppressed. Levinson mentions the four psychological functions that all personalities must exercise—thought, feeling, intuition, and sensation. By the time of the mid-life transition, a person usually has developed only one or two of these to any great extent. During middle adulthood many people tend to develop the weaker functions so as to lead a more balanced life.

Late adulthood, according to Levinson, begins in the early sixties. Because Levinson didn't include this age group in his study, he is more provisional about his comments. He notes some of the bodily decline mentioned earlier in this chapter. He points out that for many persons in this group there is increasing frequency of death and illness among loved ones and friends, and most persons have at least one major illness or impairment.

Persons in this age group experience the constant reference that they are "older" by the use of such terms as *elderly, golden age,* and *senior citizen* by social agencies and those younger. The fear for many people in this era is that they will become only dying hulks of once important and powerful young people. Moving out of jobs into retirement often leaves feelings of inadequacy and impotence.

Levinson points out that a major developmental task for late adulthood is finding a new balance of involvement with self and with society. For many persons this is very difficult.

Life-span development research is not without its critics, particularly that life-span research that focuses on a rather deterministic view of human development. There are those who simply will not accept the prediction that at a certain age we can expect adults to face particular kinds of problems and particular kinds of personality changes, simply because they have reached that age.

William Looft, for example, challenges both the developmental (organismic) and the behavioristic (mechanistic) models—both of which are deterministic and not particularly useful in helping us understand adult development. Looft suggests an alternative model that he says, "admits to a new view of reality, one that

perceives human social and mental development as the conflu-
ence of many interrelated and changing systems and subsystems,
including the biological, social, cultural, and historical. . . . the
model's unifying theme is relations; material, elemental and organismic aspects are of secondary importance. Theorists from the
mechanistic and organismic models continue to engage in be-
labored, useless discussion on causation, nature and nurture, con-
tinuity versus discontinuity, and the like. The adoption of the
relational model obviates all these debates and propels us to a
new level of understanding."[24]

Looft says that, for us to understand adult development, we
must put together what we know from biological research on
adults with historical, sociological, and demographic concepts to
form a more complete understanding of the social and mental
development of adults. According to Looft, "Each new generation will manifest age trends that are different from those that
preceded it, and thus previous empirical endeavors are reduced to
exercises in futility."[25]

Neugarten is another researcher who questions the validity of
searching for universal personality changes as one moves through
the life cycle. She believes the personality changes that occur in
adults throughout life are influenced greatly by historical and
social events.

In understanding the developmental changes that adults experience, Neugarten suggests an integration of maturational, psychological, sociological, and historical perspectives. She says we
must attempt to integrate three kinds of time: a person's life
time, or chronological age; a person's social time, the system of
age grading and expectations for age that influence the life cycle;
and a person's historical time, which is the "succession of political, economic, and social events that shape the setting into which
the individual is born and make up the dynamic, constantly
changing background against which his life is lived."[26]

But even with the criticisms of the life-span research, some
important conclusions can be drawn. Whatever we believe about
the influences, adults do change and change dramatically during
the course of the adult years. The idea that was once rather
commonly promoted—that children change dramatically until
they become adults, when there is a period of stability until one
reaches very advanced years—can be buried forever. It is abun-
dantly clear that adults change throughout their lives and for a
variety of reasons. The question facing each of us is, What are
the effects of these changes on the teaching-learning situation?

Summary

In this chapter we examined the effects of changes with age on the ability of adults to learn: changes in vision, hearing, and reaction time. Adult intelligence, memory, generational differences, and experience were discussed in relation to their effect on adult learning. Psychological barriers such as lack of confidence as a student and guilt feelings were examined. And various adult life-span theories such as those presented by Bromley, Havighurst, Jung, Erikson, Sheehy, and Levinson were discussed.

NOTES

1. Allen Tough, *The Adult's Learning Projects,* 2nd ed. (Austin, Tex.: Learning Concepts, 1979).

2. Ledford J. Bischof, *Adult Psychology,* 2nd ed. (New York: Harper and Row, 1976), p. 137.

3. D. Wechsler, *The Measurement and Appraisal of Adult Intelligence,* 3rd ed. (Baltimore: Williams and Wilkins, 1958).

4. Alan B. Knox, *Adult Development and Learning* (San Francisco: Jossey-Bass, 1977), p. 413.

5. Ibid., p. 414.

6. Ibid., p. 416.

7. Ibid., p. 417.

8. P. B. Baltes and K. W. Schaie, "The Myth of the Twilight Years," *Psychology Today,* March 1974, pp. 35–40.

9. R. B. Cattell, "Theory of Fluid and Crystallized Intelligence: A Critical Experiment," *Journal of Educational Psychology* 54 (1963): 1–22.

10. Knox, p. 421.

11. P. A. Moenster, "Learning and Memory in Relation to Age," *Journal of Gerontology* 27 (1972): 361–363.

12. Knox, p. 435.

13. Ibid., pp. 442–443.

14. Charles A. Reich, *The Greening of America* (New York: Random House, 1970).

15. Wallace D. LaBenne and Bert I. Greene, *Educational Implications of Self-Concept Theory* (Pacific Palisades, Calif.: Goodyear Publishing Company, 1969), p. 19.

16. Judith Oakey Hooper, "Returning Women Students and Their Families: Support and Conflict," *Journal of College Student Personnel,* March 1979, pp. 145–152.

17. D. B. Bromley, *The Psychology of Human Aging* (Baltimore: Penguin, 1966).

18. Robert J. Havighurst, *Developmental Tasks and Education,* 3rd ed. (New York: McKay, 1972).

19. Calvin S. Hall and Gardner Lindzey, *Theories of Personality,* 2nd ed. (New York: Wiley, 1970), pp. 99–100.

20. See the following for a discussion of Jung's views on these matters: Carl G. Jung, *Man and His Symbols* (New York: Doubleday, 1964); Carl G. Jung, *The Archetypes and the Collective Unconscious,* in *Collected Works,* vol. 9, pt. 1 (Princeton: Princeton University Press, 1959); Joseph Campbell, ed., *The Portable Jung* (New York: Viking, 1971).

21. Erik H. Erikson, *Childhood and Society,* 2nd ed. (New York: Norton, 1963), pp. 247–274.

22. Gail Sheehy, *Passages* (New York: Dutton, 1976), pp. 25–32.

23. Daniel J. Levinson, *The Seasons of a Man's Life* (New York: Knopf, 1978).

24. William R. Looft, "Socialization and Personality Throughout the Life Span: An Examination of Contemporary Psychological Approaches," *Life-Span Developmental Psychology: Personality and Socialization,* ed. Paul B. Baltes and K. Warner Schaie (New York: Academic, 1973), p. 51.

25. Ibid., p. 51.

26. Bernice L. Neugarten and Nancy Datan, "Sociological Perspectives on the Life Cycle," *Life-Span Developmental Psychology: Personality and Socialization,* ed. Paul B. Baltes and K. Warner Schaie (New York: Academic, 1973), p. 54.

Chapter 7

Exemplary Instructor Characteristics and Roles

A few years ago Ivan Illich, the author of *Deschooling Society,* lectured on our campus. As part of his visit he met with a small group of graduate students and faculty members interested in his views on adult education. None of the group had met him before, and we all looked forward to our planned hour.

Exactly at the scheduled time he strode into the room, his black cape flowing out behind him. He stopped for a moment in the front of the room, glanced at the audience, and then with a flourish pulled off his cape and handed it to one of the persons escorting him. He sat in the chair provided for him, crossed his long legs, and said with a heavy European accent, "Are there any questions?"

The room was quiet as we wondered how to respond to this flamboyant man we'd come to hear and who now waited for one of us to speak. His characteristics as an instructor did not fit what we had expected. After a pause, the questioning began and we had a most enjoyable and useful discussion that afternoon.

Over the years we all have experienced a great variety of instructor characteristics. We all can remember teachers who displayed characteristics that so annoyed us that we learned less than we thought we should have. At other times the opposite was the case. The teacher's characteristics were so positive that we learned much more than we had anticipated.

Detailed and General Descriptions

Do returning students prefer *particular* instructor characteristics? The experts differ in their answers. One group of writers and researchers advocates a very detailed listing of instructor characteristics that are most apt to enhance adult learning. These characteristics are written as competencies that the instructor should perform.

A second group suggests a more general listing of instructor characteristics that are most likely to enhance adult learning.

Competency Approach

An assumption of the competency approach is that instructor characteristics (competencies) can be defined specifically. A project conducted by a consortium of Florida adult educators and practitioners resulted in a list of competencies for instructors of adults. One category of the list related to instructional skills, which included those listed below.

Competencies Relating to Instructional Skills

Facilitates Individual Adjustment to the Changing Nature of Our Society.

Assist learners who desire to assume new roles in society.
Demonstrate instructional skills which assist adult learners in relating with peers.
Use social skills which assist adult learners in developing a positive self-concept.
Use instructional skills which assist adult learners in developing a positive self-concept.
Assist adult learners in acquiring social skills to relate with peers.

Uses Instructional Methods with Special Relevance to and Effectiveness for Adult Learners.

Communicate in a coherent and logical manner.
Utilize sequential, relevant short-range instructional objectives.
Apply basic principles of group dynamics and leadership techniques.
Apply instructional techniques which utilize talents, abilities, and experiences of group members.

Provide practical activities for learning which reinforce instruction.

Use reinforcement techniques.

Maintain interest of adult learners in educational activities.

Guide and facilitate self-directed learning in the adult learners.

Adjust instructional techniques to meet the immediate learning needs of adult learners.

Employ acceptable techniques for modifying inappropriate behavior.

Assesses Learning Needs of Adult Learners.

Diagnose entry knowledge and skill of adult learner for a given set of instructional objectives.

Provide for self-evaluation.

Use an appropriate system for keeping records of class and individual progress.

Use criteria-based assessment procedures.

Provide continuous feedback to adult learners on their educational progress.

Recognize symptoms of physical deficiencies that may be related to adult learning.[1]

The competency approach offers several advantages. First, instructor characteristics are identified as behaviors to be performed. An instructor of adults can see specifically what should be done when teaching adult learners. Second, evaluating instructor effectiveness is easier when specific competencies are identified. The evaluator need only compare performance to required competencies.

The disadvantages of the competency approach are several. First, the competencies are usually identified by observing expert teachers and then attempting to specify the acts the expert teachers perform. Arthur Combs points out the problem in doing this: "It is a fallacy to assume that the methods of the experts can or should be taught to beginners. . . . It simply does not follow that what is good for the expert is good for the novice, too. Nor is it true that the way to become expert is to do what the expert does. Some of the methods used by experts can only be used because he is expert."[2]

A second problem with the competency approach is the assumption that all aspects of education can be defined in behavioral terms. That is, the instructor defines outcomes and then prepares people to accomplish these outcomes. It is an approach that has served business and industry well for a number of years. The problem is the assumption that the production of industrial goods is similar to the "production" of intelligent human beings. Many would question the use of the word *production* in this sense and would argue that we cannot "produce" intelligent human beings, but at best only nurture, encourage, and provide some assistance for those who wish to become more intelligent.

Of course there is also the frightening prospect of the instructor confronting a long list of competencies. As Combs says, "Confronting long lists of competencies is likely to be deeply discouraging and disillusioning to the young teacher.... Discouraging and disillusioning as the behavioral objectives–competencies approach is for the young teacher—it has equally unhappy effects on the older ones. A vast complex of competencies, all of which are demanded as criteria for good teaching, leaves the individual defenseless before criticism. No matter what he does well, it is never enough."[3]

And finally, the competency approach denies the vast individuality of instructors—that some will do certain things and others will do other things and both may be equally effective as instructors, though very different from each other.

General Characteristics Approach

A broader approach to exemplary instructor characteristics comes from the field of humanistic psychology. The following instructor characteristics were developed from a review of this literature.[4]

Exemplary instructors of adult learners—

1. *Are more concerned about learners than about things and events.* They believe in the capacity of adults to learn. These instructors recognize the breadth of influences that face returning students. They believe it is important to help returning students find personal meaning in what they are studying and experiencing, and they recognize the unique qualities possessed by each returning student.

2. *Know their subject matter.* They keep up to date with what is new in their academic areas. They research and write in their discipline areas, but they are also keenly aware that, to be a successful instructor with returning students, more is required than a solid foundation in an academic area.

3. *Relate theory to practice and their own field to other fields.*
Rather than segregating information, they promote integrating
information. They search for ties among the arts, the humanities,
and the sciences. They are thus at the same time specialists in
their own discipline and generalists in many others, including,
where applicable, the field of practice—how their subject matter
applies to society.

4. *Are confident as instructors.* As Combs points out, "It is
only when persons feel fundamentally adequate that self can be
transcended and attention given to the needs of others. Inadequate persons cannot afford the time and effort required to assist others as long as they feel deprived themselves."[5]

5. *Are open to a wide variety of teaching approaches.* They do
not assume any one teaching approach is the "best" approach for
all situations, but recognize that a number of factors influence
which teaching methods are used. "The good teacher is not one
who behaves in a given way. He is an artist, skillful in facilitating
effective growth in students. To accomplish this he must use
methods appropriate to the complex circumstance he is involved
in. His methods must fit the goals he seeks, the [learners] he is
working with, the philosophy he is guided by, the immediate
conditions under which he is working, to say nothing of his own
feelings, goals, and desires."[6]

6. *Share their whole person.* These instructors do not see
teaching as but one facet of their lives, to be segregated from the
rest of their lives and the rest of their personalities. They recognize that their effectiveness is wrapped up in the totality of who
they are. This totality is communicated not only by what is said,
but also in actions, facial expressions, and the feelings that are
communicated about both students and the subject matter. Exemplary instructors are individual persons. They act natural in
the classroom; they don't try to emulate some professor whom
they admire or follow some recipe book for teaching that they
have acquired.

7. *Encourage learning outcomes that go beyond course objectives.* For instance, they encourage adult learners to experience
the joy of working cooperatively in community with each other,
with the openness to share not only experiences but also feelings.
These instructors are aware of the unlimited potentials for learning—that what happens in any classroom or other setting is but
a hint of what could happen to learners.

8. *Create a positive atmosphere for learning.* They are alert to students' reactions, both spoken and unspoken. They can read in the faces of people puzzlement, dismay, disappointment, disagreement, agreement, enthusiasm, boredom—and know appropriate responses. They know when to encourage a learner, when to provide direction, and when to allow free rein. They are constantly asking questions: Have you thought of this? Have you considered what might happen if you continued to do this? How do you feel about what you're doing? What changes have you considered making? These exemplary instructors believe learners should be encouraged to work toward their learning potential, but they also know that many factors over which the learner has little or no control often prevent a potential from being reached.

The general characteristics approach has several advantages that the competency approach described above does not have. The general characteristics serve as guidelines. Individual instructors are free to develop their own teaching approaches within these guidelines. Also the characteristics include instructor feelings as well as knowledge and skills.

The major disadvantage to the general characteristics approach to describing exemplary instructors is the lack of specific criteria for instructor evaluation. The competency approach provides for fairly easy instructor evaluation.

What Students Prefer

What do adult learners say they prefer as characteristics of their instructors? Robert Alciatore and Pegge Alciatore asked 1,593 college seniors about the quality of teaching they experienced in their four years of undergraduate work.[7] They separated the responses for those under twenty-four and those twenty-four years of age or older. Students under twenty-four agreed with the older students about the characteristics of the best and the worst teachers. However, the younger students were more critical of their teachers as a whole than were the older students.

A very high rating was given by both groups of students to teachers who allowed for discussion time, who used self-paced materials, and who often used a project approach to their teaching. (The project approach is a problem-solving process where students are given the opportunity to work through a real-life or close-to-real-life problem situation.)

Both younger and older students preferred teachers who used study guides, specified the objectives for their courses, and kept regular office hours. Both groups of students said the best college teachers are those persons who like people. They gave significantly higher ratings to teachers who were "genuinely concerned for students and their progress." Unfortunately, according to the researchers, less than 45 percent of the teachers at the college surveyed were believed to have this concern.

Both groups of students listed the following qualities for the best teachers they had during their four years of college: (1) interest in students, (2) good personality, (3) interest in subject matter, (4) ability to make subject interesting, and (5) objectivity in presenting subject matter and in dealing with students.

The worst teachers had (1) poor communication skills; (2) poor personalities, with lack of enthusiasm most often mentioned; (3) lack of organization; (4) lack of objectivity; and (5) little interest in students.

Some instructors appeared on both the best-instructor list and the worst-instructor list. One teacher in particular, who was viewed as warm, outgoing, and open but was also quite unstructured in his teaching, received fifteen mentions as a "best" teacher and twelve mentions as a "worst" teacher. This was viewed as a reflection of differences in students' expectations of a teacher.

From this research, Alciatore and Alciatore drew the following conclusions:

1. Both younger and older students prefer instructors who are student-oriented.

2. Both younger and older students prefer teachers who are organized but not overly structured. ("Organized" and "structured" referred to stating course objectives prior to the beginning of a course, posting office hours, and offering class presentations that are well organized.)

3. The type of teaching strategy or method employed is highly related to student preferences. Student-oriented methods received the highest marks by these students.

4. Although there are certain qualities that all seniors prefer to see in actual or ideal instructors, the unique learning style of students is still quite evident. The best teacher for one student may be a poor teacher for another.

In 1976, Kenneth Feldman summarized forty-nine studies where college students, both younger and older, were asked to list the characteristics they most preferred in their instructors.[8] After reviewing all the studies, the instructor characteristics that appeared most often were (1) the ability to stimulate interest in the topic, (2) enthusiasm, (3) knowledge of subject taught, and (4) preparation for and organization of the course taught.

In addition to these characteristics, students in these studies said they preferred instructors who were concerned about and respected students, who were available, and who were open to students' opinions.

Stanford Ericksen summed up the characteristics of exemplary college instructors—for all ages of college students—by raising four questions:[9]

1. Does the teacher care? If the teacher is not excited about what he or she is teaching, it is not likely the students will be excited either.

2. Is the teacher fair? According to Ericksen, students will object to unfair treatment more quickly than to excessive demands in assignments and workload.

3. How is the course relevant? This question is particularly important for returning students. They deserve to know where the course in question fits into their curriculum, why it is required (if it is), of what practical value it might be, and how it relates to their career choice.

4. Does the teacher know the subject matter?

From the research completed so far it would appear that the characteristics younger students prefer in instructors are the same characteristics returning students prefer. Unfortunately the amount of research that specifically asked returning students to list instructor characteristics is slight. The question yet unanswered: Are there unique characteristics of instructors that returning students prefer that are not mentioned by traditional students?

Instructor Roles

What does the literature tell us about the roles college instructors perform in the classroom? Writers and researchers have devised several answers to this question. Some of the roles that these writers discuss are presented on a continuum from good to bad. Others answer the question in terms of multiple roles to be performed. Joseph Axelrod has described five different roles—he calls them styles—that college instructors in the humanities perform:[10]

1. Drillmaster. This instructor is the ultimate authority. Students have no decisions to make, they are all made by the instructor, and there is only one acceptable answer to any question raised by the drillmaster/instructor.

2. Content-centered. This instructor emphasizes the mastery of material already discovered by researchers in the field. Students are viewed as coming to the content-centered instructor so they can accumulate the information that someone believes they need. Each student masters the material in essentially the same way. Insofar as possible, the content-centered instructor tries to keep the classroom an emotion-free place.

3. Instructor-centered. This instructor serves as a model, demonstrating to the students in the class what the instructor believes are the best ways of apprehending the material to be learned. The emphasis is not on the mastery of the material, but on learning the approach the instructor has to conceiving problems, defining them, thinking about them, and presenting information related to them.

4. Intellect-centered. Here the focus is also on the process of analysis and problem solving instead of on the material to be learned. But rather than the instructor modeling the "one best way," the instructor who is intellect-centered will often teach several approaches to analysis. Detailed coverage of the field is not of concern.

5. Person-centered. This instructor is guided by a philosophy of teaching that has its foundation in human development, the process by which people can achieve their greatest potentials for humanness. The person-centered instructor, like the intellect-centered, is interested in academic matters but insists it is impossible to separate matters of human development that are nonacademic from those that are academic. This instructor is concerned with personal meanings, attitudes, and feelings at the same time academic matters are considered. This instructor believes it is impossible to be an effective college instructor if the academic is separated from the nonacademic.

Though the intention of this writer appears to place these five approaches to teaching on a continuum, with the fifth approach the best, it is possible to consider certain times when the role of content-centered instructor, for instance, may be appropriate. There are times when returning instructors need to master a given content area, say some phase of mathematics, before they can go on to learning something else or before they can go on to a learning situation that is clearly led by a person-centered instructor. And there may be times when returning students would like the instructor to be instructor-centered and model how a given problem might be defined and analyzed and the results of the effort reported. So it seems possible to combine, within the person-centered instructor, some dimensions of the other roles if the situation demands.

Thomas Green talks about conditioning and training on one end of a continuum and instruction and indoctrination on the other end.[11] Training excludes the process of asking questions, looking at evidence, analyzing situations, and reaching decisions. Training aims at a change in behavior. Persons who wish to learn lifesaving skills are trained to do that, for example.

Conditioning, according to Green, is an extreme form of training, where there is no display of intelligence. A person performs some act without thinking about it. Certain types of behavior modification may be classed as conditioning.

Indoctrination deals with thinking, but thinking in a given way. People are indoctrinated to believe in a certain way just as people may be conditioned to act in a predictable way. Though indoctrination deals with thinking it does not deal with intelligent thinking—only thinking along the lines advocated by the instructor.

According to Green's scheme, the only strongly positive role on his continuum is the instruction role. The other three, with the possible exception of the training role, are dehumanizing to the learner. When the teacher performs the role of instructor, the learners are encouraged to weigh carefully evidence in a situation and are asked to give reasons for their decisions; they are, Green points out, in "a kind of conversation" with the instructor.

Kenneth Benne, concerned particularly with the education of adults, suggests four roles for the instructor, all of which may be performed from time to time as the situation demands.[12]

1. Model. The model role is performed by the educator to illustrate, for example, how a problem is conceptualized, analyzed,

and discussed. Through both actions and words the educator can demonstrate interest in and importance of the topic. Often the returning adult student can benefit from an instructor who can model various aspects of the learning process, particularly the relatively recent returning student who is having difficulty adjusting to a formal learning environment.

2. Expert Resource. The instructor serves as a source of information for the learner. This role comes closest to the traditional role of instructor as provider of information. Put into perspective, the expert resource role is an important one for instructors of returning students. But the instructor should make it clear that he or she is but one source of information for the learner and should be considered along with other sources such as the learner's experience, other learners in the group, textbooks, and library resources.

3. Counselor. The instructor of returning students often serves as a counselor when dealing both with academic and nonacademic problems of returning students. One problem that the instructor of returning students faces is knowing when to refer the returning student with personal problems to professional counselors. The problem is difficult because there is seldom a clear line between a personal problem and an academic problem. Aside from dealing with personal problems, the instructor of returning students will spend many hours as an academic counselor to returning students, particularly during the time when they are first adjusting to formal schooling.

4. Guide for the Learning Process. In this role the instructor of returning students focuses attention on the learning process itself and is constantly concerned with improving it. The instructor uses a variety of teaching methods designed to fit a broad range of situations. (See the succeeding chapter for a discussion of some of these methods.) The instructor, serving as a guide for the learning process, is knowledgeable about the total learning environment and the influences that can be modified as well as those that cannot.

According to Benne, the competent instructor of adults is able to follow any and all of these roles, as the situation demands. The focus of these roles is on enhancing the learning environment for the learner, so in effect all the roles are learner oriented.

Summary

In this chapter we looked at the characteristics and the roles of exemplary instructors of adult learners. The research and writing on instructor characteristics was explored from two perspectives—what the experts had to say and what the students themselves said. The experts are split in how they view characteristics of exemplary instructors. One group defines them as specific competencies that instructors should be able to perform. A second group cites broad characteristics that exemplary instructors should possess. There are advantages and disadvantages to each approach.

Studies of what students say they prefer in an instructor and what the experts say generally agree. Students say they want instructors who (1) are student oriented, (2) are organized but not overly structured, (3) have enthusiasm, (4) know their subject matter, (5) are prepared, and (6) are able to stimulate interest in the topic.

The education literature includes considerable writing about the roles exemplary instructors should perform. Generally, for the returning student, those roles that are learner oriented are the ones preferred.

NOTES

1. Thomas W. Mann and Arthur W. Burrichter, *Competencies for Adult Educators and an Assessment Inventory* (Tallahassee: Florida State Department of Education, 1976), pp. 7–8.

2. Arthur W. Combs et al., *The Professional Education of Teachers: A Humanistic Approach to Teacher Preparation* (Boston: Allyn and Bacon, 1974), p. 4.

3. Ibid., p. 5.

4. See the following as examples of the literature from which these general characteristics are derived: Erich Fromm, *The Revolution of Hope: Toward a Humanized Technology* (New York: Harper and Row, 1968); Frank G. Goble, *The Third Force* (New York: Grossman, 1970); A. H. Maslow, *The Farther Reaches of Human Nature* (New York: Viking Press, 1972); Donald A. Read and Sidney B. Simon, eds., *Humanistic Education Sourcebook* (Englewood Cliffs, N.J.: Prentice-Hall, 1975); Carl R. Rogers, *Freedom to Learn* (Columbus, Ohio: Merrill, 1969).

5. Combs et al., p. 85.

6. Ibid., p. 7.

7. Robert T. Alciatore and Pegge L. Alciatore, "Consumer Reactions to College Teaching," *Improving College and University Teaching,* vol. 27, no. 2, Spring 1979, pp. 93–95.

8. Kenneth A. Feldman, "The Superior College Teacher from the Students' View," *Research in Higher Education* 5 (1976): 243–288.

9. Stanford C. Ericksen, "Earning and Learning by the Hour," *Effective College Teaching,* ed. William H. Morris (Washington, D.C.: The American Association for Higher Education, 1970), p. 2.

10. Joseph Axelrod, "Teaching Styles in the Humanities," *Effective College Teaching,* ed. William H. Morris (Washington, D.C.: The American Association for Higher Education, 1970), pp. 43–49.

11. Thomas F. Green, "The Concept of Teaching," *Teaching and Learning,* ed. Donald Vandenberg (Urbana, Ill.: University of Illinois Press, 1969), pp. 6–8.

12. Kenneth D. Benne, "Some Philosophic Issues in Adult Education," *Adult Education,* vol. 7, no. 2, Winter 1957.

Chapter 8

Learning Formats and Techniques

> All are sleeping,
> just one is preaching:
> Such performance is
> called here 'teaching.'

This old German poem says all too well what passes for teaching in many college classrooms. But there is one major difference when we place returning students in the setting illustrated by the poem. They will not be sleeping for most of them are making many sacrifices to be in a college classroom. More likely they will politely put up with the "preaching" for a time, but if they think they are not gaining from the course what they believe they deserve, they will complain. And then the administration and the "preaching" instructor will have to face the question of what will be done—a difficult question to answer, particularly if no one has ever before challenged the "preaching" instructor who knows no other way to teach.

In this chapter I'll discuss various formats and techniques that instructors who work with returning students may find useful. Interestingly enough, many of these formats and techniques work well with more traditional students too. I'll also discuss some of the factors that influence which formats and techniques should be considered.

123

We need to spend a moment examining the research on teaching methods. For more than fifty years, educators have attempted to determine which teaching methods are better than others. Is the lecture better than group discussion, for instance?

Robert Dubin and Thomas Taveggia summarized four decades of this research (ninety-one studies) and concluded that there are no appreciable differences among the many teaching methods, *when an examination is used to determine whether learning has occurred.*

All this research assumed persons learned when they gained subject-matter content. The approach used to measure content gain was the examination. As Dubin and Taveggia argue, "To say that content learning, as measured by course examination is not relevant to the reasons why students are in college is simply to fly in the face of reality. Students are in institutions of higher education to learn content. We measure this learning by examinations which are content-oriented."[1] Dubin and Taveggia go on to point out that a variety of teaching approaches are equally effective "for transmitting knowledge to the next generation," which they point out is the primary purpose of education.

I do not agree with Dubin and Taveggia's assumption that the primary purpose of higher education is passing on content from one generation to another, particularly as applied to the returning student. I would agree that content is an important dimension of much learning, but learning content—particularly factual information—is a superficial and often only a beginning purpose for an educational program directed toward returning students.

Beyond acquiring content, returning students are interested in learning skills of various types—problem-solving skills, analytical skills, and communication skills. Returning students are interested in discovering and making sense out of their own experiences. And returning students are interested in relating their life experience to theoretical information.

All these purposes go beyond merely acquiring content. To provide opportunities for these broader purposes to be fulfilled, a variety of teaching methods need to be considered, including those that do not have content presentation as their primary purpose.

Philip Werdell underlines the need for a broad range of teaching methods: "While cognitive learning should continue to have high priority, the problem of integrating learning and living for the future clearly demands new emphasis on other kinds and styles of learning, as well. Specifically, the curriculum must offer experiences in creative and speculative uses of the intellect as well as analytical uses. It must offer opportunities to *act* on the basis of what one understands as well as the opportunity to theorize about ideal solutions."[2]

If we were interested only in cognitive learning for returning students—the accumulation of content—it would make no sense to have this chapter. We would simply employ instructors to develop a content-presentation approach, probably the lecture, to a high level. But teaching returning students turns out to be a more complex process than content presentation alone.

Definitions

A problem educators have had for years is lack of consistency in use of terms. In the area of teaching we toss around such terms as *teaching methods, strategies, techniques, formats,* and *approaches*—often synonymously.

Here I am using the terms *format* and *technique,* and in particular ways. *Format* refers to how people are organized for learning. I'll discuss two categories of formats: (1) those designed for *individuals,* such as the internship and supervised independent study, and (2) those designed for *groups,* such as the class and the seminar. *Technique* refers to the particular teaching approach used within a format. I'll discuss both teaching techniques for presenting information, such as the lecture and the panel discussion, and techniques for involving learners in small and large classes.

Below we look briefly at only a sampling of learning formats and techniques. Chapter 14 includes a list of resources where these and other formats and techniques are discussed.

Individual Formats

Because of the great diversity among returning students in terms of their backgrounds and their interests, the best format is often an individual-oriented format.

Supervised Independent Study

This format consists of a series of learning experiences designed for one student and supervised by an instructor. It can take a variety of forms. One form that I have used successfully with students is organized as follows: I first discuss with the student why he or she is interested in doing independent study and the possibility that some other approach might better meet their needs—attending a course, reading a book, talking with a resource person. When both the student and I are convinced that a supervised independent study approach is appropriate, I ask the student to prepare a brief written proposal for a semester's independent study activity (sometimes we map out a two-semester activity). In the proposal I suggest the student write what he or she hopes to learn from the project, what approaches will be used to accomplish the learning, and what product will be developed at the end of the independent study activity. In our discussion I suggest possible resources that might be used and possible end products that might be developed, such as a paper, a tape recording, a slide-tape, a graphic representative, or some other product appropriate to the independent study activity. We also work out a schedule of meeting times when the student will meet with me to discuss problems and progress with the project.

For instance, I recently worked with a student who was interested in learning about the history of general and cooperative extension in this country. During the course of the semester she read six or seven books on this topic and interviewed several people who had spent many years working in extension. I met with her about every two weeks to discuss the books she read and the interviews she had conducted. I also shared with her what I knew on this topic. Her final product was a chart that illustrated the major events in the development of extension in this country.

Most returning students appreciate the opportunity to do some independent study as part of their degree programs. Some will want to do more than others. I recall one of my master's degree students who took but two courses in her entire graduate program. The rest she accomplished following a supervised independent study format.

Internship

Because many returning students are enrolled in higher education with a job-related interest, providing opportunities for students to work in the jobs of their choice, as trainees, makes a lot of sense. The internship is a kind of on-the-job training where the student works with an employer, either for money or for free, but in either instance supervised by an instructor. Those involved in internships also meet occasionally with their instructors, sometimes in groups with other interns, to discuss what they are learning and any problems they may be experiencing.

Interns may work full time for a semester, or they may take classes and work part-time as interns. It is important that the internship work supervisor realizes that the intern is there to learn, not just to perform some task for him or her free of charge. This is not a problem if the instructor has developed working relationships with potential internship work supervisors prior to placing students.

Self-Study

One of the goals adult education has is to develop autonomous learners who are capable of planning their own learning activities and carrying them out, either with or without assistance of instructors. Returning students, as part of their formal educational activities, will often also take part in various self-study activities. Because self-study is entirely organized and carried out by the learner, it has much appeal to many returning students.

Self-study is used by students to enrich what they are studying in the classroom, to take them beyond what they are reading and discussing in formal classes. Self-study is also used as a way of reviewing material that was studied some years ago, in preparation for taking a more advanced course in an area.

One major category of self-study materials are the so-called programmed materials. In a programmed workbook, information is presented in tiny pieces, one piece at a time with a progression from the simple to the more complex. Each step along the way requires a response from the student and for each response there is immediate feedback. If the answer is wrong, the student is directed back to an explanation of the error.

Not all information can be fit into a programmed format. But for some information it works well. I remember when I was in graduate school and studying statistics. It had been fifteen years since I had studied mathematics, and I simply couldn't keep up with the rest of the students in my class. I went to the library and stumbled onto a statistics programmed text. If I remember correctly, we were discussing probability theory at the time. By the time I had worked through the programmed text's section on probability I had a workable understanding of the theory, at least enough so I knew what was going on in class.

There are also many self-study materials available that do not follow a programmed format, yet provide the student with an opportunity to work exercises related to the topic considered. And students who are quite adept at self-study can devise their own activities based on reading they do on their own.

Counseling

There is a fine line between what I will call counseling as a format for learning and counseling as a psychological device to relieve some distressful condition a person is experiencing.

Counseling is, of course, a one-to-one format between student and instructor. It can serve a variety of functions—to draw out, support, motivate, provide information, and help the student gain insights, to mention a few.

For at least three reasons returning students require more counseling than do traditional students. As we have pointed out earlier, most returning students are quite insecure in their role as students and often require considerable support during the first months they are in school. Second, many of them, because they have been out of school for some time, require some weeks to polish study skills and generally make the adjustment to student life. And third, they do not have the networks that traditional students have to find out the routine things about student life, including how one prepares for a test if taking Professor Smith's course, how to find access to a book that is checked out of the library, and so on. Of course, such requests as, "Tell me once more what the requirements are for a degree in this department," are common, from traditional as well as returning students. Incidentally, too many professors who are very proficient in their subject-matter fields are stopped short when a student asks them about requirements for the degree. Minimal qualifications for the instructor as counselor are having the patience and the time to listen and having routine information readily available.

It is also important to be able to recognize those situations where the student is deeply disturbed or even suicidal and to know where the student can be referred for professional help.

Another qualification for the instructor who counsels is to be available, and that does not mean routinely seeing students without an appointment. What it does mean is letting students know your office hours and also letting them know that if there is an emergency you will see them anytime. It means taking time after class to talk with students and helping to arrange informal gatherings of students, such as potluck dinners, or going out for a beer after class, or inviting students to the professor's house for a picnic. These informal situations are ideal for certain types of counseling, but more important, they provide an opportunity for students to get to know each other informally as well as to get to know the professor informally.

Interestingly enough, once returning students have been back in school for a time, they set up networks in which they do a good deal of counseling with each other. In my experience this interstudent counseling has been extremely effective.

Distance Learning

Another individual format that is receiving a good deal of attention these days is distance learning. The student may be enrolled in a course, listen to the lectures on the radio or watch them on TV, do the readings and turn in assignments, complete the examinations, and all the while never leave home. While other students may be enrolled in the course at the same time, they never see each other, indeed have no idea who the other people enrolled in the course are.

The correspondence course is another example of the individual format that is still popular, although the completion rate of the correspondence courses continues to be quite low.

Still another form of distance learning is the educational telephone network (ETN), in which a person, oftentimes several people, gather at a listening point where they listen to a class presentation and are able to ask questions of the instructor, who may be hundreds, even thousands, of miles away. Occasionally the ETN system instructors attempt to develop discussion groups of those assembled at listening posts, and when this occurs we no longer have an individual format.

With the likelihood of increasing energy costs in this country we see more distance learning practiced. We have the technology to make distance learning practical. What is missing is the interaction with other students that has always made group formats popular with learners, no matter what their age or experience. Learning by oneself can be a lonely activity—so lonely that some learners simply do not do well or are not motivated to continue learning and drop out.

Group Formats

We are most acquainted with the group formats in higher education, particularly the class—so much so that it's difficult to even consider legitimate some of the various individual formats we discussed in the previous section. Indeed, there are still graduate schools who will not accept as graduate credit those credits earned in certain individual formats. But as we shall see below, there are other group formats to consider besides the class formats that are generally not foreign to any college instructor. Let's begin, however, with the class.

Class

The single most widely used format for education around the world, no matter at what level, is the class. The basic relationship in the class is between what happens in front of the class and the class members themselves. And as Malcolm Knowles points out, the quality of the class is directly related to the quantity and the quality of the interaction.[3] In other words, the greater the amount and the higher the quality of interaction that takes place between the class and the instructor, and among the class members, the greater the learning there is likely to be.

Knowles identifies various levels of interaction in a class. The lowest level of interaction occurs when the instructor is only talking. Interaction can be increased when some visual aid is introduced, such as a blackboard, a flip chart, slides, short film, videotape, or some other visual device.

Interaction can be developed further if two people are interacting in front of the class, say an instructor debating a question with an invited resource person. And interaction moves up further when there are several people in front of the class, such as a panel presentation or role playing. But as Knowles points out, up to this point all the interaction has been passive. There has been no active involvement of the class members in the process.

The interaction changes to an active interaction when the class members have an opportunity to ask questions of the instructor or others who may be assisting with the presentation. And a still higher level of interaction is attained when members of the class are brought to the front of the class, say as part of a listening team that has responsibility for raising questions to ask the instructor or other presenters.

And finally, one of the highest levels of interaction, according to Knowles, occurs when the class members have the opportunity to interact with each other. The class can be broken up into small groups, pairs, or triads to discuss a segment of a presentation, ask questions of the instructor, react to the instructor's presentation in terms of disagreement or agreement, relate the instructor's presentation to the readings, and so on. (In the following section on techniques we will say more about how to involve students.)

Of course it is far easier to achieve interaction when the class has thirty students or fewer compared to when it has more, say up to several hundred. In the case of very large classes, the instructor is challenged to achieve the highest level of interaction possible, given the conditions under which the teaching is done.

Seminar

Everyone working in higher education knows about seminars, yet if you ask five instructors to tell you what a seminar is, you will receive five different answers. Sometimes any small class is called a seminar, even if the instructor lectures to the group and conducts day-to-day activities similar to what might be done if fifty students were present rather than twelve.

Ideally a seminar, according to Kenneth Eble, should be "a small number of intensely interested and knowing individuals letting their minds play on a common topic."[4]

In practice the seminar either operates as a regular class or, at the other extreme, has no focus to it at all and simply becomes a rambling, nondirected discussion session that wanders here and there and leaves many students, as well as instructors, perplexed and confused.

Because returning students have a rich background of experience, the seminar format, when properly used, can be a useful one. To be properly used the seminar must have a specific aim and focus. It is not enough to say the seminar is organized to deal with students' interests.

To be effective, the seminar must have a focus. That is not to say that a group of students should not meet and discuss possible topics for a seminar. Indeed, that is one way to develop topics for seminars, particularly when large numbers of returning students are involved. In operation the seminar should keep to its focus and aims while allowing the participants to contribute their experiences and reflect on how their experiences relate to other students' experiences and research available on the topic.

But as Eble points out, many seminars go wrong: "The seminar takes up discussion before an adequate base of information exists, and it ends with the delivery of formal papers crammed into the last weeks of the term."[5]

Being able to use the Socratic method often works well for the instructor in a seminar setting. As most instructors know, the Socratic method involves asking a participant a series of questions that helps the participant move from where he or she is to some broader level of understanding of knowledge they already possess.

Group Project

The group project can be compared to supervised independent study, except several persons work together on the project and meet with the instructor from time to time to discuss their problems and progress. Because returning students already have considerable experience and often have a very clear idea of their goals, this approach can be very valuable.

One form the group project can take is an action project. When I taught a course in community development, students in the course, in addition to attending the classes and doing the assignments, had the opportunity to work on group projects in the community. One group of three students worked with a senior citizen center on the problem of excessive payments by senior citizens for prescription drugs. The students interviewed pharmacists in the area, talked with senior citizens, discussed the problems with state officials, and organized a meeting for senior citizens in the community to discuss the problem.

Network Group

In some ways the network group doesn't fit into this list because the instructor is not involved. The network group is made up entirely of students who meet together from time to time, either scheduled or not, to talk about specific topics or simply to share problems.

For instance I know of a group of six returning students on our campus who eat lunch together once each week. They discuss the courses they are taking, the assignments they are working on, and even occasionally personal problems.

Another network group I am aware of meets weekly for about two hours to discuss one another's research progress. They are all returning students working on graduate degrees and have, as one of their requirements, the development and completion of a research project. They make presentations, critique one another's written research proposals, and offer a good deal of assistance and support to one another.

The network group can be exceedingly important to the returning student, particularly the part-time student who does not have the time to ferret out answers to many of the routine questions that come along, such as, What is a good resource book on basic statistics? or, How does one prepare for a comprehensive master's degree examination? Someone in the network group will likely have the answer to the question. And beyond providing information, as we mentioned earlier, the network group is often an excellent counseling mechanism for its members.

In terms of where instructors fit into a network group, sometimes beginning returning students can be introduced to other returning students who already are part of a network group, or occasionally an instructor may need to encourage students to organize a network group. But once the group is operating, it generally does well on its own. Sometimes network groups will ask instructors to meet with them to provide particular kinds of information or to help the group see another perspective on an issue they are discussing. But by and large they operate on their own.

Others

Two other group formats that should be mentioned are field trips and the laboratory. A field trip allows a group to observe firsthand and to study an object or a place of interest. If a class is studying inner-core public schools, then a visit to one will add a dimension to the inquiry that cannot be provided by books or class discussion.

And for many subject areas where hands-on experience is necessary, the laboratory is essential. In some ways the laboratory is a form of independent study with the instructor readily available when assistance is necessary.

Instructional Techniques

Within the fields of adult education and higher education, considerable material has been written about instructional techniques. Here we will mention briefly several techniques within two broad categories: (1) techniques for presenting information, and (2) techniques for involving participants.

We have tried to be neither inclusive nor complete. Readers are referred to the bibliography at the end of the book (chapter 14) for those titles where techniques are treated in considerably more depth.

For Presenting Information

The Lecture

Just as the class is the most popular format for college and university teaching, lecturing is far and away the most popular instructional technique. The technique is applauded and criticized by educators, students, and interested bystanders as much today as it has been in the past.

If the instructor's task is to present information, and the class is larger than, say, thirty-five, the lecture can be an effective technique. Many people argue the lecture became outmoded when the printing press was invented, and people had easy access to books. Eble has an answer as to why we still have lecturers and lectures: "The book did not sweep out the lecture any more than television has swept out books, for the simple reason that human beings remain responsive to all forms of intercourse with other consenting humans. The book lacks what television lacks: face-to-face confrontation with other talking, gesturing, thinking, feeling humans. Thus, the live lecture, despite its shortcomings, has reasons for its continued use."[6]

As Ralph Tyler pointed out to me, "The lecture is not primarily a technique for the student to get information because in most cases information is more easily comprehended when it is written or pictured. The lecture, however, may help to explain something and thus provide motivation; it may help to clarify a learner's objectives; the lecture may actually demonstrate the kinds of things the student could be learning."

Russell Bostert, a historian, writes about seven different lecturing techniques he has observed in his discipline, all of which have merit, in his opinion, but all quite different from one another.[7] He first describes the *scholars,* who are immersed in their subjects and who are precise and deliberate in their speech, who clear a path through the confusion of ideas and leave their classes with the idea they have witnessed thoughtful scholars in action. Second, he tells about the *flashy professors,* who enjoy themselves in a performance role, who attack a historical problem and overwhelm it with their energy, inspiration, and information. Third are those *professors who write great literature* with their spoken words, who leave quotable quotes that students can enter into their notebooks and examine, speculate about, and repeat years after. Fourth are the *no-nonsense professionals,* with their carefully organized remarks that are clear and logical and leave the students with an impression of how history can be thought about. Fifth are the *witty professors,* who have a repertoire of anecdotes and stories that keep students alert to the points discussed, yet the professors do not stray over the line of becoming entertainers versus great teachers. Sixth, the *serious professors,* who are obviously mature, concerned about history, and committed to presenting their ideas. And seventh, the apparently disorganized *meandering professors,* whose meanderings suddenly become clear and demonstrate insights that cause students to think about history in ways they never did before.

The point is, not only is lecturing an often useful technique, particularly if used with other so-called interactive techniques, but also there are many different ways of lecturing, often depending on the personality of the instructor.

We have all heard dreadfully bad lectures, a few sparkling, brilliant lectures, and thousands that are neither good nor bad. Rather than attempt to offer a list of principles for good lecturing, which all of us have seen or heard at one time or another, I would like to report on a lecturer I heard who I thought was particularly good. I was attending, for my own interest, a course on the Old Testament, and the person I am about to describe lectured most of the time, with about ten minutes at the end of each lecture saved for questions from the class. He used the chalkboard as a visual, scratching on it from time to time a few key words and a poorly drawn map of Palestine.

Not one person in the class of thirty took his or her eyes off this man during the time he lectured. It occurred to me that what kept me and the others interested in his topic was the kind of relationship he was able to develop with the group. He did follow some basic principles of good lecturing. He looked people straight in the eye when he talked. He had no distracting mannerisms such as saying "ah" or "you know" after every sentence or jingling the loose change in his pocket. He didn't preach either, but was quite conversational in his approach.

And he knew his content exceedingly well. Little time was spent consulting notes. Yet he used example upon example to illustrate the main points he was making. For instance, he shared with us how the Dead Sea Scrolls were found, how the area was excavated, and how the scrolls were marketed. He told us about the area along the Dead Sea—that the land was flat along the beach, but then rose sharply. Toward the top of the rise were numerous caves where the scrolls had been stored. He told us about the little shepherd boy who, when looking for his sheep, tossed stones into the caves, trying to scare out lost sheep. When he tossed stones into several of the caves, he heard a crash, like glass breaking. When he inspected, he found a cavern of urns, each containing scrolls.

This man shared all this information as if he were telling us a story, which he was. He was sharing with us what he knew about this topic, what he had learned from years of study, travel, and experience. During the class we could be with him, on the shores of the Dead Sea. We could share with him his honest enthusiasm for this topic. He was sincere and his enthusiasm was real. He enjoyed what he was doing. He enjoyed his research and he enjoyed sharing what he knew.

What was key in this lecture situation was not the visual aids, or even the interaction in the way of questions and answers. What was key was the instructor himself, the kind of person he was and the relationship he was able to establish with people in his classes.

Other Techniques

As we mentioned in our discussion of the class, it is possible to use a variety of approaches besides the lecture for presenting information to a class. These include films, debates, panel discussions, symposia, and demonstrations. See the bibliography for materials that describe these techniques.

For Involving Students

Many techniques exist for involving students in class activities. Below are described seven involvement techniques often used by educators of adults. Refer to chapter 14 for references that explain in considerably more detail how to organize these and other techniques.

Group Discussion

Five to twenty-five persons discuss a presentation, a problem, or an issue for not more than a half hour and then report to the total group. The group discussion technique is usually the technique used in many small classes or in a seminar—without the reporting-back feature.

Research indicates several benefits from discussion groups.[8] Students gain experience in cooperating on learning projects. The learning process is active rather than passive, which is often the case in a lecture situation. Students can quite easily relate experience to the content of what is being discussed. Students are often motivated by the discussion to go on to further learning in the areas being considered. Students tend to retain what is discussed longer than they do in certain passive learning situations. And the instructor is more likely to receive informal feedback as to how the students are doing, what questions they have about what is being discussed, and what further work is necessary.

Buzz Group

Two to five persons form a group to discuss a presentation and raise questions to ask the presenter. The buzz group usually meets for only five minutes or so.

Case Study

An incident is presented to a group in written form; on film, videotape, or oral tape; or with a skit. Participants study and discuss the case, then make recommendations. This often employs the group discussion, where several groups work on the case and report their analysis and suggestions to the total group.

Gaming

A real-life situation is replicated as closely as possible and participants make a series of decisions, either individually or in groups. Games may be manual or computerized.

Role Playing

Participants act out a problem or a situation. This is a useful technique for participants to get a firsthand feeling of being in a given situation. It is also useful to show an audience how a situation or a problem might actually appear. The presentation is usually followed by discussion.

Listening Team

Three to five members of a large group are designated "listeners." They listen to what happens at a class meeting, no matter what instructional techniques are used. One listener might look for points of disagreement in the class, one might look for what is not said, a third might raise questions to ask the presenter. Toward the end of the class, the listeners present their comments to the total group.

Reaction Panel

A small group of participants is appointed to react to a presentation. Often the presenter responds to the reaction panel, and then the total group is involved with questions and answers.

Choosing Formats and Techniques

Which formats and techniques should be used? There is no "right" answer to the question. Appropriate formats and techniques to select depend on (1) the returning student, (2) the instructor, (3) the purposes of the learning experience (the task), and (4) the situation in which learning is to occur.

The Returning Student

The returning student is the most important of all the factors to consider when selecting instructional formats and techniques. What has been the student's life experience in the area covered in the course or other learning experience? If the subject is understanding local government, and several of the students interested in the topic work in local government, this fact should influence the selection of formats and techniques. (Those techniques that allow for student involvement are likely to be more effective than those that only present information.)

What is the student's academic experience? If this is the first formal course a student has taken in ten years, the instructor should consider selecting a format and techniques that will assist in the adjustment to academic life. (A format that allows time for individual work with the beginning student is often helpful.)

What is the student's reason for returning to school? If the reason is job preparation, then an internship experience may make sense.

What is the student's formal educational background? If the

student has a background in the physical sciences and is coming back to school in a social science or humanities area, some adjustment may be necessary.

If students are accustomed to precise, single answers, which is often the case in the physical sciences, studying in the social sciences or humanities may be frustrating. The social sciences and humanities often provide multiple answers that are often not precise. Students appreciate teaching formats and techniques that take into account the adjustment problem they may be facing in moving from one discipline area to another. (Instructional techniques that give ample opportunity for these students to raise questions and interact with the instructor and other students often ease this adjustment problem.)

The Instructor

Although our emphasis in this book is on the learner and on enhancing the learning environment for the learner, when we talk about teaching we must talk about the instructor too.

With what instructional approaches is the instructor most comfortable? In most instances an instructor is able to broaden the number of approaches he or she is able to use; nevertheless, some instructors are simply not comfortable with certain approaches. Some instructors are not comfortable with audiovisual devices. Others may not be comfortable with some of the interactive approaches, where students interact with instructors or with other students, such as a student debate.

Related to this question is the confidence the instructor has as an instructor. As we have pointed out earlier, most college instructors have had little or no opportunity to learn a variety of instructional approaches. Their graduate training provided them with considerable help in designing and carrying out research projects, but almost no attention was provided on how to instruct. True, many college instructors had an opportunity to work as teaching assistants, but they usually had a supervisor who had little or no training in instructional approaches. Because of the lack of formal experiences in learning how to teach, some college instructors lack confidence in the classroom. And the instructor who lacks confidence is not likely to try a new instructional approach when there is a risk of failure.

For example, in one of the classes I teach we examine the alternative views of human nature—the Freudian view, the Skinnerian view, and the humanistic view. One activity I use from time to time is breaking the class into groups of five or six and giving each group an envelope containing paper clips, string, masking tape, pieces of paper—almost anything my secretary can find around the office. Each envelope has the same materials. Depending on the size of the class, I ask two or more groups to design one of the views of human nature, using the materials in the envelope. My classes are made up entirely of returning students who range in age from the middle twenties to the fifties. To do this project, the students sit down on the floor, discuss, manipulate, and create a design of the human-nature view on which they are working. The entire class then walks around and looks at each of the designs while the students who created it explain the symbolism to the remainder of the class. Before they begin the activity, I explain that one of the purposes of the exercise, beyond helping them understand better the particular view of human nature on which they are working, is to work in a medium other than words, at least in part. This activity is often viewed as one of the more interesting things we do in the course.

But I remember most vividly the first time I did it and how a colleague with whom I shared the idea before trying it had said, "Aren't you taking a lot of risk?" He was right. It was risky. And the first time I did it, the activity didn't work very well either, because I thought it might fail. Since then I try some new activity almost every semester, and some of them do fail.

Another variable is the instructor's philosophy of education. We discussed the importance of this at some length in chapter 5 when we discussed learning environment.

Has the instructor had experience working with returning students, particularly in classes where more than half of the students are older? Without this experience, the instructor may not be aware of the need to consider teaching approaches beyond those he or she is using now.

Many instructors who have not worked with returning students and who are comfortable only with a lecture technique of teaching will be challenged to explore the various formats and techniques that allow for student involvement. It is not enough to say, "I'm comfortable with lecturing, I have always lectured, and therefore that's the only teaching technique I'm going to use no matter what the age of the students in my classroom." Just as returning students are challenged to discover new ways of learning, instructors of returning students are challenged to discover new ways of teaching.

The Task

The tasks to be accomplished influence which instructional formats and techniques are selected. Tasks include (1) learning facts and concepts, (2) learning skills, (3) developing or changing attitudes and appreciations, and (4) responding to students' questions and problems.

For instance, those techniques designed for presenting information, such as the lecture, often serve well to help students become aware of facts and concepts. For skill learning, the internship, supervised independent study, and the laboratory are often useful formats. For developing or changing attitudes, group discussion and role playing are useful techniques. And any of the formats and techniques that allow for interaction between instructor and students, and among students, contribute to responding to questions and problems.

The Situation

Some teaching techniques are designed for small groups (the group discussion, for instance), while others work well with large as well as small groups (the lecture). The physical setting makes a difference too. If the chairs in the lecture hall are bolted to the floor, it is difficult to break a large group into smaller groups for purposes of discussion.

The amount of class time is another factor to consider. Traditionally, many colleges are organized around a fifty-minute class period. Now, with increasing numbers of returning students who are part-time, fewer but longer class periods are available. Rather than three fifty-minute class periods a week, a course may now meet but one time for 150 minutes. Many institutions are also organizing weekend classes where, rather than meeting three times a week for fifty minutes during a semester, the class meets five weekends during a semester. The class begins on Friday evening and runs from, say, 6:00 P.M. until 9:00 P.M., then meets again on Saturday from 8:30 A.M. until 3:30 P.M. The students are in the class for the same number of minutes as those attending three times a week for the semester. It is absurd to think that the instructor would lecture all this time. No instructor has that kind of physical stamina, and neither do the students. So these instructors are forced to try alternative instructional approaches.

Budget is another situational variable that often dictates the use of films and other audiovisual equipment, laboratory demonstrations, and field trips.

Ultimately, our purpose as educators is to assist returning students in such a way that they will become comfortable taking charge of their own learning, that they will learn how to learn so they can continue the learning process as effectively without instructors as with them and without colleges and universities as with them.

Paul Lengrand discusses the ultimate goals of the adult learner this way: "From being subjected to education—in principle, the situation of every learner—he became the instrument of his own education and resumed command of himself as an adult. This new individual became a person in the fullest sense of the term, endowed with his own psychological and sociological options, aware of his own individuality and engaged in a series of contests each having its own particular objective: the contest for survival, the contest for knowledge, the contest for individual and collective advancement. Instead of being condemned to an inferior status in relation to an instructor who was his 'master,' the adult pupil became a partner in a collective undertaking in which he was in a position both to take and to receive: receiving the substance of learning, he could give in exchange the irreplaceable wealth of his own manner of being a man and of accomplishing a man's destiny as worker, citizen, or other entity engaged in any one of a multiplicity of situations and relationships. From that moment the emphasis was on being rather than on having, and on having only to the extent that resources feed and sustain the individual in meeting the requirements and succeeding stages of his own development."[9]

Summary

In this chapter we have examined two categories of formats for teaching returning students, as individuals and in groups. Individual formats considered include supervised independent study, internship, self-study, counseling, and distance learning. Group formats considered include the class, seminar, group project, and network group.

Several instruction techniques were mentioned, including those for presenting information, such as the lecture and panel discussion, and those for involving students, such as buzz groups, reaction panels, and group discussion. Which formats and techniques to use depends on (1) the returning student, (2) the instructor, (3) the task, and (4) the situation in which learning is to occur.

NOTES

1. Robert Dubin and Thomas C. Taveggia, *The Teaching-Learning Paradox* (Eugene, Oreg.: Center for the Advanced Study of Educational Administration, University of Oregon, 1968), p. 47.

2. Philip Werdell, "Futurism and the Reform of Higher Education," *Learning for Tomorrow,* ed. Alvin Toffler (New York: Vintage Books, 1974), p. 290.

3. Malcolm S. Knowles, *The Modern Practice of Adult Education* (New York: Association Press, 1970), pp. 150–154.

4. Kenneth E. Eble, *The Craft of Teaching* (San Francisco: Jossey-Bass, 1976), p. 67.

5. Ibid., p. 68.

6. Ibid., p. 43.

7. Russell H. Bostert, "Teaching History," *Scholars Who Teach,* ed. Steven M. Cahn (Chicago: Nelson-Hall, 1978), pp. 16–17.

8. Mary Lynn Crow, "Teaching as an Interactive Process," *Improving Teaching Styles,* ed. Kenneth E. Eble (San Francisco: Jossey-Bass, 1980), p. 44.

9. Paul Lengrand, *An Introduction to Lifelong Education* (London: Croom Helm Ltd, 1975), p. 47.

Chapter 9

Nine Exemplary Teaching Principles

Not long ago I was talking with a fellow professor and the conversation got around to returning students. This person was emphatic when he said, "I've developed a way of teaching—a set of principles, if you will—and I'm not going to change them just because I'm seeing a lot of older students in my classes."

Other instructors have told me essentially the same thing. When I went on the road interviewing exemplary instructors of returning students, I was particularly interested in learning how these instructors worked with returning students. What they told me often applied as well to traditional as it did to returning students, with a few exceptions that I'll point out later. We could conclude from this that those instructors who do well with traditional students are well on the way toward becoming exemplary instructors of returning students. How effective an instructor has been with traditional students will determine the extent to which changes are necessary for this instructor to become effective with returning as well as traditional students.

As I listened to, and later studied, what these exemplary instructors said, nine teaching principles emerged:

1. Learn to know your students.

2. Use the students' experiences as class content.

145

3. When possible, tie theory to practice.

4. Provide a climate conducive to learning.

5. Offer a variety of formats.

6. Offer a variety of techniques.

7. Provide students feedback on their progress.

8. Help students acquire resources.

9. Be available to students for out-of-class contacts.

Know the Students

One of the widely observed approaches exemplary instructors followed was getting acquainted with the students early in the semester. This meant much more than learning their names. It meant finding out something about each student, his or her interests, expectations, reasons for returning to school, and so on.

A University of Michigan professor asks his students to write short autobiographies, three or four typewritten pages, that include such information as where the students have lived, something about their families, what work experience they have had, and something about their hobbies. Then, early in the semester, he interviews each of his students. (Of course this professor's approach becomes difficult when class size goes beyond thirty or forty students.) By the time the semester is one-third finished, he knows the students in his classes quite well. And they appreciate the personal attention he has given them and his obvious interest in them as individual human beings.

A professor of political science at North Carolina State University has each student fill out a form with addresses, phone numbers, background information, and the like. He then reproduces this information for all the members in his classes. He often has as many as seventy students in his classes, so the information sheets are very valuable. Back in 1969 he began taking photos of each of his students in his classes. He finds this not only helpful in getting to know the students, but also valuable when he is faced with writing letters of recommendation some years later.

A professor of sociology at North Carolina State spends the first day or two at the beginning of a semester going from person to person in his classes and talking to each of them for a few minutes. Of course the entire class listens in on the conversation and thus learns a great deal about the members in it. He finds out who the students are and where they are from and often kids them about secrets they'd like to share with him and with the class.

In succeeding class sessions he uses a variety of approaches to learn to know the students' names and something about them. For instance, he has a numbered sheet with all the students' names. He'll ask a student to pick a number, say from one to forty-two if there are forty-two members in the class. The student with the number picked is asked a question dealing with the material discussed in class the previous time. Then this student gets to select the next number, and so on. The students give their names at the time they respond to the questions.

In addition to finding out something about each student's personal and work backgrounds and getting to know them as persons, the exemplary instructors stressed the importance of tying class content to the experiences of the students.

Use Student Experience

Repeatedly the exemplary instructors mentioned the importance of students' experiences and the importance of tying these experiences to the class work being considered. *If there is one fundamental difference between teaching traditional college-age students and returning students, it is the need to take into account the older student's work and life experience as a beginning place for learning.*

A history professor at Temple University uses several techniques to help returning students tie their experiences to the topics he discusses in his courses. He teaches a course on Renaissance Reformation. Initially he asks students to write down what comes to mind when they hear the word *renaissance*. Then he goes through a series of steps in which he draws from the written comments themes that have been part of the Renaissance. As he points out, "This system has really never failed. If I have a dozen students, most of the theories and interpretations about the Renaissance are somewhere in their comments." After the major themes are identified, he then works with the class members to identify areas they wish to explore in greater depth.

This professor also teaches introductory history. For this course, he asks class members to do a family history, not an elaborate, sophisticated family history, but a listing of people, events, dates, and so on, that were important in that student's family history. From the histories students develop, such themes as immigration, ethnic groups, World Wars I and II, religions, and occupations are identified. He shared a specific experience to show the power and the intensity of this approach: "A black woman came up after class when I had made the family history assignment and asked if she could do something else because she didn't have a family. Well, some people are raised in institutions and don't have families. So I suggested to this woman that she do a friend's family or pick a historical family, and she thought maybe she'd like to do a historical family.

"She didn't talk to me for quite a while, and when it came time for people to report about their family histories on the board, I was surprised. Most students take twenty to thirty minutes to report on their family histories. This woman took two days. She discovered her family. She discovered her father was alive in the city. She discovered she was one of nineteen children. She'd had no prior knowledge of her father or her relatives. She had discovered just unbelievable kinds of things. And she became angry and sort of hostile toward her father, who had institutionalized her back during the Depression. When doing this project she interviewed him. I think she knew he existed before she began the project, but that's all she would acknowledge. She discovered she did have a family. She went to talk with her father, and she slowly came to understand why he did what he did. His wife (her mother) had died. He couldn't handle all those kids, and he did the best he could. She understood the circumstance better, and for her it was a real breakthrough."

Not all the family histories are as dramatic, but for this professor the technique of working out a family history is a valuable one. In addition to helping students discover major historical themes, which they pursue in greater depth as the course develops, the family history technique helps students understand and practice *doing*—interviewing, researching, and working with documents. And just as important, they have the opportunity in the course to combine experience, interview data, and document information into a useful whole that helps them understand a practical historical event. This professor emphasizes throughout the course the importance of, and how one does, analysis when pursuing historical topics. He also stresses the criteria to use in determining which historical data are valid and which are not.

Tie Theory to Practice

Returning students are not opposed to studying theory, but they do want to see how the theory they are studying relates to practical application. Because many of the returning students come back to school on leave from jobs, they are particularly looking for application of the theories they are studying to their jobs. Those students back in school with career or professional job aspirations are interested in how the theories they are studying apply to the jobs they are preparing for. So the instructor of returning students is obligated to attempt to tie theory to practice. The exemplary instructors interviewed do this in a variety of ways.

An assistant professor of family studies at the University of Wisconsin–Madison invites community people into her classes. For instance, when she is discussing family violence, she brings in a person from the Parental Stress Center or from the Women's Shelter, two agencies that operate in her community.

An associate professor of English at the University of Wisconsin–Madison encourages her students to do field projects instead of doing term papers in the library. She helps them with interview techniques and the construction of questionnaires.

An assistant professor of social work at Temple University tries to make the writing assignments in her class practical yet related to theory. She says, "When I assign papers, they have to relate to the real world, either to clients, to their agencies, or their jobs. Every single question, whether it's dealing with the life cycle or whether it's dealing with something that might be very theoretical, must be related to its implications for social-work practice or the implications for the student's particular agency. If, for instance, a student is doing a paper on homosexuality, he or she must relate the paper to social-work practice."

A psychology professor at North Carolina State emphasizes the importance of his students' participating in a work situation as part of their academic studies, as well as doing direct observation of work situations. "We have our students spend one semester full time in a job. I think they should also be involved in direct observation of political and governmental activities, because [with] the field I'm in—human resource development—the government, particularly the local government, is a principal agent. I encourage my students to watch council meetings and committee meetings and work with the legislature, get involved in political campaigns, if that's appropriate."

This professor also gives assignments in his courses that bring students in touch with practical situations. In an organizational psychology course he teaches, he has students actually analyze an organization from the perspective of bureaucratic organization concepts, general systems theory, and interaction and group organization theories. During the time the students analyze the organization, many concepts they are using in the analysis are discussed in class. For instance, the class may be discussing the problem of organizational leadership. At the time of the discussion several class members may have already looked at the problem of leadership in the organization they are analyzing. These students have many examples to share with other class members from their analysis project.

An instructor in the Department of Psycho-Educational Processes at Temple University uses a variety of techniques to help students experience the relationship of theories to practice. For example, in a course she teaches, "Research in Group Dynamics," the class looks at major social and psychological theories. Then she organizes demonstrations in the class so students can see how the theories work in practice.

Another instructor at Temple University teaches a course in human sexuality. As part of that course she requires an out-of-class weekend workshop in which students have an opportunity, in the instructor's words, "to start to get in touch with their attitudes." In this instructor's judgment, one does not teach a course such as human sexuality without some kind of practical, experiential activity as part of the course. The instructor rents a youth hostel in a park and charges students a small fee to provide money for group facilitators. Students may also bring friends with them to the workshop.

The instructor described the workshop as follows: "We start with a name-tag activity. The last time we did the workshop, students made a bumper sticker on their name tag—something to do with sexuality or with social work, a fun kind of activity. We just milled around the room and looked at the bumper stickers, and we talked about what the bumper stickers meant. Then the students worked in pairs to discuss some ideas I gave them about sexuality. Some of these topics were, What are your greatest fears about sexual issues? What turns you on? What do you think your parents' fears are or were about sexuality?

"We broke into groups of fours and then groups of eight. We take time so the students can introduce each other in the groups of eight because quite a bit of the weekend work will be in that group.

"There is a facilitator with each group of eight. At that time we put on a newsprint the expectations the students have for the workshop and what road blocks might be anticipated and how we can get over the road blocks.

"I show a short film, getting people to think about sexuality. We may do other activities too. One I've used is a fist activity. Students pair up with each other, with somebody in their group, and the instructions are to get the other person to open his or her fist first. Then we talk about what happened: How open are you to other people in terms of how willing were you to open your fist? Did the other person use force? Did the person use seduction? What did the person do?

"We do the exercise with the same sex and then with opposite sexes. Then we do something called a lifeline. One of the facilitators will go through their own lifeline as a model, and what you do is get a piece of newsprint and draw a line down the middle. Then I ask the students to think back to their earliest sexual experiences. Maybe it is when they played doctor as kids, or they had a contest and the loser had to pull down his pants. They mark different ages on the line. And they identify the significant experiences they can remember. If they remember the experience as a negative experience, it's placed on the bottom of the line. If it was a positive experience, it is placed on the top side of the line. After persons finish identifying experiences on the sheets, they begin to look for themes that may have been involved, like guilt, power, control, whatever they might be. The participants have about a half hour to put together the lifeline and begin to identify the themes. They do this individually, this development of their sexual history.

"Then they pair up with each other and share as much of the lifeline that they are comfortable sharing. Students have told me that they have shared things with other persons that they've never shared with anyone, not with their partners, their wives, or their husbands. Sometimes they chose to share this information with their husband or wife or the friend they brought with them to the workshop; sometimes they will choose someone else to share this with. That's about what we accomplish on Friday evening. We stop and break out the wine: it's usually quite late.

"The next morning we may start with some physical exercises, something to help us wake up. We begin talking about how people feel about the previous night's activities. The first topic of the morning is masturbation. We have everyone lying on the floor, just touching different parts of themselves, nonthreateningly—how does it feel?

"We show a film next, an explicit film of a male masturbating and then a female masturbating. Then we get into small groups and we talk about masturbation. The purpose of the film is to trigger a discussion of people's feelings about masturbation.

"After masturbation the next topic is homosexuality. To introduce the topic we do an activity I call body painting. A student teams with a partner of the same sex and the instructions are to paint the other person's body. The other person can communicate only nonverbally in terms of what is allowed for you to paint. Some people will actually touch the other person, and some people won't touch.

"Then we spend some time talking about this. We deal with such questions as, Did you touch things you didn't want to touch? especially for a man who may never have touched another man before. After that we do brainstorming about all of the words people think of when we say 'homosexuality.' We talk about stereotypes and usually get very negative words. Films are next: one on two male homosexuals and another on two female homosexuals. After the films we break into our small groups and we discuss what we have done and what we have seen; this is usually an extremely heavy discussion. Often during this discussion, one or two people who are homosexuals will come out; they will begin to talk about their experiences as homosexuals.

"After lunch we show a heterosexual film and we talk about relationships. We'll usually do a fishbowl to get at some of the relationship problems. We put the men in a circle with the women gathered around them. The women aren't allowed to talk. We usually start the men discussing such questions as, What do I like most about being a man? What do I like least about being a man? What do I like most about women? What do I like least about women? Often it's locker-room talk, and the women can't talk but they are listening. Then we switch, and the women are in the circle and the men are on the outside watching and listening.

"The discussions following this exercise are fascinating. The women get much more angry than the men do. The women are angry with the men. The men, when they talked about the women, they talked about the ability of women to be emotional, to be soft, to be giving. And what the men said they didn't like about being a man was the competitiveness, the inability to cry. Some of the men will say, 'What I like about women is they can give me a son.'

"The women don't have much to say about the men, so then the men feel angry because the women haven't acknowledged them as much as the men have acknowledged the women. But it's just fascinating because what you also see is a lot of men who are coming out as being very sensuous and very soft and very emotional, and many are at least wanting to be more that way. People haven't seen that side of men.

"So that's it, that's the workshop. We do some evaluation of the entire activity, and that's the end of the day."

After the workshop experience the various concepts discussed in the classroom setting have considerably more meaning for the students in the course.

Not every instructor would be comfortable in carrying out this type of activity, and not every subject-matter area lends itself to such an intensive, personally involved activity. All of the exemplary instructors I interviewed stressed the importance, in whatever way possible, of presenting opportunities for students to see the relationship of theory to practice. These instructors have worked out approaches that work for them. They have no particular suggestions about which approaches to use, only that relating theory to practice should be emphasized.

Provide a Climate for Learning

As the exemplary instructors said to me often and in a variety of ways, there is much more to teaching older returning students than standing in front of them and delivering a lecture.

Fundamental to a conducive climate is an attitude of support for the returning student as a student. As one of the exemplary instructors said, "Some professors find it difficult to support students. They think it's more important to obstruct so that only those students who really have the motivation and intelligence can make it . . . but I can't operate that way. I want to support students and my attitude has changed over the years too. I've always been supportive of students but recently I've shifted to be supportive of all students, men and women, and of all ages."

Another attitude expressed by several exemplary instructors concerns their views on students and subject matter. A more positive learning climate results when students come first and subject matter comes second. The instructor starts with students and their interests, their problems, their reasons for coming to school, their experiences, and then ties all of this to the subject matter of the course. Also, the students' experiences become subject matter. Often the college classroom is where the instructor's subject matter is the primary emphasis. In order for a conducive learning climate to develop, the students must be recognized as important.

It's often not easy for a professor interested in students to build a learning climate. Many returning students have not experienced a student-oriented learning climate in their formal schooling. So they don't know what it is. Other students either don't believe what is happening or view the teacher as someone who is manipulating them when an instructor attempts to develop a student-oriented learning climate.

As one exemplary instructor explained, "What do you do with a student who comes to your classroom where the word *I* is acceptable—*I* think, *I* feel—from a classroom where if he or she said it they would be slapped down? You try to make them relax, you tell jokes, and you even refer to your own wife, or home, or children in order to make them feel that you welcome personal experience in the classroom. And then you have to make them believe. They think you're just putting it on, and you'll jump down their throats if they refer to their personal experiences."

Another instructor tells stories both to help relax his students and to help them see his subject matter in a different light. This instructor teaches a course on research methods. One of the stories he tells his students early in the semester is this:

"There was a lion who wanted to do some research in the jungle. The lion thought he was king of the jungle. So the lion said, 'I'll go out and carry out this little research project to demonstrate that I am indeed the king of the jungle.'

"The lion meets a number of different animals as he walks through the jungle and he asks each one, 'Who's the king of the jungle?' And each one quickly answers, 'You are,' as they wish to escape with their lives.

"Finally the lion meets this huge elephant. Three times the lion asks the elephant, 'Who's the king of the jungle?' but the elephant ignores him. But the lion is insistent. 'Who is the king of the jungle?' the lion roars in his loudest voice. The elephant has had enough. It reaches down, picks up the lion, and thumps him against a tree several times, and then tosses him aside.

"The lion drags himself off into the jungle. When he thinks he is at a safe distance, he turns back to the elephant and says, 'You didn't have to get so mad because you didn't know the right answer.' That story usually breaks the ice."

Several instructors said how important it was to create an accepting learning climate early in the semester, during the first class if possible. Some instructors plan potluck dinners or picnics with their students early in the semester. Some have after-class get-togethers where students and faculty can talk informally. All these approaches help to create a learning climate that says to the returning students they are accepted, they are important, they have something to contribute to the learning situation.

Offer a Variety of Formats

At many colleges and universities the fifty-minute class period is the norm. Students and professors down through the years have proclaimed the virtues of this time length as ideal for learning and for teaching. Fifty minutes probably does fit the lecture well, for that is a comfortable length of time for a professor to talk; and if he or she is not too boring, fifty minutes is a reasonable time to expect a student to stay awake. Of course not all professors are able to keep a lecture room of students awake and alert for fifty minutes, but that is another topic.

In addition to the fifty-minute class, another time-honored format at many colleges and universities is holding classes two or three times a week, say Monday, Wednesday, and Friday, at 8:50 A.M.

A moment's reflection about returning students and we see quickly that these time-honored formats must be changed, or the working part-time student will not become part of the college scene.

Several types of format shifts are taking place on those campuses where increasing numbers of older returning students are attending. Many courses are now offered once a week for 150 minutes, in the late afternoon or in the evening. At a number of institutions weekend courses are offered in a variety of formats. Here at the University of Wisconsin, we offer weekend courses for graduate students in continuing and vocational education (see chapter 12).

Another format shift is to move the courses off campus to a location that is more easily reached by students. At Temple University many courses are offered downtown in the evening so students can travel easily to them. Here at the University of Wisconsin, many courses are offered off campus and at various locations around the state, such as in public schools.

These shifts in approaches for offering courses require some shift in the thinking, and doing, of the instructors who offer the courses. One of the Temple professors, in describing the evening class schedule, said, "We meet once a week for six hours, and it's grueling for the students and for the faculty. But for many of the students we have it's the only way they can go to school. They often have kids at home and a job, and the evening is the only time they can come to school."

Of course professors find it impossible to lecture for three or four or more hours in a row, and students likewise find it impossible to listen to lecturing carried on for that length of time. So some different teaching techniques are required.

Offer a Variety of Techniques

The exemplary professors I interviewed use a variety of techniques in their teaching. Some of them do quite a bit of lecturing, primarily those instructors who are still teaching courses where the number of returning students is not great and the traditional format of a fifty-minute class can be followed.

Malcolm Knowles told me of a procedure he has worked out in working with returning students that has several identifiable stages to it. The first stage emphasizes climate setting. As he explains, "In my estimation the opening session, the opening hour or two or three in any activity, is the single most critical time of the whole period in which I engage learners. It is at this time that we become acquainted with each other. It is during this time we surface the resources the students are bringing to the class. It is during this time we begin to build a collaborative rather than a competitive relationship among the students in the group. It is during this time we build an atmosphere of mutual trust, mutual respect, supportiveness, and I present myself as a human being. I also explain my role as facilitator and resource person, and what theoretical framework underlies the approach I use. I tell them I am a trout fisherman from Montana, things like that.

"The second thing I do relates to helping learners diagnose

their own needs for learning. Here I've developed competency models for all the courses I teach in which the learners see what the competencies are that the course is designed to help them develop. The students go through the process of diagnosing which of these competencies they already have developed and which they haven't. Then we talk about procedures for involving the students in the planning of their learning, and here the main tool I use is the learning contract. Every student contracts with me what he or she is going to learn as a way of organizing a plan for learning. The learning contract does several things. It helps the student identify the objectives of what he is planning to learn. It helps the student identify the resources, the printed materials, the peers, the resources out in the community. The learning contract also is a guide for evaluation for the students to specify what evidence they are going to collect to demonstrate that they have in fact accomplished what they said they wanted to accomplish."

In terms of in-classroom activity, several of the professors used various kinds of group activities. Details of these were discussed in the previous chapters.

I assumed that all of the exemplary instructors, or at least most of them, used audiovisual aids of one kind or another. The literature of adult education suggests audiovisual aids are often useful adjuncts to learning. But I didn't find a universal use of audiovisual aids by the exemplary instructors. In fact one of the instructors, when I asked him what place educational technology had in his teaching, replied, "None. I can use projectors, movies, and so on, and I've done several lectures on our TV series here. But I really think teaching is an interpersonal thing, and the less you mediate that with gadgets and gimmicks, the better."

Several of the exemplary instructors said they used a film or two during the semester, when it fit well with what they were doing. Some said they used slides and overhead projectors. Several said they liked to use and found most effective the flip chart or the blackboard. As one instructor said, "I much prefer a blackboard or a flip chart to an overhead transparency, for the simple reason that, if I go to the trouble and give the energy to developing an overhead transparency, I'll have pressure on myself to use the transparency, whether it really turns out to be the best thing or not."

This same instructor also commented on the use of teaching machines and other types of inanimate, individual-oriented teaching equipment. "When we consider teaching machines and programmed instruction units, I have found that the learners really have trouble dealing with the isolation that goes with this equipment. It's awfully hard for an individual to stick to an inanimate teaching machine for very long sequences. So when I use that kind of hardware, I always try to find some way of introducing some interaction, some human interaction . . . having two students use a teaching machine together, or five use it together."

Another instructor often encouraged her students to use various kinds of educational technology in developing class projects. Videotapes seemed to work well for this purpose when students went out into the field on some class project. They videotaped something and then took it back to the classroom for discussion. She also encouraged students to use color slides and audiotape recordings for the same purpose.

An instructor who did use several films during the semester explained the problems of students sitting in the dark, not being able to take notes, and often not knowing what to look for in the films. She was developing film guides for each of the films she used in her classes to hand out to each of the students. In the guide she gives clues to pieces of dialogue, narration, or background music, or to particular cuts that are symbolically important for the interpretation of the film. She said it was very difficult for students to deal with both the information of the films and the symbolic content at the same time and believed the film guides handed out before viewing the film would help.

An English professor I interviewed used slides extensively in her teaching. She told me about a course she was teaching on myths. She took slides in England and France and then in New York to illustrate Greek and Roman sculpture that centered on gods and goddesses. She gave each student slides, and the student then went to the reference library to find out the story behind what was represented on the slides. Back in class, the students told the story they found about the slides while she projected the slides on the screen. This instructor often used slides of great paintings to illustrate her points. When the slide of a painting was projected on the screen, and the students told the stories they had researched about it, the instructor raised questions about the artist's perceptions during the classical period in which he painted. She found this approach a very useful one for involving students in their learning and also a way for students to share experiences with one another.

But there was no unanimous statement that every instructor

of returning students should use audiovisual materials such as films, slides, overhead transparencies, educational TV, and the like. As a professor of education said, "Use educational technology if it works for you. But don't be afraid to try various kinds of educational technology. Try it and see if it works for you within the settings you have."

This professor also pointed out that sometimes the administration has strongly encouraged instructors to use more educational technology in the classroom. He believes this is wrong. In certain settings the educational situation may be enhanced with educational technology. In other settings the use of various kinds of equipment may obstruct learning. There are no universals.

Provide Feedback

Returning students want to know how they are doing. They want feedback from their instructors about their progress and their problems as students. They also want the opportunity to provide feedback to their instructors about teaching effectiveness and the contribution of courses to their learning expectations. So the returning student sees feedback going in two directions, from instructor to student and from student to instructor.

Let's first look at instructor-to-student feedback. Examinations and grading are as controversial for the returning student as they are for the traditional student. Many of the same questions are raised for both groups of students: Are the grades equitable from one professor to another? That is, does Professor X essentially use the same grading procedures and come out with comparable ratings as does Professor Y? Are colleges and universities experiencing grade inflation? Is a B in 1960 an A in 1981? Are we putting too much stress on grade-point averages for fellowship and scholarship and other financial aid considerations, for graduate-school entry, and for ranking the worth of students? These are the questions that perplex higher education instructors no matter what age their students.

As one of the instructors I interviewed said, "I dislike the formal procedure of having to evaluate students based on an examination. I guess that's where my skin is the thinnest, particularly with the older returning students. They're back after ten years away from studying and examinations. And they often have difficulty with their first examinations. I hate to see their disappointment." This particular instructor, if given the opportunity, would like to see alternative ways used to evaluate the progress of students. He said, "I think if we had time there are other good ways to evaluate students' progress. But in a class of forty-two people you can't go to an individual-type format. The numbers game we have to play at a state university, at least when we're funded on a basis of full-time equivalents, forces you into some standardized procedures. And you lose some of the individuality you're trying to create."

Another instructor questioned the whole idea of grades and grading in higher education. He questioned why higher education today still uses the antiquated approach that is based on comparing one student with another. For him a better approach is to determine performance criteria for a learning experience and then determine the extent to which each student reached these performance criteria. The present educational grading system, according to this professor, "is one of the most anti-educational inventions in all of the history of education."

Still, according to another instructor I interviewed, grades mean a great deal to the mature student. According to this instructor, grades are an indication to students as to whether they are getting anything out of the learning experiences in which they are participating. This instructor had some suggestions for the grading process and the instructor doing the grading: "The professor needs to make it quite clear to the students what the grading system is he plans to use. He also should tell them whether or not he is grading on a curve, that is, being compared with each other rather than against some standard. He should help them understand what the various grades mean. Many of the returning students are accustomed to positive feedback on their jobs, and if they get a C on an examination and don't understand the grading system, they may feel they've done very poorly. What's important is that the student understand the meaning of the grades and what is expected to reach a certain grade—amount of work, quality of work, and so on."

A variety of approaches are used to help returning students adjust to and prepare for examinations and feedback on their learning performance. For instance, one instructor tells his students at least a month ahead of time what they can expect on an upcoming examination so they can prepare for it. He believes that not only does this procedure reduce a lot of the test anxiety that often builds in returning students, but also it is in itself a good learning experience.

Another instructor I talked with about the question of feedback and testing said he took time at the very beginning of the course to tell the students what the goals and objectives of the course were, as well as the expectations and the requirements of the course. He said, "In the Renaissance course I teach, I first expect a general knowledge of the material of the field. Second, I expect a demonstrated ability to deal with the material, that is, demonstrate some of the basic skills of organization, criticism, and analysis. Third, the course emphasizes the content and context by which values change in specific social settings. I expect students to be able to demonstrate in one or two test cases that they understand what that means or how that takes place in a specific setting."

But even with preparation at the beginning of the course, this professor is not comfortable with the process of grading. He shared a specific instance: "I've got a student coming to see me the week after next, when I come back from Maine, to talk about a B+ which he thought should be an A. In his case he wrote a play and produced it in class and it was really a good play as a dramatic work. One of the things I emphasize in the course is for people to work together and cooperate on a project, to learn how to deal with each other, to work with people they don't like, so that's part of what I expect. It's those parts of the course, the working together, the cooperative aspects of students' activities, that are most difficult to grade."

Aside from the feedback that comes from grades and grading, from scores on examinations and on term papers and class projects, several of the exemplary instructors mentioned the need for the instructor to provide honest, informal feedback to returning students. They pointed out the importance of simply saying, "Hey, you're doing a good job," to a returning student from time to time (assuming it is true).

Returning students, particularly during the first semester they are back in school, are often extremely insecure. They are in need of feedback from their instructors about the progress or lack of progress they are making. To wait until the first major examination or the completion of a major term paper before feedback is provided is unfair to the returning student. Some feedback approach, either formal, informal, or both, during the first six weeks after a student returns can make a real contribution to the student's mental health.

The experienced, continuing student knows he or she can do the work because they have been doing it. But the returning older student who may have been out of school for ten years isn't so sure. And not having the feedback about progress can itself get in the way of further progress.

In terms of student-to-instructor feedback, several approaches can be followed. Many instructors use a formal evaluation form at the end of a course to receive feedback from students about course content, teaching approaches, and general feeling toward the course. This feedback is obviously too late for the students currently enrolled in the course but is useful for the instructor as he or she plans the next offering of the course.

An informal approach many instructors follow is to encourage feedback by students throughout the course. This approach assumes excellent rapport between students and instructors, so that students do not feel uncomfortable or threatened by sharing concerns they perceive.

Still another approach some instructors follow is to ask a class to elect four or five of its members to serve on a steering committee. Students are asked to share concerns and suggestions with the steering-committee members, who in turn meet periodically with the instructor. For classes larger than twenty students, this approach works very well.

Help Students Find Resources

For any student, access to resources is an important part of the learning process. Of course, the traditional resources for learning are reading materials, and they continue to be so. One of the differences between returning students and traditional students is how returning students view reserve lists and extended library use. In recent years, with the tremendous increase in the cost of textbooks, many professors use a minimal number of required textbooks in their courses, but long lists of reserve materials are available at the library.

The problem for the returning students, particularly those who attend school part-time and work full time, is having sufficient time to spend in the library. In my experience, many of these students would spend the extra money for textbooks so they have them easily available. Some instructors make multiple copies of research reports and other reading materials available to students so they can avoid spending the time in libraries looking up the materials and reading them at the library. (Check on possible copyright restrictions.)

A technique one of the instructors I interviewed uses is to ask students in his courses to bring materials that they have come across that relate to the topic on hand. He then puts those materials together in a central location outside his office so students can have access to them without going to the library. Students often stop by the professor's office before or after class to read these materials.

Other professors have made their personal libraries available to students on a check-out basis to provide them more easy access to written materials.

Two other types of resources that returning students often overlook are their own communities and their fellow returning students. Many of the returning students are employed and have many community contacts; these are often rich sources of information for many of the topics being studied. This is particularly so in such disciplines as psychology and sociology, and the professions such as engineering, law, health, social work, and education.

The most obvious and often overlooked source of valuable information is other returning students. Through various kinds of informal arrangements such as lunching together, after-class meetings, and informal seminars, returning students can gain much valuable information from each other on a variety of topics. But first, the returning student must move past the notion that only professors and books have valuable information.

Keep Out-of-Class Contacts

Most college and university instructors, no matter what the student's age, recognize the value of out-of-class contacts with their students. This is particularly so for returning students. Instructors who come onto campus only for their courses, then sneak back to their offices or their laboratories to avoid any out-of-class contact with students, are quickly challenged by returning students. For returning students, what happens outside of class is often as important to them as what happens in class.

The exemplary instructors I interviewed agree. They recognize the importance of working with returning students outside of class and schedule major blocks of time to do it.

That is not to say that these instructors aren't heavily involved in ongoing research projects; they are. What they do is schedule times for work with students and then make this known to their students. A time-honored procedure followed by many professors is the so-called open-door policy. Students with problems stop by anytime and can expect to find the professor there, waiting to talk with them. Though this may sound like the most compassionate and student-centered system, it often is not. The student who knows he or she can barge in on a professor anytime often doesn't take the time to carefully sort out the questions he or she has or doesn't seek other obvious answers to the problem (another student may have the answer they are seeking, or the answer may be in the textbook). In some ways the open-door policy is a disservice to the student because it can create a dependency relationship with the professor. If the professor has assigned office hours, and students need to make appointments, the students have the opportunity to reflect on their problems and perhaps work out answers themselves, which in most instances is the preferred way. The open-door policy is not fair to the instructor either. Most professors are expected to be involved in, and indeed are interested in, research and scholarly writing. To do this they need to have major blocks of time set aside for such activity.

Even with scheduled office hours and an appointment system, most instructors clearly make it known to their students that, for any serious problem, they are available.

Some instructors abuse the appointment system. They make themselves so unavailable that students sometimes have to wait three or four weeks to see them. This is as unacceptable to the returning student as it is to the traditional student.

The key is, of course, a balance—sufficient time set aside and communicated to students for out-of-class contacts, and sufficient time for the instructor to perform the many other tasks that go with the position of college or university teacher, including writing and research.

The amount of time instructors spend with students outside of class varies greatly from instructor to instructor. One of the instructors I interviewed organized her course so students met in committees outside of class to plan class activities. Sometimes, she reported, these committee meetings will take as long as four or five hours each. But she says, "The learning that goes on in those sessions is great. We're looking at a lot of alternatives. And it's a setting where I can become part of the group."

This instructor also meets with her students in a variety of other settings. She says her students come early for their classes and stay late, and they talk through lunch. After class she and her students often continue the sessions informally at the cafeteria, a pizza parlor, or wherever it is convenient for them to get together to rehash the recent class session.

An important learning activity for the returning student is what happens with the professor in out-of-class situations. Often, as viewed by the returning student, the one-on-one contact with the professor is as valuable or sometimes even more valuable than what happens in the formal class situation. In the one-to-one situation the returning student is often more free to share problems and concerns and share experiences and background related to the course. Sometimes a student wants to talk with a professor about a learning style that the student has discovered is comfortable for himself or herself, but the student fears the professor may misunderstand. For instance, one of my own students recently stopped by to talk with me about her reluctance to do much talking in class. We do a great deal of group discussion in the course I teach, and I had noticed she seldom, if ever, contributed. She stopped by to tell me that this was not her style. She really was gaining much from the group discussion, but her learning style was not to say much in a large group discussion. She also indicated that she wanted to consider changing her behavior but didn't know quite how to do it. So we talked about various things she might do to make sharing in a group discussion a pleasant experience for her. Slowly, as the semester went along, she began to contribute.

Summary

From interviews with exemplary instructors, nine principles for teaching returning students emerged:

1. **Know the Students.** Learn their names. Find out about their life experiences, the jobs they've had, the interests they have, and some of the reasons why they have returned to school.

2. **Use Student Experience.** Returning students often already know something of the content of the courses they are taking. Much of their information is practical information they have gained through their work and other activities. Starting with this experience base, the instructor can help returning students quickly see a tie between their experiences and the academic course they are now taking. Using students' experience in the classroom is also a motivational device, for returning students are usually interested in sharing their experiences.

3. Tie Theory to Practice. One of the reasons many students return to school is to improve themselves for the job they now hold or to prepare for another job. Returning students enjoy studying theory when they can see its relationship to the practical and often to occupational application. Returning students expect the instructor not only to discuss theories but also to show the relationship of the theories to practice. They are put off by instructors who concentrate only on theory, and they are also put off by instructors who concentrate only on practice. They want to see a combination of the two.

4. Provide a Climate for Learning. The nature of the learning climate influences the quantity and quality of the learning that occurs, particularly when we consider returning students. Fundamental to a positive learning climate is an instructor's support for returning students.

5. Offer a Variety of Formats. For most returning students, particularly those who work full time and are in school part-time, the traditional three times a week for a fifty-minute class is not satisfactory. Returning students require more flexible formats: evening classes, weekend classes, late afternoon classes, classes that meet once a week for an hour and a half rather than three times a week for fifty minutes each, supervised independent study opportunities, internships, and network groups.

6. Offer a Variety of Techniques. There is no one way to teach classes for returning students that is automatically better than another. Some of the exemplary professors lecture; some use group activities such as group discussion, panel discussion, and buzz groups. Not all agreed that audiovisual aids enhance learning all the time. Instructors should be careful to consider when to use audiovisual aids, realizing that, at times, an audiovisual aid may prevent learning.

7. Provide Feedback. Returning students want to know how they are doing. Returning students also want the opportunity to let the instructor know how he or she is doing. Thus feedback is a two-way process, involving examinations and grading, informal contacts, and the possibility of class steering committees.

8. Help Students Find Resources. Returning students often have difficulty using libraries to the extent traditional students are able to. Alternatives include providing multiple copies of

written materials and placing more emphasis on purchasing text-books. Many returning students are willing to pay a little extra to have written materials readily available. The community and fellow students are often overlooked as valuable resources for the returning student.

9. Keep Out-of-Class Contacts. For many returning students and for their instructors as well, the contacts with students in out-of-class situations is often as valuable as what happens in formal learning situations. Providing ample office hours for student contact is an obvious way for professors to make themselves available to returning students.

Chapter 10

Problems Instructors Face

Every instructor I interviewed for this project enjoyed working with returning students, without exception. Many said they preferred returning students to the younger, traditional students.

But that is not to say there aren't problems. As I listened to these instructors tell me about the problems returning students presented them, I discovered five major categories: (1) counseling time—returning students required a great amount of counseling time, far beyond that demanded by traditional students; (2) teaching-research tension—inadequate time for both; (3) problems related to the classroom—particularly in classes with both younger and older students; (4) problems related to career preparation; and (5) problems related to monetary support.

Time

Returning students require an extraordinary amount of instructor time for counseling, both in formal and in highly informal settings. This counseling generally falls into two broad areas: (1) that related to personal problems, and (2) that related to academic problems. The reality is often a combination; personal problems affect academic situations and academic problems create or contribute to personal problems.

For instance, one of the instructors said many returning students came to him with an emotional overload. First, he said, there was emotional overload because of lingering cultural guilt many of these returning students felt. Some of them still questioned whether they should be going back to school at their age; many of them are in their thirties and forties. Some students this instructor worked with were divorced women. Therefore, a second emotional overload they brought with them to the classroom and the professor's office concerned problems related to their divorce. According to this instructor, some of these women saw going back to school as a way to work out the personal problems associated with their divorce. Often the instructor referred the student to a professional counselor, but nevertheless they often came to the instructor first because he was available.

A third type of emotional overload many returning students face is wondering whether they can make it as a student. Even though, as we explained earlier, research clearly shows the remarkable abilities of adults as learners, many come into degree programs with doubts. Very often the counseling they need is simply reassuring them that they can make it as students.

Because returning students are older, they are wrapped up with all the problems, and sometimes more, that adults living active lives face: supporting families, working, and all the rest that goes with being an adult in our society. The course instructor is often available as a person to share personal problems related to everyday living. Many of these problems do get in the way of learning and are legitimate concerns for both the returning student and for the instructor to consider and do something about.

It seems that women who have families and return to school have more than their share of problems—many of them related to lack of acceptance of what they are doing by their husbands and by their children. Feelings of guilt often run high for these women, and they often search for a sympathetic ear for their concerns. Again, their instructors are often logical choices. For some women who return to school, family responsibilities continue at the same level as before. For instance, one of the instructors I interviewed told about a student who had thirteen children to care for. She was not an academically strong student either, so the instructor found herself spending vast amounts of time with this student, trying to help her with both the academic and the many personal problems she faced.

Related to the often heavy family and job responsibilities that many returning students have is the problem of time scheduling. Students often come to their instructors with questions about how they could manage their time demands now that they have added one other responsibility—coming back to school. Listening to their concerns and helping them work through alternative plans for time management often becomes the responsibility of the students' instructors.

The second broad area requiring counseling time relates to academic problems. These problems take a variety of forms, from failure to understand readings and what is going on in class to feelings of mistrust toward the instructors and sometimes toward other students. One of the instructors talked about a student who she said was taking up a tremendous amount of her time and emotional energy. She said she couldn't get this student to do any work, and she thought it was because the student didn't trust her. She said he kept promising to turn in his written assignments but then didn't. The student couldn't drop the course because he was a senior and it was required for graduation. She was concerned about failing the student and preventing his graduation after all the effort he had put into his program up to that point. So she spent much time working with the student, encouraging him, trying to work out a relationship so the student would trust her enough to turn in the written assignments and thus complete the course and graduate.

Another interesting problem shared by one of the instructors relates to student networks, the informal contacts students have with one another and by which they gain much information about instructors, courses, requirements, available resources, and so on. Traditional students know the networking system very well and use it to great advantage. But the returning student, particularly if attending school only part-time, is outside this system. The returning student often comes to instructors with questions traditional students answer themselves by talking with one another. This instructor decided one solution was to attempt to help returning students work into the existing network of information shared by traditional students. He went a step further by helping returning students set up networking approaches that were unique to the returning students and specifically dealt with many returning-student problems.

He provided all the students in his classes with the names, addresses, and phone numbers of the class members so the students could get in touch with one another easily. He helped students who were experiencing similar problems contact one another. He helped arrange for a student lounge where students could come together before and after classes if they liked. He made certain to provide breaks in his classes so students could talk informally. He offered to meet informally with groups of students to discuss any academic problems they were facing. And finally, he encouraged his classes to hold social activities such as potluck dinners or picnics so the students could learn to know one another better.

Another instructor said many returning students with whom she worked, particularly the female students who had been out of school for many years, looked to the instructor as a role model. She said, "It gets to the point where they have to project you into your forties, even though you're not there yet, so they can have a role model. Many of these students go through a period of adjustment that is really terrifying. Some of them tell me they feel like their brains have died, and they're not going to be able to make it as a student. And they look at me as a role model, as someone who is learning."

And finally, in a somewhat lighter vein, one of the instructors shared an anecdote with me about one of her older returning students who was having some difficulty with the course the instructor was teaching. She tells the story: "I was lying in my bed one night on the third floor of my house, and I heard this timid little knock on my bedroom door. It was a student who happened to live in my neighborhood, and she was having trouble with a paper she was writing. That really blew my mind. I wanted to say, 'What are you doing, can't you leave me alone, even when I'm sleeping?'

"But I got up, got dressed, and went downstairs. And I worked with the woman. She was a woman who was going through a divorce and was feeling a little shaky. And I didn't think she was going to sleep that night. And I knew I wasn't going to sleep. So what the heck. Those kinds of things happen."

Teaching-Research Tension

Because of the extra time returning students require, some instructors feel a tension between doing an adequate job as a teacher and counselor and keeping up with research and scholarship. But nearly all the instructors I interviewed stressed the importance for instructors of returning students to keep up with their research and writing. As a relatively young instructor at Temple University said, "I don't know how you can be an academic without doing some kind of research. And being young in this profession and hoping to survive here, I also feel that I must do research. But most of that is really internal pressure in that I think you have to be on top of what you're doing in order to be an effective teacher. So teaching and research merges for me. It's often difficult to handle both, especially when we're talking about the older returning student who is much more assertive about calling you up and saying, 'Look, I want to talk to you and it's going to take some time, let's go out and have a beer.' They often call you at home with questions . . . so the pressure of fitting research into a busy schedule is sometimes a problem."

A mid-career instructor from the University of Michigan had obviously thought about the relationship of research to teaching a great deal. He said, "My basic view is that in the United States we have a rather unique integration, an institutional integration of teaching and research. This is one of the few countries of the world where the major institutional centers for research are our universities. That's not true in western Europe, the Soviet Union, and that's not true in Asia. I've seen lots of ways in which our teaching is beautifully informed and made lively and current by our research. I think our best teachers are some of our best researchers. Not all the researchers are good teachers, and not all the good teachers are good researchers. But there is, as I see it, some close correspondence between the two. I think some of our best teaching here comes out of people who are in the forefront in research, and their research then informs their teaching. This can happen whether one is teaching an introductory or a very advanced course. Then I think, too, our research is, in some important ways, well informed by our teaching. I must say though, in part of the equation, research is helped somewhat less by teaching than teaching is helped by research. There are two ways I think that this happens.

"One, the pressure that teaching lays upon us to turn our research into exposable statements makes our research better. The kinds of questions we get from our students always brings the research up short—and we say there's something I haven't considered here, I better take a look at it. That happens at the undergraduate level and the graduate level. Somewhat more at the graduate level, of course, where one actually involves the students, the more experienced students, in the research and they do help push it on a little more. They contribute instrumentally and specifically to it.

"There are costs, certainly. Teaching takes a substantial portion away from the research in time and energy. And in order to promote research you have to sit on your rear and at your desk and push things along. Teaching means you have to prepare lectures, prepare curriculum, prepare reading lists, meet with students, spend a lot of time with students, and that all takes time away from the research. So that's a cost. I think research has its cost for teaching too; certainly some people, and we see this not infrequently, neglect their teaching. One of the causes for this is the emphasis on research for promotion and tenure. In our promotion in the university we look at research, teaching, and service—in that order. And the research is most critical. Of course to a certain extent we can evaluate research more objectively than we can teaching or service. We get people outside the university to comment on the research. Also, people get rewarded for their research. They are not rewarded very much for teaching and not very much for service. But even with the heavy emphasis here on research, our promotion system also places considerable emphasis on quality teaching."

A retired professor of education who continued to teach on a part-time basis had an interesting perspective on the relationship of teaching to research. He observed that some teachers get very involved in their teaching and neglect their research, and likewise some researchers may get heavily involved in their research and neglect their teaching. But he saw a relationship between the two functions. He said, "I think the sense of inquiry and the sense of testing hypotheses is a style of thinking and a style of work that contributes to the teaching process." He went on to explain that he believed many of the same approaches, particularly the logical approaches of conducting research, could be applied in teaching-learning situations. Such processes as identification of a problem or question to be answered, the exploration and testing of a number of possible answers to the question, and making decisions about the answer that seemed most appropriate because of the available evidence were procedures that worked as well in the classroom as they did in research projects.

In this professor's opinion, professors have made too much of the gap between research and teaching and have in many instances created a gap that logically and even practically doesn't exist. Very often teaching and research can be closely integrated, certainly closely related both in terms of approach and content, if professors would reflect on how to bring the two processes together rather than focusing on them as separate entities.

By talking with an instructor it is easy to determine how he or she sees the relationship of teaching and research. If instructors tell you about the courses they teach and the kinds of students they attract and then tell you about research they are doing that seems to bear no relationship to their teaching, you have an inkling that perhaps they are having some problems in seeing the relationship of teaching to research. But if they begin telling you about their work and mention research and teaching together as an integral part of their academic program, you have at least an idea that they are able to work out the relationship in some type of satisfactory way.

Even though the majority of the instructors I talked with thought that it was important for instructors to do both research and teaching and that it was possible to relate the two in an integrated academic program, nevertheless some saw problems.

More than half the professors mentioned time pressures as the biggest problem in continuing to do high-quality teaching as well as carrying out a research and scholarly writing program.

When I asked her about the possibility of tension between teaching and research, a psychology instructor replied, "Only in terms of time. If one wants to do a good job on both—teaching and research—then one spends more time doing it than people who opt for either one or the other. Only in that sense is there a tension between teaching and research for me."

Some of the instructors I interviewed were involved or had recently been involved in administrative activities, so they were also aware of the time problems associated with administrative assignments. For instance, a geography instructor commented on the tension between research and teaching this way: "It's certainly real as far as time commitment. One of the reasons I haven't been productive in research for the last four years is I've been in administration and have been doing a lot of innovative teaching, and that's taken a lot of time. I do a good deal of troubleshooting in my administrative job, and that's very time consuming."

Closely related to inadequate time was personal energy. As an education instructor said, "I don't have energy enough after taking care of my teaching assignments to write the proposal to do the big project. And at our university, the expectation and the rewards go to the administrator of a large research project who hires people to help with the task. And I don't want to do that kind of research, and I'm not ready to do that kind of research. That's not where I want to put my energy. I end up not wanting to do the kind of research that is recognized and rewarded at this university."

In addition to the problems of time and energy, it is obvious from this professor's comments that her ideas about how research should be done differ rather dramatically from the institutional expectations. As I talked with her further, I learned that she wanted to be involved in much smaller projects, many of them growing out of the courses she taught. She was working toward an integration of her research and teaching, and working toward making maximum use of her time and energy.

In terms of solving the time problem, a professor at North Carolina State University told me, "When I first started teaching back in 1969, I almost lived here on campus. I jokingly said this was my home, and it was. I worked on my teaching during the day and my research at night. I wrote at night. Some of my colleagues try to take a couple of days out of the office, but I've never been able to do that. I think I should be here as much as I can to work with students. It means I have to move a lot of my research over to my family time."

Another North Carolina State professor commented on the difficulty in obtaining funding for research projects. The specific point he made is the need to have some research completed before funds can be obtained; doing the necessary "pump-priming" research often presents a time problem for professors who are heavily committed to doing excellent teaching. He said it this way: "The old idea that the university community supported the research activities of scholars along with their teaching has long disappeared. As a result, what you've got is a new system. And I didn't fit into that system very well, and so it was a question—if you want to get a grant, you can't get it by saying you want to do these things. Even if it's the best idea in the world, you won't get the grant. In order to do the spade work to even make the first move towards qualifying for a grant, something's got to give. If you're teaching a half-time load, sometimes it's very difficult to get the chunks of time because research can't be done a little at a time. You can't turn it on and off between two classes. You've got to have chunks of time like a half a day or a day, or something like that to be able to work out good research. So I've been faced with a problem: Do I slight my teaching duties to some extent so I can steal some time so I can write a proposal and maybe get a grant? Usually you've got to have external support to do research. That's the tension for me."

Still another time-related problem for a University of Wisconsin professor was with her extension appointment. A considerable amount of her time was devoted to activities off campus, and the travel time alone used up huge chunks of her time. For her the tension was between extension and research, and she was able to integrate her teaching and research to a considerable extent.

One of the instructors had worked out a system allowing her to have considerable blocks of time available for doing her research activities. Her classes met on Monday and Wednesday evenings and Tuesday and Thursday mornings, which allowed her to essentially have all of Monday and all of Wednesday free to work on research.

In addition to time contributing to a tension between teaching and research, several other problems were mentioned.

While the majority of the instructors I talked with saw a rather strong relationship between research and teaching, one of the instructors did not. In fact he believed that research and teaching were growing further and further apart on college and university campuses. In this instructor's opinion, researchers have become increasingly more specialized, working in greater and greater depth with more narrowly defined topics. On the other hand, this instructor pointed out, the teacher in the classroom must of necessity be something of a generalist. "I don't think that there is an organic relationship necessarily between research and teaching," this instructor said.

According to this instructor, increasing emphasis on highly specialized research activities by instructors on college and university campuses will make it increasingly more difficult for excellent teaching to take place in the college classroom. In his judgment, before instructors are hired and placed in the classroom, they should be evaluated not only on their knowledge of subject matter but also on their self-knowledge, their attitudes toward human beings, and their understanding of the relationships between themselves, their subject matter, and the students with whom they will come in contact. He underlined that we continue to employ college instructors who are highly trained in a subject-matter area but often have little or no training and experience as teachers. According to this instructor, until some changes are made in this system we will continue to see a cleavage between teaching and research on college and university campuses. More emphasis must be placed on the importance of the teaching role beginning from the time that decisions are being made about hiring a professor and continuing as decisions are made about that professor's promotions and his or her salary increases.

Still another perspective on the teaching-research tension was presented by a mid-career instructor. In her opinion women instructors have particular kinds of problems with the relationship between teaching and research that are different from those experienced by male instructors. She said, "We are socialized in a different way toward our careers, toward how we interact with other people, how we interact with young people. We come from a very different subculture than do male instructors."

She shared with me a specific example of what she meant: "I started teaching in 1957, and I have what you'll see from my vita is a very typical vita for a woman faculty member in her late forties. That is, I have periods of unemployment. I've got a split appointment. I'm not wholly in the department of my research specialty. I had not taught in my research speciality until a year ago. I taught other kinds of courses. I have an interest in teaching innovations, which I find much more characteristic of women faculty members, at least that is so at this institution. Some of my male colleagues learn to manage hundreds of students; they lecture two hundred students with a minimum of time involvement or emotional commitment and still get good teaching evaluations. They are able to encapsulate their teaching effort and still do their research, if they are really interested in doing it. I think this approach is harder for women."

She was saying that because of the reality of a woman's career she believed women were more committed to teaching (often by default) than some of their male colleagues. Because of a career that meant in and out of university life for many women, the opportunity to build a long-term research program was more difficult. Thus, without the long-term research program and long-term commitment to research, there is more time for teaching and more of an emotional commitment to teaching.

Classroom Problems

The returning student in class often presents a particular set of problems, especially if the classroom is made up of both traditional and returning students.

For instance, a professor of history said a mixed class with students of varying ages, varying experiences, and various reasons for being in the class does not have a common language. Without a common language each student hears and reacts differently to what the professor is saying and, just as important, to what other students are saying in the classroom. In his history courses, several of which had large numbers of older returning students as well as traditional students, many of the older students had a sense of their own place in history and could relate their lives to particular historical events personally, while some of the younger students had great difficulty doing this. Thus it was difficult for returning students, traditional students, and the professor to have a common discussion.

Another instructor I interviewed also saw this diversity as a problem in his classes, but he worked out an approach that at least for him not only helped solve the problem but made a potentially negative situation a positive one. He explained what he does this way:

"One of the basic principles of effective group collective work is to identify the roles for each of the persons in the group so they don't find themselves in competition with each other. If the instructor can make it clear that the class is lucky to have persons in it who have a great deal of experience in this field, it helps lessen the competition that may develop between the more experienced and the less experienced students. It's good group dynamics and this approach helps to improve the effectiveness of the class a great deal.

"Students will listen to each other if they understand that each of them has an important contribution to make to the class discussion and that no one person's contribution is more important than another's, only different.

"If the instructor doesn't do this, doesn't take some time to explain that the class has a variety of people and can expect a variety of contributions, the first person to make a suggestion, say in response to a problem situation the instructor might pose, will be put down simply because the suggestion was made. But if ahead of time the instructor can make clear that we have a person in our group who is unusually skillful in applying mathematics to situations like this, people in the group look at this person differently then. They see the person not as a competitor but someone who can help the group with its problem-solving task.

"Of course this whole approach assumes that the instructor understands how much students can learn from each other and that the instructor doesn't have all the answers."

The instructor having all the answers raises another point that several of the instructors I interviewed mentioned—the older student as a threat to the younger instructor.

A professor of social welfare said that, when she first began teaching, some of the older students were a threat to her. She believes two factors contributed to the situation: her age (she was younger than most of her students) and her inexperience as a professor (not knowing how to involve older, experienced students in the class discussions). Today she says, "I don't think that it's an issue because I feel confident about myself as a teacher. Sometimes when we talk about life cycle, or talk about children, I'll ask the more-experienced students to explain what it was like to have children or to even tell the class about their own children. At this point in my career, older students aren't a threat at all."

One instructor, a professor of psychology, said, "In my younger days as an instructor some of the older students were actually hostile. I think part of it was based on my youth and their age. Some of the problem related to exam grading. If they did not do so well on an exam, some of them resented a much younger person grading it, and thus grading them down."

More recently her experience has been somewhat the opposite. She is concerned that many of the older students are reluctant to come to her with an exam on which they may have done poorly and discuss it. They are reluctant to ask how certain examination questions were graded and what they missed, what they did wrong in response to a particular examination question. For this instructor today, many of the older students in her classes are not assertive enough to raise questions with her about how they are doing and how they are being evaluated. For this instructor this is as much a problem as the former situation, when some of the older students were openly hostile.

Simply being younger than many of the students presents a particular set of problems. As one of the female instructors said,

"I'm thirty-two, which makes most of my students older than I am. And I'm also single so there are all kinds of issues that have to be dealt with that don't apply if you are teaching undergraduates. You really have to try to keep your roles straight—your hats straight—What hat am I wearing now? and When is it appropriate to put on which hat?"

Another point that is easily overlooked in this discussion of problems is the matter of required energy. Several instructors pointed out how much easier and how much less a drain on their physical and psychic energy was the younger, more traditional student. As one instructor said, "For the kinds of interactions with older students that I know are productive and helpful both to them and to me takes a lot out of me. It drains me. It's hard to do."

Career-Preparation Problems

In terms of career interest, two types of students are represented in the returning student group. One group of returning students is interested in employment, either in getting a job for the first time, which is true of many women returning to school, advancing on a job now held, or making a career or job change. The second group is more interested in education for its own sake rather than for its employment relationship.

According to several of the instructors I interviewed, people in the first group are often overly aggressive about finishing their education in the shortest possible time and, for some of them, with the least amount of effort expended. This poses a problem for the instructor who is concerned about providing quality educational offerings, related often to employment but not single-mindedly related. Single-minded students with a goal of finding employment as rapidly as possible present problems to the instructors as well as to those students who have a different reason for being in school.

Some of the instructors felt it was their responsibility to help these "hell-bent on employment" students see a broader perspective in their educational activities, and even in some instances to counsel them out of higher education into vocational or technical education, where they were likely to achieve their employment aspirations more quickly. This problem is discussed further in chapter 13.

Financial Support

Several instructors were involved in making decisions about which older returning students should be eligible for financial aid.

One of the instructors told me about a returning student who had two children, was divorced, and was not receiving any support money from her ex-husband. Not continuing her financial aid would mean she would have to drop out of school. Yet if one used purely academic criteria, aside from life situation, to judge her eligibility, she probably shouldn't have continued on financial aid. As a result of the situation, this instructor was quite concerned about having to make this kind of decision and about what the best way of making the decision might be. As she said, "It really is a concern of mine, and I think that these people have unusual problems, and sometimes there need to be unusual solutions . . . and this takes a lot of my time and energy."

Another instructor told of the difficulty he had in convincing his administration that financial aid should be provided to a returning student when the family's income was, say, $15,000 a year or even more. "But when the wife in that family decides to come back to school, the costs of her doing that just don't fit within that family's budget," he said. "And she needs some kind of financial support."

Summary

To sum up this section, instructors who work with returning students are faced with a number of problems that these students present to them. Many of these problems relate to the particular circumstances of the returning student: employment, need for financial aid, family problems, adjustment to school after several years away, and so on. The point is, though, these problems cannot be ignored. The instructor of returning students is often the first person the returning student goes to when he or she has a problem, whether it be a personal problem or an academic problem. Also, because of the great amount of time returning students require, many instructors feel a tension between their teaching and counseling responsibilities and their research and scholarship responsibilities. Unfortunately, there are no easy solutions, no pat formulas to be followed by instructors in working with these problems. But work with them the instructors must, if they are to be effective with the older returning students in their classrooms.

Chapter 11

Descriptions of and Advice from Exemplary Instructors

I am sometimes asked, "Does it take a particular kind of person to be a successful instructor of returning students?" With that question in mind, I tried to find out what kinds of persons the exemplary instructors I interviewed were. Was it possible that these exemplary instructors fell into categories that made them different from instructors who work only with the younger, more traditional students?

So I asked these instructors about their leisure-time activities—Were they all workaholics who spent all or most of their time working? I asked them about what they liked and didn't like about college teaching in general. I asked them about their research interests. I asked them what they had planned for five years from now, and finally I asked them if they had any advice for other instructors who were, perhaps for the first time, working with returning students.

The instructors I interviewed ranged in age from the mid-twenties to the seventies. Two were retired but still actively involved in teaching. One of the instructors, an assistant professor, had not yet completed her Ph.D., but she was working part-time toward it while teaching full time. All the rest had completed the doctorate.

Leisure-Time Activities

These instructors were extremely active in leisure-time pursuits in a wide variety of areas.

Six mentioned vigorous activities such as tennis, squash, swimming, flying, and handball. A professor nearing retirement age said he played handball every noon. "And I guess I'm the second oldest handball player on this campus. There's a man in the math department who is a year or two older. But I still play, if not well, enthusiastically. I began playing handball in my mid-forties, and I really enjoy it. Keeps me slim too."

A female professor of psychology was the aviator in the group. She belonged to a flying club where she flew regularly, even though the flying club was located some distance from her home. It was an expensive enough leisure-time activity that she had to skimp on many other things, including a newer car.

Several of the professors mentioned their children and their families as being included in their major leisure-time pursuits. Some mentioned attending concerts and plays; two played the piano. A retired professor who was still actively teaching said he considered himself quite a good amateur piano player. He plays Chopin, does a lot of improvising, and plays hymns. At the time of the interview he was seventy-nine years old.

Cooking, photography, sewing, wine making, and candy making were some of the arts and crafts leisure-time activities these professors mentioned as occupying major parts of their nonwork time.

Twelve of the eighteen professors mentioned nature and outdoor activities as high-interest areas for them. They mentioned hiking, hunting, fishing, camping, gardening, traveling, sailing, bird watching, chopping wood, working in the yard, managing a woodlot, canoeing, enjoying a place in Maine, and azalea propagation as examples.

Reading was mentioned by nine of the professors as a major leisure-time activity. Contemporary novels, best-selling novels, poetry, political biography, books on spiritualism, and books about the Arctic region were specifically mentioned. Two of the professors said they like to read a good "trashy novel" on occasion. One said she liked this kind of reading occasionally because "you can do it without engaging your brain."

Within this group there were not many collectors. Only one of the professors said he collected stamps as a major leisure-time activity. Three participated in various kinds of service activities in their spare time. These varied from involvement in political campaigns and serving on political boards to giving slide talks on the trips the person had made.

Both of the retired people interviewed (they were still actively involved in teaching and research) mentioned their work as one of their major leisure-time activities. But both of them had a long list of other activities in which they participated.

One could conclude that, though these persons were identified as exemplary instructors of returning students, they were also persons with broad interests who participated in a wide array of activities in their leisure time. They enthusiastically shared what they were doing. There were no overtones of guilt—that time spent on leisure-time activity might better be spent on preparing for teaching, working on research projects, or engaging in writing activities. There was none of this attitude expressed. It was obvious that these people knew the importance of leisure in their lives.

To obtain some perspective on how these professors saw their jobs as instructors, I asked them to share what they liked about being a professor and what they disliked. They were very candid with their comments, sharing many examples of what they didn't like as well as what appealed to them. It is difficult to summarize information like this. But one point seems clear. Those professors who have worked for at least ten years mentioned an increase in what they didn't like about university life from when they first began their academic careers.

What Is Liked About University Life

Teaching and Student Contact

As might be expected, these exemplary instructors mentioned most often that they liked teaching and contact with students. As one of the professors said, "I really enjoy teaching a whole lot. I mean, that's what I wanted to do, and I do it."

Another said the thing she enjoyed most about college and university work was coming in contact with interesting students. "I get a lot of gratification out of my students," she said. Still another said, "I find a personal recharging, a personal keeping myself straight, keeping myself together, which comes from being with students who are dealing with the same kinds of issues and who share in the resolution of these problems with me." This instructor worked only with graduate students, and all of them were returning older students.

In addition to liking to work with students, several of the instructors talked about the positive feelings they have when their students begin to grasp new ideas and grow. "I get a big kick out of seeing them light up and get excited about learning and doing things and feeling good about themselves because they've done something productive and useful," one of the instructors said.

An instructor shared with me the example of Vicky, one of his returning students. Vicky had married as a teenager and then later came back to college. This instructor kept in touch with Vicky after her graduation. "She's lived in three communities since then, and I have watched her grow in confidence. Not in intellect—that's been there all along—but in her assurance. She has applied for a very responsible job, and I'm trying to help her get it."

Watching student advisees grow and develop and watching a class become a unit and learn how to work together were two things mentioned by one of the instructors as particularly satisfying to him. He said, "I especially like seeing students grow, whether or not I have anything to do with it. Students grow intellectually because of the environment they are in, of which I am just one small piece. I particularly enjoy watching my advisees change. You are really close to an advisee and you can see the changes over a period of time, from month to month, over a year or more of time. You know that they are doing this and this and this. You confer with them on research proposals; you have them in your classes.

"The other changes I enjoy are in the classes themselves. I enjoy observing a class become a cohesive working group with self-determined objectives and products. I had an example of this just yesterday with a mix of traditional and returning students—a small group of five. As an experiment I broke the class into eight such groups. I show up in classes as a resource—no lectures—if they want help from me I'm there. The first couple of weeks they weren't even around, they didn't need any help." For this instructor one of the real joys of teaching was to structure his class in such a way, and build an attitude about teaching and learning in such a way, that the class, through its small groups, was able to organize its own learning projects and carry them out. A positive satisfaction for this instructor was being able to take the risk of teaching in a rather unusual way and see it work.

And not only did he take pleasure from seeing his unusual teaching approach work (some would label it a nonteaching approach), he thoroughly enjoyed observing the class groups come together and learn how to work as groups.

Finally, a psychology instructor said, "I really get a great deal of pleasure out of shaping minds, that is, seeing people learn something new and use that in getting their heads turned on—I get a lot of kicks out of that."

And at an even deeper level, several of the instructors said they liked what they were doing because they dealt with the most basic dimensions of human existence—that part of education concerned with what it means to be a human being. A professor of history said, "The thing that has kept me working as a professor is the joy of assisting in lifting the human spirit. I think that's what keeps any serious teacher on the job—when the breakthrough occurs and somebody lights up. Or people come and tell you things are happening. That's the primary reward. In fact, sometimes the only reward. I'm often puzzled about the senseless self-satisfaction that one gets from teaching, as against the satisfaction one gets from publishing books (which is something very tangible) and you get reviews and you get paid. Once you finish teaching it's all gone out, and students go off, and although you may remain in contact with them, your relationships change. But your part is over, and you have really nothing to show for it, nothing tangible."

This professor went on to explain how empty an experience teaching must be for those professors who do not recognize the importance of the intangible contributions: the contributions of the instructor to improving the human condition through helping students see new perspectives, learn new ways of thinking, and new ways of dealing with problems, and introducing them to writers and thinkers who can stretch their minds beyond day-to-day existence. For him it was the nonmeasurable outcomes that kept him teaching day after day and year after year.

Several of the instructors commented on how much they enjoyed working with classes made up of both traditional students and returning students, as well as other mixes of students. As a Temple University instructor said, "One thing that I really enjoy about working at Temple is the kind of mix that I have in the students in terms of age and in terms of race and background. We have at least half of our majors who are black, and we have rural [people] (not too many, we're mostly city people), but the old and the young and the black and the white mix I find a real challenge. And that's something I don't think I'll find at most other schools. It's very unique to here."

A University of Wisconsin professor particularly liked the mix of older and younger students in her classes. She was very frank with her comments. "I get really bored sometimes with twenty-year-olds," she said. "But with older students in the class it is a richer experience. When I'm talking about the 1920s, and there's somebody in the class who can remember the twenties, it's really good. One year I had a sixty-two-year-old man in my writing class. I often heard the students down the hall clustering around him and just talking to him. These younger students liked having him there. And he added a lot to the course."

A professor of sociology I interviewed had spent some time working in government prior to coming to work for the university where he now taught. For him the greatest satisfaction comes from "the great diversity of energetic people; compared with those big bureaucracies this is the place that's just absolutely alive, with everybody questioning everything and fantastic numbers of new ideas coming in. And all sorts of real intellectual explosions, and personal explosions coming up too—it's very exciting. It's just a marvelous thing to be with people who are performing intellectually and constantly questioning. This goes for undergraduate through graduate students."

An instructor nearing retirement said one of the long-term benefits he saw from teaching was watching many of his former students progress in their careers. He was obviously and for good reason very proud of his former students. "The present governor of this state was a student of mine; so was the commissioner of agriculture for our state," he said. Then he went on to share an anecdote: "One time not long ago the commissioner of agriculture here was talking with four or five of us, including some other faculty members, and he said, 'I want to tell you something about this man.' He was talking to me. He said, 'The first course I had from him I made an A, the introductory course, and I thought he was the greatest teacher I ever saw. I took a second course and I made a C. I'll tell you he turned into the worst teacher I ever had. Just like that.' "

Then the man I was interviewing laughed, and his eyes twinkled, and I could see he shared the story to illustrate the excellent relationship he has maintained with his students over the years.

Research and Writing

After teaching and contact with students, the reason most often given for liking college and university life was the opportunity to research and write. For some people this may come as a surprise, for there is a myth that good teachers are not interested in research and writing. That was not the case with the exemplary instructors I interviewed. It didn't make any difference whether the instructor was male or female, young or old; nor did the discipline that was represented matter. Of course the reader is reminded that the number of professors interviewed for this project was relatively small, only eighteen, so no sweeping generalizations can be made. But for the group interviewed there was no question that these professors not only enjoyed teaching and contact with students but also enjoyed the opportunity to work on research projects and write the results. As one of the instructors said, after he had spent some time describing what he liked about teaching, "I've always liked to do research. I've also been blessed with opportunities to get money for research almost anytime I needed it. I've just automatically got to be involved in research. I'm not particular about the type of research, but I do hate to do the same kind of research over and over again."

Another point made by several of the instructors that should be underlined is the integration of teaching and research into an instructor's work. These instructors did not see teaching as just one aspect of what they do, divorced from research, but rather saw the two closely integrated. (Refer back to chapter 10 for a discussion of teaching-research tension.) Problems and concerns expressed by students, particularly the older returning students, were often triggers for further research. The findings of research often fed directly into the instructor's classroom teaching.

Freedom to Choose One's Tasks

Freedom to have control over a major part of what one does was cited by several of the instructors as a reason they enjoyed college and university life. As a sociology instructor said, "I don't know how long it will last, but now we can teach the courses we want, and we can investigate the questions we want to investigate. There's a kind of freedom that just blows one's mind, really. You don't have to do a lot of things people in big organizations do. I've seen this particularly in federal government and the

United Nations. People get stale. They spend their lives shuffling papers from in-basket to out-basket and going from one meeting to the next over and over and over again. There's nothing really changing. The university affords a freedom to change in a tremendous way."

Another professor, commenting on the freedom she had as a university instructor, said, "It's almost embarrassing because people pay me to do something I would do for free. I have the freedom to think, to talk to people a lot, to do a lot of reading."

Relationship to Other Faculty

The relationship to other faculty members was another reason for enjoying college and university life. A professor of sociology said, "I like being in a community with other academics. It's just a delight. Every day I see people I know only casually, and I wish there were times I could get to know them better, know the kinds of things they are doing. I do work in South and Southeast Asia and we have a South and Southeast Asia Center which draws together a tremendous diversity of people in linguistics and music, geography and history—everything. I meet with an exciting group of people who are doing so many different things. It's certainly better to be frustrated from having too much of that than by having too little of it."

Application of Learning

Some people have the impression that college and university instructors are interested in teaching students and doing research, but they are usually not interested in how their work relates to problems in society, or what might be called the practical aspects of life and the world.

That was not the case with the instructors interviewed for this project. Several of them were very interested in seeing how their research and their teaching related to real-life problems. For instance, one of the instructors told how she enjoyed seeing students, most of them in school part-time and at work full time, getting turned on to ideas that they were trying out in their jobs. These students brought back to the classroom the results of their efforts, and this provided the class with opportunities to examine real-life problems and offer suggestions for changes that the person who had been trying out new ideas at work could introduce.

Another professor, working in the area of public administration, shared some of the experiences he had had in attempting to relate his subject to the community. He shared the example of a female probation officer he had in class several years ago. Those were the days when people were discussing dress codes. This probation officer had wanted to appear in court in a pantsuit. Her supervisor said he would fire her if she did. She asked her supervisor if she could wear a pantsuit if she first asked the judge whether it would be all right. She went to the judge with the question, and the judge told her that his wife wore a pantsuit everywhere and he didn't see any problem if she wore a pantsuit in his court. This incident became a point for discussion in his class.

What Is Not Liked About University Life

It was not difficult for the exemplary instructors to list what they didn't like about college and university life. In fact, when I asked them about what they liked, some of them interrupted me to make sure I planned to ask what they didn't like. They didn't mince words either. Heading the list of what they didn't like about college and university work was bureaucracy, committees, and rules.

Bureaucracy, Committees, and Rules

Nearly every instructor I interviewed mentioned this category as his or her major dislike of academic life. As one instructor said when I asked her what she liked least about academic life, "Committees. Endless committees. Committees upon committees. Most of these committees I serve on are concerned with one question: What do we do with 10 percent less money in the coming year? How do we allocate our resources? Professors haven't figured out who they really are. They should be fighting for their rights, and what they do is to respond to external decisions by meeting in committees."

Committees were mentioned by several of the instructors as what they disliked most about university life. But the instructors were quick to point out that they approved of committees that had a real purpose and that met to move forward the idea of faculty governance and faculty decision making in academic policy. It was the many committees that met with no apparent purpose or direction that instructors were concerned about. For instance, one instructor said, "What I dislike the most about university life is committees which cannot make any kind of contribution to anything, and committees to which I am in no position to make any contribution."

He went on to explain that one problem with committees was the purpose for which they were formed. In his judgment many committees met to make decisions and to carry out what an individual could do more effectively and efficiently. He also was highly critical of standing committees that met because they were supposed to but seldom did anything except to agree to meet again. This same instructor, however, was highly supportive of committees that involved faculty governance and met with that purpose in mind. He said, "Where the involvement makes a difference, I don't object to it."

A professor who was about to retire noted the great increase in rules and regulations over the years that he taught. He pointed out that professors may often get caught up with spending more time interpreting and carrying out rules and regulations than they do working with students and carrying out other activities that are supposed to be the primary roles of professors.

An assistant professor also recognized the same problem. In response to my question about what she didn't like, she said without hesitation, "Dealing with administration, dealing with forms and rules and not knowing what the forms and rules are for. We don't know what a particular form is; we don't know how somebody plans to use it; we don't know why it is necessary. Consequently, it is pretty hard to be enthusiastic about filling them out."

A mid-career instructor had thought about the problem of bureaucracy, committees, and rules and had put the problem into a larger context. From her perspective, she believed her university had developed into a corporate hierarchy patterned after some of the larger corporations in our society. The consequences of that change, from her perspective, meant that faculty members were in a powerless position and getting more powerless. She was particularly concerned about the powerlessness of the women faculty members. She pointed out that, at her institution, there had never been a departmental chair who was a woman.

Following closely behind a dislike for bureaucracy, committees, and rules, university politics was noted by several of the professors as something they disliked. Of course in many ways university politics is related to the bureaucracy and the rules. So some of the professors went immediately from talking about bureaucracy and their disdain for it to how the bureaucracy of the university dealt with them.

Campus Politics

As a tenured female professor said, "I'm a token woman. I'm the only woman working right now with an academic degree and with tenure. There are thirty-two men with tenure and me. So it's very lonely, very isolated. They believe in the combat model of classroom behavior—a great many of them do—and I believe in the cooperative model. So there's not very much of a meeting of ways. I'm a democrat, small *d*, and the place is run on conservative lines, so I find it very isolated."

Another female professor pointed out, "I worry about the people who get promoted because they sit on a lot of university committees and are not that concerned about classroom activities." For her it was a political thing. It was clearly a case of who you knew, not how you performed, that made a difference at tenure time. As an untenured professor with a great concern for teaching and working with students, she was concerned and often upset by this.

Economic Problems

With decreasing enrollments already upon many colleges and universities, the economic picture for many institutions does not look bright. Instructors I interviewed admitted freely that they were concerned about the economics of higher education in the future, and they were particularly concerned about their own institutions.

Not only were they concerned about the long-run effects of budget problems on their institutions, but they were also concerned about the problems presented right now. As one of the instructors said after she described to me the reality of less state support for her institution, "Just justifying every piece of paper and little or no support for students because there isn't enough money bothers me." All the instructors who mentioned the economic problems conceded they would likely get worse before they get better. Because not only are institutions faced with the possibility of dwindling enrollments, particularly among the age group that ordinarily attends college in large numbers (18–22), but also the high level of inflation the country has faced and will likely continue to face makes budgeting more complicated.

Surprisingly, only a small number of instructors mentioned salaries as a problem and as something they disliked about teaching at a college or university. Only one of the professors really made a strong point of the salary situation; in fact he mentioned relatively low salaries as his first answer to the question about what he disliked about college and university work. He said, "You don't make much money. When I look at the people in Aid for International Development and the United Nations (he had consulted with both these agencies) who are making two and three times as much money as I'm making, that's not pleasant. I wish we could make more. But we get enough to get by."

Evaluating Students

In the last chapter we discussed some of the problems faculty members faced when working with returning students. Not surprisingly, the second most mentioned dislike of college and university life in general was grading and evaluating students, no matter if they were younger traditional students or older returning students. Almost to an instructor they did not like to do this, yet most of them saw the need to provide feedback to students about the students' progress. Many of them mentioned the necessity of maintaining high standards in academic programs. When pressed to say more about academic standards and whether there might be alternatives to tests and grading to maintain standards, only one instructor had really considered alternatives. This instructor thought we should try to move away from comparing students with each other, the normal-curve approach to grading, and begin comparing students against some standard that might jointly be determined between the professor and the student prior to the beginning of a semester's work. Thus, within any class, there might exist as many standards as there are students in the class.

Other instructors I talked with were far less clear about alternatives. Several implied that they both compared students with each other and compared each student with some set standard they had in mind.

Tension and Anxiety

Although it sounds like a contradiction, several of the instructors mentioned tension and anxiety as dislikes. An apparent contradiction is mentioned because most instructors listed the freedom they had in their jobs to do the things they wanted to do in the way they wanted to do them as a plus. Yet they still experienced tension and anxiety.

As one of the instructors said, "I don't like the kind of fractionalization of your life that goes on here. For example, I teach two and sometimes three kinds of courses. I'm on several committees. My day gets cut up into all different kinds of patterns, and it's really very difficult to put in solid chunks of work on particular kinds of things. And I find that disconcerting."

Interestingly, this instructor was in mid-career, with tenure, and was one of those who replied to the question, What do you enjoy most about being an instructor? with, "The freedom to choose to do what I want to do."

A professor of history said he disliked the personal disruption and the fact that "the strains and tensions and anxieties that are an inherent part of this intellectual life rub off on a person."

So even though most of the instructors recognized and enjoyed the freedom associated with academic life, several of them recognized also that university life is not without its tensions and anxieties. Recognize too that the instructors I interviewed were special people. They had all been recognized as exemplary professors in terms of teaching returning students. This would seem to indicate that they had little to fear in terms of how their departmental chairpersons and deans viewed their performance. They did not need to worry about being judged inadequate and putting up with the pressure of forced improvement, as may be the case for some professors on university campuses. Forced improvement obviously can lead to feelings of pressure, tension, and anxiety.

Given the relatively secure positions of these instructors and the recognition they have gotten for good work, several of them still mentioned tension and anxiety as things they disliked about university life.

Another tension creator, for at least one of the instructors, was related to the free and open nature of the university where this professor was employed. When we talked about what he really liked about university life, he mentioned to me the free atmosphere for inquiry, the liberal position the university had taken toward student views and student activities, and so on. But when we were talking about what he disliked, he brought this point up again, but from quite a different perspective. He said it this way: "The university is an open and free community, and we get a lot of nuts. And nuts take time. I'm talking about people who really are off the deep end, hallucinating about all kinds of things. And you have to deal with them.

"I had a very unsettling experience last year in teaching a large introductory course. One young woman student accused me and the administration of experimenting with the class and trying to warp and shape her mind. Well, we went through the whole review process with the university review panel; it had both students and faculty on it. It came out fairly clearly that the woman had some personal problems of her own, which she was projecting on others and trying to solve those problems that way. It was an unsettling thing. It took time and a lot of personal energy. She was a person.

"That sort of thing comes up constantly, the political disruptions, the personal and intellectual disruptions, which are an integral part of this life. They are stressful and tension producing. But you wouldn't want to do without it. You wouldn't by any means try to avoid that."

Problems Related to Students

As I indicated earlier in this chapter, all the instructors mentioned their love for students and for teaching. Yet, when I talked about what these instructors disliked about university life, nearly half of them mentioned some aspect of their contact with students.

At least two of the instructors said they were impatient with all students who lacked basic skills and lacked the motivation to improve. For instance, one of the professors who worked primarily with graduate students said, "I must confess I am working on some theses where the writing quality is doubtful. I must be frank about it. I find myself a bit impatient with having to help someone with English."

Another instructor couldn't understand why all the students with whom she worked weren't highly committed to the subject area she taught. She said, "I get very frustrated with students who don't seem to take this seriously, and part of that is my own problem because I guess I'm really invested. I had a class last year where papers were late, and people just didn't come, and it really bothered me personally because I'm invested and I want them to be invested." Later she mentioned she had few problems with older returning students concerning interest and motivation. The returning student, to use her words, "is usually 100 percent invested in academic work."

A political science professor agreed with the motivational difference between traditional and returning students and expressed concern that a growing number of traditional students "are much less motivated than the returning students and they don't want to do what they don't want to do." He gave an example of a young woman in one of his classes who said, "I don't want to study that because I don't know anything about it."

This same political science professor shared another concern he had about students, primarily the younger, traditional students. He believed there is a growing adversary relationship between teachers and students. Even though he worked to avoid it, he noted larger numbers of students each year turned in extremely negative reports on him on the end-of-class evaluations. He said, "I find that out of two sections of seventy students I'll get five who obviously deeply resent me. They don't like me, and they don't like a lot of other people." He said he seldom got this reaction from returning students. He also compared what is happening now with what happened in the sixties and seventies. He said, "In those years we had students who disagreed with teachers. We had some faculty members who felt the Vietnam War was the right thing and said so, but the students, though they disagreed, did not seem to resent the professors. This increase in resentment toward professors bothers me. And I don't expect everybody to like me either; that's not it."

Five-Year Plans

To gain another perspective from these instructors about their lives and how they viewed their roles as instructors, I asked them to share with me what they had planned for five years hence. I listened to the responses very carefully, trying to determine whether any of these exemplary instructors was plateauing. I had assumed that exemplary professors were alive people with many aspirations and ideas for future activities. Without exception this was the case. It didn't matter whether the person was retired and teaching only part-time or an instructor with only a few years of experience and most of a career ahead.

I was also impressed by the spirit with which these instructors answered the question. As one of the younger instructors said, "I hope in five years to be doing what I am doing now, and even enjoying it more than I do now."

With one exception, all the instructors I interviewed said they wanted to be teaching and researching five years from now. The exception was a sociology professor who said he had two plans for five years from now. One of the plans was to be doing what he was doing now, with two or three more books completed. The other option he was considering was working in another institutional setting such as the United Nations or the federal government. He had done consulting work with both and had many contacts. He ended by saying, "If I were to bet on what I'll be doing five years from now, it will probably be almost exactly the same thing I'm doing now."

Interestingly, the retired professors also said they planned to do part-time teaching and researching, just as they were doing now. One of the retired professors, a seventy-nine-year-old man, said, "I have a whole flock of things on the back burner that I would like to do. I'll keep on teaching. I want to do a book of readings on community colleges. I'll continue to do work on educational gerontology."

According to some standards this man was well beyond retirement age and should have been thinking about retirement activities that sounded less like work. Yet it was obvious this professor enjoyed what he was doing and wanted to keep at it as long as he could.

I got a similar reaction from one of the instructors who planned to retire within five years. What this instructor had in mind was part-time teaching and consulting, with the rest of his time spent writing books. And he added, "When I have some time to work on it, I'd like to spend time seeing what can be done to improve education."

The younger instructors, particularly those without tenure, mentioned receiving tenure as one of their goals for five years from now. As one of these instructors said, "I hope to be tenured. And I would like to be doing more undergraduate teaching than I do now. I would also like to have a giant grant to look at the relationships of families where members of the family are going back to school. I think that higher education has largely ignored the human part of being a student."

Advice for Other Instructors

Because all the instructors I interviewed had considerable experience working with returning students, I thought it would be interesting to ask them what advice they had for instructors facing returning students for the first time.

Several mentioned the need for instructors working with returning students to be acquainted with contemporary life, particularly the relation of contemporary life to the subject matter the instructor taught. For instance, a professor of psychology said that college and university instructors should be encouraged, at sabbatical time for instance, to go out into the field to see what was going on. He believed that on some campuses relating to the field of practice was seen as being beneath the role of the instructor. Some instructors, in this psychology professor's mind, did not want their theory contaminated with practice. And, according to this professor, that sort of attitude feeds upon itself. If there are several professors who do not want to relate to practice, they talk to one another and reinforce one another. If this is carried to an extreme, a campus can have entire faculties who become increasingly removed from the field of practice.

Malcolm Knowles shared an example from his own career to emphasize the importance of real-life experience for the college or university instructor: "I keep realizing over and over again how fortunate I was that I myself was a returning student. I was a traditional student as an undergraduate. Then I worked for twelve years before coming back and starting my master's degree. I graduated from college in 1934 and started my master's work in 1946. First I worked at the YMCA in Chicago and then as the executive director for the Adult Education Association. I had a family, a mortgage, insurance to pay, and so on. So I could only study part-time. Fortunately, the University of Chicago, where I did my graduate work, had the kind of flexibility where I could take one course that required residence on campus and then two courses of independent study which also met the residence requirement. I didn't receive my doctorate until 1960. So from 1934 to 1960, twenty-six years, I worked as a professional and went to school part-time for several of those years. I did all that before I became a college professor."

Not every instructor of returning students needs to have twenty-five years of experience in the field before coming into college teaching. But having some years of practical experience is obviously very important, whether it be before a terminal degree is completed or as time taken as leave away from teaching positions. Practical field experience, for many disciplines, helps the professor become a more successful and creditable teacher for returning students.

Again, to quote from Knowles, "If college and university instructors are going to be successful with returning students, we'd better find some way of giving them all some work, some internship, some life-work experience other than teaching that will enable them to experience what it's like to be a returning student. In addition to that, many college instructors have little or no understanding of how adults learn. For many of them their lives have been devoted to teaching young people. They just don't understand the developmental stages that help us understand the differences between traditional students and returning students. They don't understand the psychological foundations of adult learning, and so on. So in addition to having some actual field experience, they need to have some intellectual preparation."

Several exemplary instructors emphasized being patient with returning students. One said, "From an instructional side we professors ought to slow down a little and try to be better counselors and teachers for returning students and try to help them become reacquainted with the educational process."

A sociology instructor offered a very practical bit of advice: "Let's learn how to accept returning students as adults because that's what they are. I think most of us, at various points in our careers, have all been frightened at the notion of a person older than we are in the class. I believe we've got to learn to overcome this fear that often leads to problems in the classroom and learn how to work together with these adult students." This instructor went on to discuss how the returning students can make positive contributions to a class, if the instructor can learn to bring them into the class discussions.

Ralph Tyler, who has had many years of experience, offered the following suggestions: "First I would remind these instructors that they should find out as much as they can about the returning students—why they've come back to school, how they are different from traditional students. Then my counsel would be to re-examine your courses, what you're teaching. Try to find out, either by your examination or by discussing with others, where your courses will be especially helpful to the returning student and where they may present some difficulty.

"One of the things that turns up in my experience is the problem of instructors who have very long reading assignments, and the traditional students have learned just to skim them and pick up things. More mature students take these reading assignments quite seriously, and they try to read everything. Soon they're bogged down, and finally they may decide that there's too much here, that they can't do it. So you must be clear about every assignment—why the assignment is important, how much of it is important, how it's to be attacked. This is to help the returning student learn what the successful younger students have already learned—that not all that's assigned is really expected to be read.

"I think the failure to consider how a mature student takes an assignment is one of the common causes of students' dropping out, saying, 'College work is too difficult,' that 'there's too much to do,' or 'It's irrelevant to my purposes.' Another thing: grades mean much more to the mature student. I mean the older students take grades more seriously because they are an indication to them if they really are getting anything out of what they are studying. I think the instructor of returning students needs to make it quite clear to students what grading system will be used. The grading system itself may knock them out of school. These returning students are accustomed to doing quite well in their occupations, and say they get a C which they think, unless they understand the grading system, means they are not doing very well.

"Finally, I would say the instructor of returning students needs to be aware of how much can be learned from these older students." In Tyler's judgment, the classroom made up of returning students provides the opportunity for returning students to learn from the instructor and the instructor to learn from the students, a most interesting and provocative learning situation.

Summary

Does it take a particular type of person to be a successful instructor of returning students? In this chapter we shared comments from the exemplary instructors who were interviewed for this project. They talked about their leisure-time activities. They described what they liked and disliked about academic work. They shared their aspirations for the future, and they offered suggestions to instructors who were working with returning students for the first time.

Chapter 12

The Need for
Institutional Changes

Institutions vary greatly in how they respond to increasing numbers of part-time students aged twenty-five and older returning to their campuses. Historically, many higher education institutions developed extension divisions for older students. In some of the larger urban centers, institutions developed evening colleges, particularly after World War I and again after World War II. Extension divisions and evening colleges continue to attract many adult students. But in addition, institutions are responding in several ways.

Some institutions continue their programs as if their student body was made up entirely of traditional-age students, those eighteen to twenty-two. They allow returning students to attend classes and even pursue degrees. But the returning students must adhere to the same admission and entrance procedures as the traditional students. The returning students attend the same classes as the traditional students and at the same time, which usually means daytime. Some of these institutions have extension divisions that offer wide varieties of noncredit programs for adults, from programs that deal with national issues, liberal arts topics, and vocation-related subjects, to leisure time and self-development topics. Often the degree-granting units of these institutions look down on the noncredit adult education facets of the institution's offering as superficial and lacking academic rigor.

A second group of institutions offers traditional programs with all their manifestations, similar to the first group described above. Except these institutions make a special effort to recruit returning students into their programs. Many of these institutions assume their traditional programs are of high quality; many of them are. They believe changing what now exists will somehow lower the quality of the offerings. These institutions emphasize the quality of their existing programs and the importance of returning students' meeting traditional requirements and participating in the traditional structure.

A third group of institutions, growing in number, continue their traditional programs but have made some major adjustments. They offer courses on weekends, in the late afternoon, and in the evening, often at satellite locations. Rather than three times a week, many of the courses are offered once a week for a longer time. They have worked out special registration approaches and have worked with support facilities such as libraries to make materials available at nontraditional times. These institutions are more open to accepting transfer credits from other institutions. They have also established special counseling centers for returning students that provide assistance with career planning, study-skills development, and a broad range of problems related to adjusting to academic work.

A fourth group of institutions does all the things the third group does in addition to offering special curricular materials designed for returning students. Some of these institutions design entire degree programs, such as a master of liberal studies program, with the returning student in mind. Returning students are found in their traditional degree programs as well, but even in these programs considerable adjustment has been made in the curriculum. To a considerable extent these institutions have initiated faculty-development programs aimed at helping the faculty understand the returning student and the teaching-learning approaches that may be more applicable for the returning student than for the traditional student.

Finally, a fifth group of institutions, a much smaller group, is developing degree programs for older returning students only. These programs are planned entirely with the returning student in mind and are innovative both in terms of content and the teaching and administrative approaches used.

Later in this chapter, when we discuss various structural forms, we will look at examples of how specific institutions have developed new programs or modified old programs to meet the needs of returning students.

Before we come to that, however, we will explore several areas of change that institutions should consider when they wish to attract returning students and provide quality programs for them. These considerations include administrative procedures and rules, structure, support systems, curriculum, and faculty development. Many of the suggestions for change included in this chapter were those offered by the exemplary instructors interviewed. Others come from the literature and from my personal experience.

The suggestions for change are on at least two levels: (1) those that deal with changes in rules, procedures, facilities, and content of courses and curriculum at one level; and (2) those involving attitudes of administrators, faculty, and other decision makers such as governing boards, boards of regents, and in many instances state legislatures.

Administrative Procedures and Rules

Many of the administrative rules and procedures found on college and university campuses were designed historically with an implicit attitude of youth discipline in mind. (Students should learn how to respect authority. They should learn to accept the judgment of those older and more experienced than they.)

It's extremely doubtful those assumptions make any sense for today's traditional students. They certainly make no sense for the returning student.

The registration and entrance procedure is often the first formal contact the returning student has with the institution. (Returning students are encouraged to work with the institution's returning student center prior to registration—many institutions have these centers—but many students do not take advantage of, or are not aware of, this opportunity.) Often the first indicator of the acceptance of returning students by the institution is in how the registration procedure accepts or fails to accept them. An instructor I interviewed pointed out how institutions have fixed their parking to accommodate the handicapped and therefore should be able to fix their registration procedures to accommodate the returning students. Another instructor said it this way:

"I think one of the silliest traditions this institution has is its registration system. Registration could be handled by phone or by letter—take avantage of the communication systems we have. There is just no reason for standing in line for registration. No reason whatever why we can't register well in advance of the session start."

Many institutions also require an extended time for full-time, on-campus study. This is particularly true of many graduate programs. As one of the exemplary instructors said, "For a person who's been working for ten years, has a family, a home, a mortgage, insurance to keep up, taking off for a full year is a burden that many of them can't, just can't, afford."

Test taking is also an entrance requirement of many institutions, "as a way of sorting out those who may not be qualified for academic work." Entrance examinations such as Miller Analogies and the Graduate Record Examination have been quite controversial for traditional students. Many have challenged their effectiveness in predicting academic success. Their usefulness in predicting the success of returning students is even more questionable. Research on adults as learners quite clearly shows that many adults are poor test takers. As we have pointed out earlier, three things are happening with adults that can cause them to do less well on examinations than younger students:

1. Adults tend to put more stress on accuracy than on speed and will thus not work fast even though the test is timed.

2. Reaction time slows somewhat with age, and though an adult may not have lost any capacity to respond to test questions, the speed of response is slowed. On a timed test this can be a serious detriment.

3. Because adults have had a wide range of experience simply because of their age, they often read into test questions nuances that were not intended.

Many instructors have rules about having assignments in on time. Often the instructor will lower the grade a few points for each day that a term paper is late. Because returning students have many other responsibilities, they may at times find it impossible to turn in a particular assignment on time, even if they made a real attempt to do so. Sometimes a child is sick; sometimes an unexpected work assignment comes up. The returning student has less control over schedules in most instances than does the younger, more traditional student.

Turning in papers on time or receiving a punishment harks back to an attitude that students really aren't mature enough to control their own time management and must be forced to do so or be punished. The mature adult student who may have some problems with time management resents an instructor trying to discipline him or her because an assignment is late. This is particularly true if some unforeseen circumstance makes it impossible for the returning student to comply with the time deadline.

Structure

As mentioned at the beginning of this chapter, it is possible to find a variety of structures within colleges and universities responding to returning students. These structures vary from no change at all to entire programs developed for returning students. For instance, at Temple University many of the classes begin at 4:30 in the afternoon and go until 10:00. Classes meet for three hours at a time so it is possible for a returning student to take two courses in an evening. And the classes meet only once a week. As a professor at Temple pointed out, "It's a grueling schedule for students, but for many of them with kids at home and a job, it's the only way they can do it. Temple has a day-care center—we should also have a night-care center for returning students' children."

A University of Michigan professor pointed out the need for new approaches to scheduling courses: "Right now, particularly in a major research university like this, the schedule of courses is set up for the professor's convenience, not for the student's convenience. That's not too bad when you have full-time students living on campus, but when you have students moving on and off campus with other time constraints, we should work out class schedules to take into account these time constraints."

The University of Wisconsin–Madison developed a weekend graduate program for returning students interested in a master's degree in continuing and vocational education. Each semester one or two courses were offered, each meeting for five weekends. The courses began on a late Friday afternoon, continued into Friday evening, and finished on Saturday afternoon. Many of the students enrolled in the weekend program commuted from outside of Madison, some from more than a hundred miles. Both the content of the courses and the instructors were the same as when the courses were offered in the traditional format. The only difference was that, rather than meeting three times a week for 50 minutes, or perhaps once a week for 150 minutes, the course met for five weekends. Arrangements were made with the library to be open early on Saturday morning so students could read prior to attending the Saturday session. Arrangements were also made so the students could borrow books for three weeks, which was the time between weekend sessions. To supplement the courses taken in the weekend format, students also enrolled in field courses taught in their communities, courses taught by other institutions, or in summer-school programs at Madison. In something less than three years, most students were able to complete a master's degree.

An interesting aside for the University of Wisconsin's weekend program is the interest in it by full-time graduate students. Many full-time students could easily attend regularly scheduled classes but preferred the weekend format because it gave them more flexibility in their class schedules. Some full-time people also said they enjoyed interacting with the part-time weekend students because of the day-to-day work experience that they brought with them to the classes.

Moorhead State University, Moorhead, Minnesota, has developed a new Master of Liberal Study program at their institution. This program is specifically designed for the older returning student who wants a broadly based degree. Rather than simply developing a new system for scheduling existing courses, Moorhead is developing a new set of interdisciplinary courses, many of which are centered on contemporary issues.

Examples of Moorhead's new courses are "The Human Spirit in Art," a study of selected great painters and sculptors to probe the depth and richness of the human spirit; "Genetics and Society," an exploration of such contemporary social issues as genetic counseling, genetic engineering, and the influence of genetics on aging, behavior, social structure, and the food supply; "Gender Role and Sexuality," a study of the process of sexual differentiation, development of gender identity, and the learning of gender roles; and "Imagination, Reform and the Urban Transformation," an investigation of the imaginative response to cultural change with a focus on 1880–1920 in the United States. The

Moorhead program is designed for the person who is employed and already has at least one college degree.

At Wayne State University in Detroit, the University Studies and Weekend College Program was developed specifically for working adults. The curriculum is organized around three major focal points, as follows:

Social Sciences: Ethnic Studies, Work and Labor, International and Domestic Conflict, and Theory and Methods in the Social Sciences.

Humanities: The quality of life: folk, classical and mass culture; arts of the imagination: the Faust legend; the performing arts: the film, and criticism and cultural history.

Science and Technology: Science and Energy, Life and Ecology, Science, Technology and Values, and Planning the Future.[1]

In the College of Continuing Education at the University of Southern California, degree progams have been developed with the adult student in mind. One program is their Master of Liberal Arts degree program. A recent annual report from USC's College of Continuing Education described the program this way:

"The humanities, the social sciences, and the natural sciences come together in this program to give students more than one intellectual approach to understanding the forces that shape society and the self. The Master of Liberal Arts (MLA) program is one of the best examples of the College of Continuing Education's ability to pull together resources from several academic areas to create a rigorous, innovative program. True to continuing education guidelines, the degree is designed to be earned on a part-time basis, with classes held at times and locations convenient to adults. Classes are offered at satellite locations in Beverly Hills, Newport Beach, and Santa Barbara. In conjunction with the faculty of Cambridge University, the program also combines instruction with excursions for a three-week summer course in the arts of Britain."

The University of Wisconsin currently offers three extended degree programs. A Bachelor of Arts–General Studies is offered at the University of Wisconsin–Green Bay. This is a broad-based liberal arts program that incorporates elements of problem solving and lifelong learning. The program is designed for persons who wish junior-senior level studies through a competency-based curriculum and in an extended format. At the University of Wisconsin–Superior, an individually designed major resulting in a liberal arts bachelor's degree is offered. Working with a faculty advisory panel, the student designs a program from at least three disciplines. The University of Wisconsin–Platteville offers a Bachelor of Science–Business Administration degree in the extended format. It is an extension of the existing bachelor's degree program in business administration in the university's College of Business, Industry, and Communication.

Features of these three degree programs include competency-based course modules, independent study courses, transferable course work from nearby institutions, field experiences, radio or TV classes, study with an approved tutor, an apprenticeship or internship, a research project, programmed learning using cassettes, an on-the-job learning situation, and other learning activities agreed upon by the student and the degree-program faculty. There is no set time span for completion of these extended degrees. A student contracts for completion of a certain number of credit-units each year. Students may also receive university credit through assessment of their prior learning and achievements. Academic credit possibilities include union- or company-sponsored courses, job training, studies completed during military service, experience gained from work on a volunteer project, or running a business.

Nova University, Fort Lauderdale, Florida, offers yet another structure for degree programs designed for the adult student who is working and who must study part-time. In Nova University's Center for Higher Education it is possible to earn an Ed.D. for community college faculty, an Ed.D. in vocational, technical, and occupational education, an M.S. in institutional development, and an Ed.D in leadership of adult education.

Nova's "Face Sheet" for the Ed.D. in leadership of adult education describes the program this way: "Participants are drawn from the adult educational and training personnel in business and industry, the military services and other government agencies, public schools, colleges and universities, religious institutions, voluntary organizations, health agencies, agricultural extension, and other institutional settings from a given geographical area and clustered into groups of from fifteen to thirty participants. Each cluster is managed by a Cluster Coordinator— a part-time Nova staff member—who is responsible for the logistics and administrative services of the cluster, academic student advisement, and coordination of visiting resource persons. Each cluster meets all day Saturday for three Saturdays about a month apart with a National Lecturer for each seminar. One seminar meets during a summer institute. The national lecturers are drawn from among the most distinguished professional leaders in the field of adult education and training."

The mission for the Nova program is twofold: the development of the students, who gain "theoretical and practical foundations for their practice," and the "improvement of the institutions and organizations in which the participants are employed."

To complete the Nova Ed.D., participants are required to complete five core seminars, two specialization seminars, five practicums, a "major applied research project," and two one-week summer institutes during the three-year program.

Still another approach is one devised at National University in San Diego, California. This university is designed for business executives, government and military career employees, and professionals. Students in this program work toward bachelor's and master's degrees in public administration, business, education, and the behavioral sciences. Law courses have also been added recently. The founder of the school, Dr. David Chigos, a former management consultant, says the school is designed for those persons who are climbing career ladders and need degrees to climb higher.

Its more unusual aspects include the following: (1) 95 percent of the classes meet at night; (2) it has no tenured faculty but draws on 400 mostly part-time instructors who are employed in their fields and hold doctorate degrees; (3) there is no semester system but students, through a computer system, can enroll anytime during the year; and (4) classes are often held close to where the students work. Through an elaborate computer system, students are usually able to schedule classes as far as two years in advance.

For additional information and insight into external degree programs, refer to Cyril Houle's 1973 work.[2] One of the most widely known external degree programs that Houle discusses is the Open University at Great Britain. He also mentions the programs at the University of Oklahoma, Goddard College, Minnesota Metropolitan State College, and several others.

Donald R. McNeil, president of the University of Mid-America, a consortium of eleven state universities and land-grant colleges in seven midwestern states, calls for yet another approach.

Dr. McNeil believes that millions of adult learners are blocked in one way or another from acquiring formal degrees. He says, "The barriers differ, depending on the area, the economic level of the inhabitants, and the location and character of the surrounding institutions; but they exist—mostly because of the attitudes, perceptions, leadership, and commitment (or lack thereof) of the institutions themselves."[3]

McNeil would like to see the present system of colleges and universities supplemented with an "open university" to meet the needs of the part-time, credit-oriented adult learner. "Such a university would serve as a credit bank for adult students throughout the country, with a system for aggregating all types of credit: credit earned by competency-based testing, correspondence courses, independent study, life experience, or any other acceptable means, in addition to traditional classroom credit."[4]

The New York State's Regents External Degree Program began in 1972 to award credit to persons who, for one reason or another, could not attend regular degree programs. Gene Maeroff believes the New York State Regents program is the most radical experiment in nontraditional programming.[5]

Other institutions that have similar programs include Thomas Edison College in New Jersey and the Board for State Academic Awards in Connecticut. The Board of Governors Bachelor of Arts Degree Program in Illinois is similar, but it requires that at least 15 of the 120 credit hours needed for an undergraduate degree be obtained at a cooperating state university campus in Illinois.

In the New York State program, the Thomas Edison College program, and the Connecticut program, students put together enough credits for a degree in three basic ways: (1) by completing examinations, (2) by receiving credit for "life experience," and (3) by submitting transcripts for regular college courses they have taken.

Maeroff, in a description of the New York program, tells about a student who wished to become a lawyer. This student passed the Law School Aptitude Test with a high score but was refused admission to every law school to which he applied because he had never attended college. Over a period of nine months this student took nine long examinations that qualified him for a bachelor's degree from the New York State's Regents External Degree Program. He received the degree without ever setting foot in a classroom. He then applied and was accepted into Harvard Law School.[6]

Support Systems

As pointed out earlier, returning students often need a period of time to adjust to academic life. Particularly during the adjustment period, returning students are often insecure about the decision they made to return to school, about their ability as students, and about the relationship with their families. It is during this initial adjustment time that these students especially need support.

Support systems can take various forms. Many women and some men as well experience math anxiety—a fear of taking math courses. If their study program requires math, many of these persons are invited to attend math anxiety workshops that help students deal with their anxiety about numbers. Instructors teaching courses involving mathematics often find they need to spend more time with certain returning students.

Many institutions now offer study-skills programs for adult students where they can polish their skills in exam taking, writing papers, organizing their time, learning concentration skills, learning to use the library and other resources, learning to use their reading time effectively, and learning to listen and take notes. Returning students drop in and out of these programs as they have need. Not only do the programs help returning students sharpen rusty study skills, but they also help students regain their confidence and self-image.

Some returning students have to shed the idea that because they are older they can't learn as well as younger students. As a professor of education told me, "Returning students have to develop a faith in their ability to learn. My experience is that once the person does come back to school and does recover some study skills, the person goes sailing right along with few difficulties."

The National Science Foundation has sponsored reentry programs for women intent on gaining jobs in science. Anne Roark reports on a student who completed an undergraduate degree in 1955 and, more than twenty years later, entered a science program at American University. She first enrolled in a so-called reentry program that included two hours of laboratory work and two hours of lectures, five days a week for a full year. The schedule was equivalent to twelve graduate hours in physical chemistry, organic chemistry, biochemistry, and inorganic chemistry.

In addition to sharpening her science skills, this student stressed how the program taught her not to be afraid—it developed skills and confidence at the same time. Another student who was enrolled in a National Science Foundation reentry program said the most exciting thing that happened to her was discovering her brain was still functioning.[7]

Moorhead State University in Minnesota offers an educational brokering service for adults. This is particularly related to those adults who anticipate returning to school with a career goal in mind. When a person has made some type of career decision, either general or specific, he or she meets with the education broker for assistance in determining how to reach that career goal. A person who feels tentative about the career decision or who would like more information about the career is encouraged to talk with at least one person working in that career area. The broker makes the initial contact and helps arrange the first meeting. These sessions with a person in the career area help the person learn about the career area and in addition provide a contact for someone who may wish to enter that employment area.

Other kinds of support can be more subtle: a kind word from an instructor, a word of praise when a comment is offered in class (not phony or artificial, but an honest comment about someone's contribution), a positive comment about written assignments along with suggestions for improvement, a suggestion of someone to talk with who has a similar problem—these are the kinds of support returning students appreciate.

Adequate counseling systems must also be available for returning students, and at several levels. During the time a person is trying to decide whether to return to school, counselors can be of great assistance—to point out alternatives, to suggest persons to talk with, to share information about costs, requirements, and the like.

As I mentioned earlier, returning students bring with them a host of personal problems and counselors must be available to listen and help. Often a student's academic advisor or class instructor is the first person to whom the student comes with problems and these persons must know when they can be of assistance and when they should refer the student to someone else.

Curriculum

Curriculum questions have confronted educators for years: What content areas should be included in the curriculum? Who should be involved in developing the curriculum? Should the potential learner be involved? If so, how? How should the curriculum be organized? What about requiring parts of the curriculum · for all students while having parts of it organized as electives? What provisions are there for keeping the curriculum up to date? Should the curriculum focus on discipline areas, or should it focus on societal or life problems?

These same questions confront educators in institutions with increasing numbers of returning students. Although teachers and administrators in a wide variety of educational institutions have wrestled with these questions for years, the returning students are increasingly pushing for answers. Increasingly the returning students will not accept answers to the curriculum questions that they believe are historical rather than contemporary, or answers based on the assumption that someone knows best for a student, without any input from the student.

In my conversations with Ralph Tyler, he spoke to several of the questions I listed above: "I think institutions need to make much clearer what the real objectives of each course are and how they relate to any total program. With the case of nursing, for example, I think institutions need to reexamine the question of how chemistry fits the curriculum and what chemistry has to do with being a nurse. Because very often the institution employs a person whose only interest is chemistry, and the nursing students are frustrated. Somebody ought to be able to develop a rationale for every course in the curriculum to show that it's sensible—it isn't just a hurdle for the students to climb over.

"And the objectives of courses must be stated more clearly, that which is expected of students. Returning students need a clear notion of where they're going and why they're going there.

"Returning students must also have more opportunity to demonstrate competence in things learned without repeating courses and studying areas they already know. There must be a sincere effort to identify what returning students already have learned.

"Once we know what students have already learned, they are counseled into courses or parts of courses that have content that is new to them. This approach requires quite a change because it may be only parts of courses that students need to take, rather than the entire course.

"When I was university examiner at the University of Chicago, an institution that depends on comprehensive examinations, we had placement tests that enabled us to say to students, 'Well, you don't need the first two parts of this course, much of what you still need to learn will be in the third part of the course,' or, 'You've already attained so much that a little brushing up with some reading or discussion may be all that's necessary.'

"I think many institutions have taken the opposite view, that the more they can keep the student taking courses the better it is for the institution. Of course it increases their enrollment, and often, if tax supported, it will increase their appropriations.

"I think a different attitude has to be developed and this may require some part of the institution to devote itself to helping mature students make the most of their college or university education. For instance, Radcliffe has an institute for returning women where counselors help these women find and use Harvard's resources most efficiently, help them decide which parts of courses they may need.

"Yet, this approach where students only take parts of courses goes against the grain of those instructors who feel that any part of their course left out is a serious loss. These instructors have this view that it's like the priesthood, the laying on of hands in their program . . . 'You can't really have learned a given content area unless you've had a course under me.'

"What is required is some unit of the institution, such as a center for returning students, continually finding out what students need, where the problems are, so that students don't waste a lot of time taking what they don't need. If what you learned on the job, or at home, or elsewhere from your reading, if that's pretty well covered by the first two parts of the term, and it's the last part where you need help, I see no reason why you shouldn't come in at that last part."

How should a curriculum be planned with the returning student in mind? Tyler responded this way: "Well, if it's an occupational program, it ought to have been designed in terms of dependable evidence about what persons in that occupation need that the institution can provide, the kind of theory that helps these returning students understand what they are doing. For instance, when a returning student is moving from a job into a profession, one of the more important things that the institution provides is an understanding that this is a profession, not a job. It isn't to be judged with just how much pay do you get, how much status, but how much you can help—if it's a physician, helping a person get well; if it's a teacher, helping people learn; if it's an engineer or an architect, designing a building that has the utility required."

In my conversations with Malcolm Knowles, I discovered some of his strong feelings about changes necessary in curriculum for returning students. He said, "The curriculum provided by most institutions is not geared to adults' learning characteristics. The traditional curriculum is very content centered, very course oriented, very credit oriented. Adults return to school not to accumulate credits; on the whole that's not their central purpose. What they want to do is gain competencies that will enable them to cope more effectively with their life situation. So the curriculum ought to be organized around life-centered areas of study, life applications. This is particularly so in the education of professionals. I see the health professions particularly going in this direction."

Knowles shared an example of McMaster University School of Medicine in Hamilton, Ontario, where the curriculum has been restructured around problem areas and competencies. As Knowles explained, "It is a totally modular, self-directed medical education program. And McMaster doesn't have a single course; there are no lecture sessions at all. They've identified the problem areas that physicians have to be able to deal with and, for each problem area, the competencies within that problem area. For each competency they've developed what they call a learning package. The package includes both preassessment and postassessment instruments and all sorts of resources for learning, including videotapes of lectures, clinical exercises, readings—this sort of thing."

Knowles is also opposed to the "lock-step" curriculum that is part of many institutions' programs—first you take this course, then this one, and so on. Knowles said it this way: "I feel so bad when a returning student comes in with a rich background of experience and self-study and is told, 'You have to take the following required courses.' And very often I know, and the student knows, that either the required course is not at all relevant to his or her life goals, or the content has already been gained through rigorous independent study, previous training, workshops, institutes, and so on, that don't carry academic credit. But unless the student has the academic credits, the learning can't be counted toward his or her degree. Well, that's childish, I think.

"Another aspect of the lock-step feature is the system of the course that meets once a week for fifteen weeks, three hours per week, and covers a prescribed, predetermined body of content, and requires a kind of time pace that may be totally out of kilter with where the student is. I'd much prefer and be happier in an institution in which the curriculum was organized according to units or modules, more self-directed and more flexible in terms of time commitment."

A Temple University professor pointed out another dimension of curriculum that is exceedingly important for returning students. She emphasized the need for returning students who are interested in obtaining jobs to acquire job-related experience (internship-type experience) as part of their formal study. It is often the internship experience that provides the credential for successful job placement. She said it this way: "Just being aware that a woman who is fifty-five doesn't just want a master's degree or a doctorate but wants other credentials too, so at the end of her program she gets a job. She doesn't have the time to go out and spend the next four or five years building up credentials that would lead to a job. Students who are looking for career changes need vita entries, so we encourage their involvement in all kinds of things, from coordinating noncredit kinds of activities in the community to getting involved in community activities in lots of ways, so when they leave here they've got more than a degree, they've got some credentials."

In the paragraphs above I've shared some lengthy quotations from people who have strong feelings and beliefs about how curricula for returning students should be developed. In summary, what these persons have said is as follows:

1. The objectives of every course, every module—every learning activity—must be clear to the student in terms of where the particular offering contributes to the total curriculum and how it contributes to the expectations the returning student has for the curriculum.

2. Returning students should not be required to take courses where they already know the content of the course. This means an extensive counseling-assessment-placement program is needed so returning students can be correctly placed in those courses or parts of courses where they need further work.

3. Following the second suggestion, many courses must be more flexibly designed so students can take selected parts of them, when necessary, rather than the entire course.

4. Occupation-related curricula should be closely related to the requirements of the occupation for which the returning student is seeking employment.

5. Curricula for returning students should put more emphasis on life-centered areas of study than on traditional discipline, particularly in occupation-preparation programs.

6. Returning students, insofar as possible, should have the opportunity to study in the curriculum at their rate of speed. Thus, the curriculum should be designed so that students need not move through it together.

7. Related to the above is the opposition to the lock-step curriculum, where everyone takes the same required course even if they know much of what is contained in many of the courses.

8. A curriculum for returning students who are interested in job placement should include opportunities for practice in the job, so the students can have broadened vitae when they seek employment, and so they have a chance to practice what they learn in the more formal parts of their academic program.

Not all these suggestions are without controversy. There are particularly strong feelings on the part of many persons, both in and outside of academia, as to what occupation-related academic programs should include. In the next chapter we will examine some of these issues and controversies.

Financial Aid

Many financial-aid programs are based on the assumption that the student is studying full time. This is not the case with most returning students, and thus they are not eligible for aid.

There is also a rather strong attitude in this country that adults should be required to pay their own way if they wish additional education. Unfortunately, many returning students cannot afford to pay their own way. And this is ironic, because additional education may help a low-income person find a higher-paying job; yet, because he or she can't afford the education, the opportunity for possible new employment is blocked.

If financial aid were more readily available, we might not see as high a proportion of returning students studying part-time. We might also see less family financial stress.

As the number of returning students increases, decision makers will have to face the question of financial aid for these older students, particularly if larger numbers of low-income and minority students are to participate in academic degree programs.

Teaching Approaches

We have already written considerably about the teaching approaches that are preferred by returning students. Here we would only underline that one of the changes that is necessary on many campuses is a shift in the teaching approach that many younger students have passively accepted to a teaching approach that is consistent with improving the learning environment. Returning students, as we said in earlier chapters, will not accept shoddy teaching. They will insist that changes be made.

Attitude

The attitude of administrators, faculty, and other decision makers who affect policy and procedures of colleges and universities often determines the effectiveness of the institution's program for returning students. And though improving, many of the attitudes toward returning students expressed by faculty and administrators are often negative—particularly when we identify the returning student as someone interested in enrolling in a degree program.

A professor of sociology from North Carolina State University whom I interviewed believes much of the negative attitude many instructors have toward older returning students is based on fear. "Many instructors fear they will not be able to communicate, and they fear putting their discipline on the line and saying, 'Well, okay, I know some things, you know some things, let's put them together.' I think there's fear on the part of many of them that they'll get caught up out there and perhaps be made an ass of, or they'll make it out of themselves."

Donovan Russell summarizes very well the attitudinal changes that must occur on college and university campuses as we look ahead to the end of this century: "Perhaps the rich resources of our great universities can still be organized so as to offer strong competition for the clientele [of the future]. To do so will require that academics put aside the comfort of the monastic life and get out from the shadow of ivy walls. It will require that academics stop worrying about security mechanisms (tenure, degree granting authority, etc.) and begin worrying about the educational needs of people. It will require that academics be willing to share planning for the redesign of the educational establishment with those who would use its services. There is hope that the great resources within Ivy Walls will continue to be used in meeting societal needs if the academic community can begin to see education as a mission rather than to continue seeing it as a blessing bestowed by the all knowing."[8]

Faculty Development

The words *faculty development* are negative to many college and university instructors, for they smack of required attendance at boring meetings where someone talks to them about something they already know or they don't want to hear. Yet, faculty development is often a key ingredient in providing learning environments accepted by and useful to returning students.

The faculty development to which I refer is not the "everyone must attend a seminar" type. It may take a variety of forms, including seminars that are available but not required. Faculty development may also include providing a list of instructors who have had experience in working with returning students and who are open to assisting instructors who have questions. Faculty development may be a slide-tape presentation available to instructors who wish to learn more about the characteristics of adults as learners or about the differences between traditional and returning students. Materials on the subject of returning students may be available for instructors to review at their leisure. Videotapes of exemplary instructors in action may be available for instructors to watch. These are but a few of many activities that may be part of a faculty-development program.

What about those instructors who absolutely refuse to make any changes, who do not attempt to adjust to working with increasing numbers of returning students?

When these instructors are evaluated, they should be alerted to the fact that their performance in working with returning students is not adequate and that their merit increase will reflect this inadequacy. At this time they should also be offered, as they no doubt were offered before, a list of faculty-development opportunities that they may find useful in improving their work with returning students.

The most difficult instructors to work with are those who do not recognize that they have a problem and who see no reason for participating in faculty-development programs of any type. When students complain about their teaching approaches, these instructors blame the students for not spending enough time on assignments, for being too caught up with outside interests such as work and family, and for not knowing how to be students. Sometimes there is truth to the statements, but seldom is a bad teaching-learning situation solely the students' fault.

Related to faculty members' adjusting their teaching approaches and work habits to accommodate returning students is the problem of "burnout." As Jill Tarule and Rita Weathersby pointed out, "The programs [for returning students] are enthusiastically designed as person-centered. They are organized on the basis of personal commitment and excitement of the designer. To serve the nontraditional student, the program is often year-round or meets at convenient evening hours. One outcome is that we are creating a 'new faculty professional' in higher education, one who is able to develop alternatives and appreciate student needs. This often leads to the unfortunate phenomenon of 'burnout,' in which programs are well designed for the adult faculty, leading to high stress and high turnover. In this new faculty role, the usual and expected privileges of teaching in higher education have slipped away: the summer vacation, the time to write or do one's own research, and the general feeling of competence-as-teacher that accrues from simply being older than one's students. The developmental dimensions can indicate faculty needs as well as students' needs, and can thus help to divert essentially self-destruct designs."[9]

Tarule and Weathersby's point is well made. A program for faculty development not only must focus attention on those faculty members who lack the skills and understanding in working with older returning students, but also must focus attention on the problems experienced by those faculty members who are successful and, as a result, experience other problems. One of the issues I will discuss in the next chapter is the instructor time required when working with returning students and the drain on time for research and writing.

Summary

We have explored several changes that institutions might consider as they enroll increasing numbers of older returning students. I discussed changes in the area of administrative rules and procedures, including a suggestion to rethink registration and entrance procedures, full-time study requirements, and procedures that are designed to "discipline" students.

In the discussion of structural changes to be considered, I mentioned times for offering courses as well as special programs for returning students, such as those at Moorhead State University in Minnesota; Wayne State; the College for Continuing Education at the University of Southern California; Nova University; National University, San Diego, California; the University of Wisconsin extended degrees; and New York State's Regents External Degree Program.

I pointed out the need for support systems for returning students that might include study-skills programs, various types of reentry programs, and the more subtle support that is offered by instructors and administrators.

In the discussion of curriculum changes I quoted extensively from conversations with Malcolm Knowles and Ralph Tyler and summarized these conversations with eight suggestions for curriculum improvement.

Other changes touched on included the need for financial aid for returning students and attention to teaching approaches instructors use when working with returning students.

One of the more difficult general changes that often gets in the way of specific changes involves attitudes. Certainly not all instructors and administrators hold negative attitudes toward returning students, but many do and they get in the way of change.

Finally, I discussed the need for faculty-development opportunities, both for those who have difficulty working with returning students and for those who are successful but may be facing burnout.

NOTES

1. Otto Feinstein and Frank Angelo, *To Educate the People* (Detroit: Center for Urban Studies, Wayne State University, 1977), p. 12.

2. Cyril O. Houle, *The External Degree* (San Francisco: Jossey-Bass, 1973).

3. Donald R. McNeil, "America's Adult Students Need an Open University," *The Chronicle of Higher Education* (May 5, 1980), p. 64.

4. Ibid.

5. Gene I. Maeroff, "Colleges Without Walls," *Phi Delta Kappan,* vol. 60, no. 8, April 1979, p. 573.

6. Ibid.

7. Anne C. Roark, "Re-Entry Programs Enable Women to Resume Careers in Science," *The Chronicle of Higher Education* (February 11, 1980), pp. 3–4.

8. Donovan Russell, "Looking Beyond Ivy Walls: An Assault on the Traditional," *Adult Leadership,* November 1974, p. 154.

9. Jill M. Tarule and Rita Weathersby, "Adult Development and Adult Learning Styles: The Message for Nontraditional Graduate Programs," *Alternative Higher Education,* vol. 4, no. 1, Fall 1979, pp. 21–22.

Chapter 13

Issues and Controversies

I don't want to leave the impression that everyone agrees on the direction colleges and universities ought to take in responding to increasing numbers of returning students. That is far from the case. In this chapter we'll explore some of the issues and controversies debated by faculties, administrators, and other decision makers about various changes to consider. The issues range from practical considerations, such as what the curriculum ought to be and how teaching should be carried out, to more theoretical and philosophical considerations, such as the future for colleges and universities, the effect of increased emphasis on credentials in our society, and the effect that changes in college and university programming will have on the dream for a society of self-directed learners.

Curriculum Content, Structure, and Development

Content

Should the curriculum be changed to reflect increasing numbers of experienced adults returning to the classroom? Decision makers seem to be answering that question in at least four different ways: (1) The curriculum as it now exists should not be changed to accommodate returning students. No matter what the age or experience of the student, all take the same courses. (2) Much of the curriculum for returning students, if not all, should have a strong career orientation. (3) The curriculum for returning students should combine traditional elements with a career orientation. (4) Alternative degree programs should be available for returning students, some emphasizing career preparation and some emphasizing a more liberal arts orientation.

Traditional Curriculum for All

Proponents of this position argue that colleges and universities, to maintain their unique position in society and to maintain standards of excellence, should not tamper with the present curriculum. These persons concede that the curriculum is constantly changing as new knowledge is discovered, but the discovery of new knowledge should be the basis for curriculum change, not a change in the characteristics of the student body. Many proponents of this position fear colleges and universities will become vocational schools—not that they are opposed to vocational schools, but they see a distinct difference between a college or university education and vocational education.

Career-Related Curriculum

This position is the opposite of the first. Its proponents argue that all parts of the curriculum for returning students should have a career orientation. These persons point out, correctly, that the majority of returning students are in school for occupation-related reasons—to obtain jobs, advance in jobs, update themselves in their present jobs, or change jobs. Therefore, these proponents argue, the curriculum should be related as closely as possible to the returning student's career aspirations. These curriculum changers argue that returning students have limited funds for education and have a great many pressures on them to finish their advanced schooling as quickly as possible. The curriculum should thus contain only "essential" content.

Combination Curriculum

A more middle-of-the-road position is the modification of certain elements of the curriculum to put more emphasis on career preparation but to maintain elements of the more traditional curriculum as well. As Gordon Godbey argues, "Adult education will serve mankind best if it refuses to become a docile, sterile system only to feed the factories, offices, and homes of production and consumption. Adult education will serve best if it teaches principles, foundations, habits, and attitudes which question, which test on logical and intelligent criteria; if it makes millions aware of the great gift to us from heroic minds and souls now gone—or still living. Its promises must not be exaggerated nor sugar-frosted at those times when truth offers only bitterness."[1]

One of the exemplary instructors I interviewed, a history professor, believed that career preparation and broader educational goals could be combined in the same curriculum for returning students: "My sense is that, while we'll obviously need to continue to help people prepare for careers, we're going to have to take a lot more seriously the individual identity question . . . a person's search for meaning, a search for some kind of life plan or life patterning."

This professor believed strongly that it was possible to combine elements in the curriculum that emphasized career with the deeper, more foundational elements of what a college or university education could contain. He continued his discussion with me to suggest some approaches for designing and carrying out such a combination curriculum: "First of all, the goal of education is to move away from a knowledge factory to working with people and assisting them to find their way, to develop their own plans. And second, this requires a different kind of approach, an understanding of the purpose of a college or university and how that purpose is carried out. This means a whole reorganization of the structure of the college or university, involving everything from grading systems to the other kinds of incentives for learning we provide students. This reorganization should start with a recognition of what the university has been, and I mean all the way back to the twelfth century. I think we are at a turning point, a major turning point concerning the purposes for a university, and we need to begin doing something about the situation."

Alternative Degree Programs

A fourth possibility is for colleges and universities to offer a career-related degree for returning students as well as a more liberal arts–related degree. The graduate liberal studies program at Moorhead State University, discussed in the previous chapter, is an example of an alternative degree program for adults who are not interested in the career-preparation route. The Moorhead

State people describe the objectives of their liberal studies program this way: "The objectives of this program include offering non-traditional graduate level courses to the increasing number of college graduates in our service region; emphasizing the cultural, social, political and scientific dimensions of human experience, maintaining a forum for the critical examination of human values, achievements and prospects; and the furthering of competencies necessary for responsible participation in a global community of unprecedented social and technological transformation."[2]

Another instructor I interviewed believed strongly that colleges and universities were making a serious mistake if they modified their curricula totally in the direction of career preparation. "It concerns me," she said, "to encourage adults to enter higher education given their often-held definition of higher education—to teach some kind of career for employment. Sometimes I wonder if higher education won't go back to the model, developed in the early twentieth century, of colleges and universities' being rather elite places for small numbers of highly intelligent people who want to be sort of renaissance people, who want to be 'educated people.' *Many people coming back to school should probably go to technical and trade schools, which are designed for career and job preparation* [emphasis added]."

This instructor believed that colleges and universities that pushed for some kind of total career-preparation emphasis in their curricula not only were steering away from the time-honored purpose of higher education—dealing with fundamental questions of the human condition, learning how to be analytical and solve problems, exploring the place for values in living, and so on—but also were opening themselves to criticism when people go through a career-related program and aren't able to find employment. "If every adult returns to a college or university with the notion that this is going to get them employment, we have a serious problem on our hands." She believed that if enough returning students become disgruntled with the career dimensions of their education, the college and universities will change back to a more traditional purpose.

This instructor also believed that the adult who is contemplating returning to school should think about the decision from two perspectives. "Either go into a kind of technical education with training for employment, or go back to a model of education for its own sake. I see fairly large numbers of older students wanting to come back to school just to learn something. They just want to go to 'college'; they like to go to classes. They like to learn things, and they are enjoying it. Can we as a culture believe that education can be for its own sake, for the purpose of acquiring information about the culture, about history, about literature? A society really can't fail to give people an opportunity to work toward a degree just because they may not be able to put that degree to work in an employment situation."

Another dimension to the question of curriculum change is whether the curriculum should be discipline centered or problem centered. A discipline-centered curriculum is what is most common today—the institution offers courses in mathematics, history, chemistry, sociology, and so on. A problem-centered curriculum deals with problems related to career or living, and the content from the disciplines is integrated as it relates to the problem being considered.

For example, in Wayne State University's University Studies and Weekend College Program, the curriculum is interdisciplinary. Its proponents argue that such a curriculum "avoids waste of mental energy that comes from the switch-on, switch-off method used in the traditional curriculum where the student is working on four totally different disciplines each day. The smorgasbord nature of the current undergraduate curricula also does not satisfy the adult worker's desire for a highly nutritional educational experience."[3]

At Moorhead State University, an interdisciplinary approach is used for the curriculum for returning students enrolled in the Graduate Liberal Studies program. Both the Wayne State and the Moorhead State curricula are designed so returning students can make considerable inputs from their own experience into what is being discussed in the classroom. This is one of the unique aspects of this curriculum approach.

On the other side of the issue are those faculty and administrators who believe the traditional, discipline-oriented curriculum should not be tampered with. They use several arguments in defense of a traditional curriculum. On the practical side they argue that getting people from several disciplines, or even as few as two disciplines, to work together on a course is next to impossible over any length of time. University and college content is organized around discipline themes—chemistry departments, history departments, sociology departments, and so on. To suggest an interdisciplinary approach is simply impossible from a practical perspective.

At a deeper level, they argue that each discipline has its own way of discovering and organizing its content. One does research in history in a particular way, and the content of history has a unique organization. Likewise, one researches in chemistry in a particular way, and the content of chemistry is organized in a particular way. When we begin to combine these disciplines, we attempt to combine two often very different approaches for discovering and organizing knowledge. We are putting together, in a same course or learning experience, that which really can't sensibly be put together, except at a superficial level. If we want to consider the content of discipline in some depth, we must look at it from a single discipline approach, not from an interdisciplinary approach, these persons argue.

Structure

How the curriculum and the courses within it are organized for returning students is a problem facing many curriculum builders.

First, the question of course integrity. On the one hand some people argue that a course is an entirety. Its total is more than the sum of its parts. Thus, it is not possible to break courses into modules for the convenience of students who may have had some contact with certain aspects of the course. The opposite viewpoint advocates modules within courses, so that the returning student who may have already taken courses at three or four different institutions doesn't have to repeat material he or she has already taken. A convenient and more practical way is to find out what courses the returning student has already taken (and the content of those courses) and then have the student sign up for only those modules of courses that are new to the student. This releases the student's time for taking other modules that will contribute to the overall degree program rather than spending excessive time in courses that are partially old and partially new to the student.

A second problem relates to course sequencing. Many degree programs require students to spend at least half their time at the institution granting the degree, thus assuring that they have some of the sequenced courses in that degree program. The argument for this approach, beyond the requirement that a student earn the majority of his or her credits at the degree-granting institution, is the intricate relationship of courses to each other. The totality of the courses in the degree program is more than the sum of the courses that make it up—the same argument used in advocating the integrity of courses.

On the other hand, because returning students do often attend several institutions, it is argued they need to be able to take courses and parts of courses without an overall concern for the relationship of these courses to each other. Here, the argument goes, the sum of the courses taken equals what is required for the degree. It is impractical to even suggest that the relationship of the courses to each other might create a curriculum that is more than the sum of its parts. Returning students simply do not have the luxury, in many instances, to do their entire degree program at one institution. Even those who do attend but one institution usually have to do so as part-time students and thus have courses spread out over a longer period of time than traditional students.

A third problem is the relationship of courses to the degree. Returning students should be able to see clearly the relationship of every course they take to the overall degree toward which they are working, goes one side of the argument. For instance, if a student is required to take a basic chemistry course, this student should have answered how this basic chemistry course relates to the overall scheme for the degree requirements. Returning students should not be expected to accept the reply, "The chemistry course is a prerequisite to other courses you are taking, and you can't take these courses without chemistry." The relationship of chemistry to other courses and to the degree should be sufficiently clear so the returning student can decide whether it is even necessary to enroll in chemistry.

The other side of the issue often revolves around practical concerns of colleges and universities. Many of the basic courses such as chemistry, mathematics, introductory sociology, and introductory history are taught to students who are pursuing a variety of degree majors. It is impossible for instructors of these courses to know, or even be concerned about, the possible connection of what they are teaching to every degree represented by the students in their classes. Furthermore, these instructors are usually specialists in their discipline areas. Expecting them to know the relationship of their discipline areas to many often career-related majors has the potential for reducing their effectiveness as specialists in their discipline areas. If a chemist is expected to know in some detail the various applications of chemistry to, say horticulture, nuclear physics, nutrition, and pharmacy, the chemist would have to study all these majors—an impossible task.

Development

Many issues revolve around how the curriculum for returning students should be developed. There are at least two approaches that I see followed, with no argument that one or the other should be followed.

The first approach followed by many institutions, indeed written into the policy and a part of the tradition, is for the faculty to design the curriculum for their institution. Sometimes the faculty will involve students in the curriculum-development process in a nominal way, and sometimes the faculty will invite an advisory group, made up of former graduates or people who represent fields where graduates of the program are expected to find employment, to offer suggestions for curriculum modification. But ultimately, the faculty designs the curriculum.

There is, of course, considerable variance within this approach, depending on the amount of student input and the amount of advisory committee input. Many curricula for returning students are designed without any student input and without any advisory committee input.

A second approach is for students to have an equal say with faculty in what the curriculum will be. This is the case in some of the departments at Temple University. Students on the curriculum committees have a vote equal to the faculty, and some attempt is made to balance the numbers of faculty members and students on these committees.

Advocates for the first approach—the faculty having complete and total responsibility for the curriculum—argue that it is proper for faculty members to have this role because they are content experts and because, in the past, students were immature and quite unknowing about majors and degree requirements. Returning students are not immature, and they often do have considerable insights into what they want to get out of their degree programs. Thus increasingly, returning students will insist on some involvement in curriculum-development discussions.

Higher Education and Adult Education

Until recently higher education and adult education have been separated from each other. Higher education was for youth who are pursuing undergraduate degrees after high school, with some of them going on to pursue graduate degrees. Adult education was noncredit activity offered by a host of institutions, including higher-education institutions. Adult education offered by higher-education institutions was clearly something different from the rest of higher education. We can see this difference clearly if we reflect on the traditional functions of colleges and universities: teaching, research, and public service. It was in the area of public service that adult education was placed. Thus adult education had separate funding approaches, often separate faculty, and certainly an image different from traditional higher-education teaching.

Now with the advent of increasing numbers of older students returning to the classroom, we begin to see a blurring of the once-clear distinction between higher education and adult education. Now we see increasing numbers of adults who are enrolling in regular degree programs in the teaching departments of colleges and universities.

Several issues have resulted from this shift. One of the major issues is the image adult education has as a broad field of educational endeavor in the eyes of those who are responsible for the planning and development of degree programs in higher education. Unfortunately, adult education and adult educators' image have not been, and are not now, positive in the eyes of many college and university professors. For instance, William Rogers says, "Adult education is too important to be left to Adult Educators. One look at the dismal quality of the public schools should convince anyone of the danger of turning any kind of education over to specialists in education. Their low level of competence and their disrespect for subject matter (since their own is so watery) makes them particularly dangerous in dealing with educated adults . . . those who are returning to universities and other institutions often have their bachelor's degree or master's degree, and won't stand still for the subcollegiate kind of offering with which educationalists feel most comfortable."[4]

Many academics in traditional college and university degree programs view adult education as a place where students who can't succeed in "regular" programs enroll, or where those who want something to take up their time enroll. The critics also claim that many adult-education programs are taught by teachers who wanted to teach on college and university campuses but were unable to meet the rigorous hiring requirements. In the eyes of many traditional faculty members, adult-education instructors are of considerably lower quality than "regular" academics.

Many college and university faculty members are not so sure they want to become involved with returning students. Some of these people do not want to be in the same group as those "adult educators" who teach basket weaving at retirement centers, who instruct women about the complexities of belly dancing, and who teach horseback riding as a weight-loss approach.

Quality and Standards

Many college and university faculty members and administrators are concerned about academic quality if adjustments are made in entrance procedures, in curriculum requirements, in residency requirements, in how and when courses are taught. Returning students are insisting that many of these changes be made, and some colleges and universities are worried about the effects on their reputations as high-quality institutions.

For instance, many institutions have entrance requirements that are supposed to screen out those who do not have potential for college-level work. Often these entrance criteria emphasize grades earned when the person was previously in school or are based on the results of various examinations. Graduate-school admission policies at many institutions put considerable emphasis on the grades earned as an undergraduate. The problem, of course, is that returning students have great gaps of time between when they last did undergraduate work and when they return, or many years since they completed high school and want to begin college.

The institutions argue that their entrance requirements have stood the test of time and should be applied to students no matter what their age. The returning students "cry foul" and point out that what they did ten or fifteen years ago in the classroom has little to say about what they can do today. Increasingly, faculty members are supporting returning students who are attempting admission to programs with traditional entrance procedures. Alternative procedures are tried. The student is allowed to study as a special student and use the evidence of successful completion of courses to build a case for admission to graduate study. But much more needs to be done. Some argue for an open admissions policy and then careful screening of students along the way to screen out those who are not able to do the work. Others argue that this is unfair to the institution and to the students, and that students who do not have potential for college study should be screened out before they begin. The problem is that there is no good way to accomplish the screening.

The matter of residency requirements is another concern, particularly for graduate study and most specifically for Ph.D.-level study. There are strong arguments made by institutions for the importance of full-time study on campus without the distraction of outside work responsibilities. Students have the opportunity to delve deeply into their graduate programs. They have the time to discuss questions with other students in informal settings. They have time to discuss what they are studying with professors in out-of-class situations. They have time to spend much time in the library or the laboratory, as their program requires. They have time to think about what they are doing in their graduate program and not just meet a set of requirements.

These are strong arguments and time-honored policies that have been developed to assure a high level of quality in graduate programs. Yet many returning students, for a variety of reasons—economic, family, and others—do not have the time to spend weeks in full-time study. (Many graduate programs require a year of full-time study to meet the requirements for residency in a Ph.D. program.) If returning students are required to spend large blocks of time in full-time study, many are effectively excluded from these programs. What are the alternatives? Is it possible to organize smaller blocks of time for full-time study, say three weeks in the summer? Is it possible to shorten the amount of time required in full-time study and still effectively maintain the same high-quality program and the advantages that go with full-time study? These are the questions that must be examined by colleges and universities with increasing numbers of returning students.

Of course another alternative is for the traditional colleges and universities, those with the traditional requirements, to continue them as they are and encourage the returning students to enroll in the various types of external degree programs that we will discuss below.

A number of external degree programs have sprung up across the country (refer to the preceding chapter for examples of some of these programs). Many of these programs began with quite different assumptions from those associated with the internal, more traditional degree programs. In a 1973 report from the Commission on Non-Traditional Study the differences were mentioned: "One of the most accepted and revered traditions in academic life—that success in college is measured by the number of courses taken, credit hours earned, and information assimilated—is in the process of being overturned. Today the feeling grows in many quarters that regardless of the individual's credits and courses of study, what really should be measured is competence, adaptability to change, and, in such cases as career education, performance."[5]

Many external degree programs were built on the premise that practice can inform theory. As Peter Cowden and Frederic Jacobs point out in a discussion of external doctoral degree programs, "Unlike conventional doctoral programs that emphasize research, external doctoral programs are practice oriented. In this light, criticism that external degree doctoral programs fail to meet traditional standards in financial resources, facilities, library volumes, and full-time resident faculty is inappropriate. It assumes that the same standard must apply, despite a professed difference in approach."[6]

Cowden and Jacobs believe that, because external degree doctoral programs are based on assumptions that are different from those of traditional, internal doctoral programs, they "should be allowed to determine their own standards, content, and curricula, responsive to their educational philosophy and the needs of their students."[7]

The position taken by Cowden and Jacobs is not universal, however. There are those who argue that if the external degree focuses on practice, its title should reflect this focus. The critics argue that to call a degree that focuses on practice a doctorate, to be equated with a research doctorate, is misrepresentation and dishonest.

Besides a criticism of the degree title, many more persons, both those inside and outside of academia, find it difficult to believe "that a part-time, off campus, Saturday scholar is the equivalent of a regular, full-time, on campus scholar."[8]

On the other hand, why do they need to be viewed as equivalent? The kinds of students who enroll in external degree programs are certainly not equivalent to the traditional students who enroll in on-campus, internal degree programs. External degree students are usually older, are usually already working full time, and for one reason or another cannot take part in traditional campus-based programs. A survey of the New York State's Regents program revealed that persons who enroll in this external degree program are likely to hold a full-time job, and their average age is thirty-three. If these students are not equivalent to traditional students, then why must external degree programs that are designed for them be equivalent to those available for traditional-age students?

But aside from the equivalency question, there are many other concerns about external degrees. External degree programs make assumptions about adult learners that likely do not hold for all adult learners. Not everyone is able to learn effectively in a piece-meal, catch-as-catch-can fashion.

Some adult students need the close contact with other students and faculty over time to help them keep focused on what they are doing and help them maintain a sense of direction for their degree-program goals.

Cyril Houle raises the question of the external degree itself, from the perspective of employers and society generally and from the perspective of the campus on which the external degree is located (assuming the campus also offers internal degrees). The specific question Houle asks is, "Will the external degree be regarded as cheap and unworthy?"[9]

Houle answers, "Judged on past American practice, the answer is no. Some of the most outstanding American leaders of government, business, social, and academic life are the products of evening colleges or hold other extension degrees. Once the degree is awarded, it stands as a symbol of accomplishment and is usually accepted as such by an employer, by the individual himself, and by his associates."[10]

But when Houle answers the same question from the perspective of local campuses, the answer is somewhat different: "The reputation of the external degree on the campus itself depends largely on local circumstance. If the degree is reaching a merito-cratic elite, has a reputation for excellence, or pays faculty well on an overload basis, it may have high standing with much competition among the academic staff to teach in it. In other cases, it is viewed with reserve, withdrawal, indifference, or scorn; and even the enthusiasts who support it may have dubious motives."[11]

Another issue that must be mentioned because it is often an unspoken yet pervasive reason why many adults are returning to school is the society's extreme emphasis on credentials. At first glance it seems to make sense that a society should be able to judge the amount of education its members have by the degrees or other evidence of academic achievement they hold—the continuing education unit, certificates of participation, and the like.

It also seems to make sense that employers establish certain levels of educational achievement as a basis for job entry, for job retention, and for job promotion. The assumption is that evidence of participation (the degree, for example) is a symbol of what the person has accomplished in academic study and is thus an indication of what the person is able to do.

Particularly in the professions, this attitude of the importance of continued study with visible symbols of participation and accomplishment has led to forced attendance, or what is commonly called mandatory continuing education. Interestingly enough, there is no clear research evidence so far to show that, because someone has been forced to participate in continuing education, he or she performs any better on the job.

Even without mandatory continuing education, many adults feel the need to earn a degree as a credential that is related to their job status. And unfortunately, some of these adults see the credential as the all-important reason for enrolling in a degree program. If they learn something, if they are able to develop some new skills and some new approaches to thinking, that is a fringe benefit.

And also unfortunately, there are some administrators of degree programs for returning students who are so anxious "to meet the needs" of these returning students that they are, sometimes unwittingly, seduced into providing shortcuts to degrees that do indeed speed up the degree process for the returning student but end up prostituting what might otherwise be a quality educational program.

There is need for a balance between providing quality programs with high standards and at the same time designing programs that fit the unique requirements of returning students. This is often not an easy task, for it is difficult to obtain consensus from academics as to the meaning of "high standards and quality programs," particularly when we begin talking about a different clientele from what colleges and universities have worked with for the past many years.

Relation to Business and Industry

Because many of the returning students, well over half at most institutions, are interested in job and career opportunities, it would make sense to explore what the relationship of programs for returning students should be to business and industry. And furthermore, increasingly over the past ten or fifteen years, business and industry themselves have begun providing many continuing-education opportunities for their employees, without any contact with colleges and universities.

A new trend in higher education is to allow students to receive academic credit for noncollegiate-sponsored instruction. The American Council on Education (ACE) offers credit recommendations for courses sponsored by a wide variety of organizations such as Trans World Airlines, the U.S. Public Health Service, General Motors Corporation, and the Communication Workers of America. Some eighty organizations and 1,000 courses were listed in ACE's *National Guide to Credit Recommendations for Noncollegiate Courses.*

Companies and organizations that want their courses accredited pay for a visit by an ACE evaluation team. The particular course is evaluated and a credit recommendation is offered if it passes muster. For instance, a course offered by the Bank of America titled "Business English" has the following credit recommendation: "In the lower division baccalaureate/associate degree category, 2 semester hours in Business Communications."

Academic credit for noncollegiate-sponsored instruction is not without controversy. According to J. W. Peltason, president of the American Council on Education, "There's no evidence that the quality of higher education is deteriorating because of the acceptance of noncollegiate-sponsored instruction. Some of it is good, and some bad—but some kinds of traditional education are bad, too. So as a category, nontraditional education is no worse and no better than other kinds of education."[12]

Of course, a worry of some in higher education is how much this so-called outside learning will cut into course enrollments at colleges and universities. But many believe higher education is being improved rather than damaged. Many of the courses offered by noncollegiate organizations are often too technical or too specific for a college or university to offer. And thus it makes some sense for colleges and universities to work together with organizations offering courses.

Some professional organizations, such as state bars, set up their own continuing-education programs without contacting colleges or universities for any assistance. Some businesses and industries are also moving toward offering their own degree programs. As William Griffith points out, "It is almost certain that business corporations will increasingly take over education and training. Some of the larger companies can already grant degrees. The American Society for Training and Development is a much larger and more aggressive group of adult educators than a combination of the membership of AEA [Adult Education Association of the U.S.A.], NAPCAE [National Association for Public Continuing and Adult Education], and AACJC [American Association of Community and Junior Colleges] would be. So far as these adult educators are concerned, we are really overlooking business and industry, which have clearly moved into the education business."[13]

Not long ago I had dinner with the vice-president of a major corporation in New York City. His rather blunt comment to me was "You people in colleges and universities have dropped the ball so far as continuing education is concerned. Your old traditional programs, your outmoded admission policies, your insistence that many of your courses be taken on campus, keep many of our people away—people who I think could benefit from what you have to offer."

I asked him what we ought to be doing. He proceeded to tell me how we should get up out of our chairs and go visit some businesses and industries and talk with their people about their continuing-education needs and how we could best serve them.

He has a valid point. Without question colleges and universities could be doing a better job in relating to business and industry. But let's look at the other side of the issue too. How should business and industry relate to colleges and universities?

The traditional relationship is for colleges and universities to prepare employees for business and industry and to provide continuing-education opportunities for their employees. But many people in higher education argue for more than the traditional functions. These people believe higher education should serve as a conscience for society, raising value questions pertaining to business and industry, questioning some products being produced, and questioning certain corporate decisions. So to an extent colleges and universities must remain separate from business and industry if this function is to be carried out.

Some higher-education institutions are making special attempts to relate to business and industry; Central Michigan University at Mount Pleasant is one that is. They follow seven principles they believe have made them successful in reaching the business community through their Institute for Personal and Career Development. (Since the establishment of the institute in 1971 they have awarded more than 6,000 degrees.)

1. Corporate Input. They ask corporations how they can best serve them—what are the needs of their employees?

2. Individualized Curricula. Though there is a core curriculum, programs are tailored to various clientele groups.

3. Individualized Advising. Each person who enrolls in the program prepares a program plan with the assistance of an advisor.

4. Location of Program. Most of the classes are taught in the facilities of the corporation.

5. Scheduling. First consideration is given to those times appropriate both to the corporation and to the prospective students. Most courses are offered in a concentrated format—a regular semester course may be offered over four to eight weeks, for example.

6. Experimental Learning. In addition to the classroom, learning takes place through independent study, travel, volunteer work, and through job-related activities.

7. Library Services. Corporate libraries are supplemented with materials from Central Michigan University.[14]

Though considerably more cooperation is possible between colleges and universities and business and industry, Fred Harrington warns how easy it is for the institution to lose control. "Continuing professional education even on campus tends to slip out of the control of higher education. Pressure for continuing professional education comes mainly from outside—from practicing professionals, companies, government agencies, and trade associations. Often a college or university is asked to sponsor a course with a specific title and is told that the requesting agency will supply the students, pay for fees, and provide the teacher and the in-plant classroom. What is wanted, in such cases, is the university's imprimatur, its name and reputation, and perhaps some professional assistance in preparing the outline or assembling background material."[15]

Business and industry are a rich source of potential students for colleges and universities. Much more can be done to provide educational opportunities for these students, but there are cautions to consider.

Research

This is, of course, not an issue for those institutions that have as a principal responsibility teaching and public service. But what of the major research institutions that not only teach and do public service but also have the discovery of knowledge as a major responsibility? What are the possible problems for the research function of these institutions as the number of returning students increases?

One of the problems relates to faculty time for research, as I mentioned earlier. Because returning students take much out-of-class time, there is less time left for faculty research projects. This, of course, could become an even more serious problem as the number of returning students increases on the campuses of research institutions. To do an effective job in counseling returning students, professors do need to spend the extra time with them, sometimes at the expense of their research projects.

Perhaps one partial solution to the problem is for administration to provide decreased teaching loads for research professors, or semesters away from teaching so research interests can be pursued. It is asking too much to expect that research production will continue as usual and that an adequate job of teaching will be accomplished at the same time, when we consider the requirements of returning students.

Another issue is whether it is realistic to hope an outstanding researcher can ever be even an average teacher. The prevailing assumption on many college and university campuses is that, if one is an outstanding researcher, there is little time left for students and the preparation of class materials. Sometimes the argument goes so far as to suggest it takes a particular kind of personality to be a researcher—the desire to be alone, a general dislike for people, high motivation in terms of individual achievement and writing production, and a general disdain for intellectually immature people such as might be represented by college students, whether of traditional age or older returning students. And furthermore, the professor with the "research personality" is not one who can or wants to do a good job as a teacher and counselor of students.

This attitude about the separation of scholarship from teaching is enhanced by institutions when they put nearly all emphasis on research production to determine whether a faculty person is promoted or given tenure. The message is out to many assistant professors that, unless they concentrate almost all their efforts on research, scholarship, and writing during the first years they are on a campus, there is no hope for them to be granted tenure and they will have to seek employment elsewhere. Many institutions continue to put heavy emphasis on research and scholarly writing as evidence for tenure decisions. On the other hand, in recent years some institutions have modified this rather extreme position and look for balance. They look for evidence that an assistant professor is both able to do a creditable job as a classroom teacher and able to produce quality research and scholarly writing.

Let's look for a moment at the reverse of the question raised above. Is it possible for the outstanding teacher to be also a creditable or even an outstanding researcher? Some of the same arguments used above are used to answer this question. Often the answer is no, it is not possible for an excellent teacher to be also an excellent researcher. The personality question comes up again. An outstanding teacher is one who has a "teaching personality." That is, teachers are oriented to people, they like students, they like working with students individually and in groups, they like presenting ideas to others, they enjoy the interaction that often takes place, and so on.

From these arguments, at least, it would appear that universities are asking for the impossible when they expect an instructor to be both an outstanding teacher and an outstanding researcher. The arguments presented above suggest that the two roles are nearly incompatible and that universities should strive to have outstanding researchers and outstanding teachers, but not in the same person. Of course this avoids the position of tenure review committees who require high-level competence in both teaching and research. By implication, the larger, research-oriented universities would almost by definition not be places where good teaching could be found. (Only researchers survive the tenure process, and assistant professors are working hard on research and therefore aren't interested in teaching.)

The instructors I interviewed for this project reside at universities that are large, nationally and internationally known research institutions. I discovered that not only are they exemplary instructors, but also they are researchers. Some of the instructors I talked with are clearly exemplary researchers. They all expressed interest in research; they were all doing research; they said they liked research and writing. Although my sample is admittedly small, these exemplary instructors of returning students did find time to combine teaching with research and enjoyed doing both activities.

A related problem is graduate-student involvement in faculty research. Traditionally, research professors have worked hand in hand with their graduate students on research projects. Often a research-project team was made up of a professor and three or four graduate students, at both the doctorate and the master's levels.

Three factors complicate the tradition. Many returning students are not interested in a so-called research degree but want a practical degree they can immediately use in the job world. Many will work only on master's degree programs and will resist any in-depth training and experience in research.

Second, many returning students are part-time students who come to their classes and then leave campus for other responsibilities—job, family, or community. They are thus not available for work on research projects that require interaction among the researchers and extended time on campus. Also, even if offered a research assistantship, many returning students will not accept because they can make more money in their regular jobs, and they need more money than what a half-time research assistantship provides to support their families.

And third, those returning students who are interested in a research degree have research projects in mind that come from their own work experience, or perhaps relate directly to their work. Sometimes their employers even provide money for conducting the research. These students are usually reluctant to tie into a professor's research project, which may be on a topic far from the one they are most interested in pursuing.

The advent of increasing numbers of returning students presents many unanswered questions for research institutions, questions that must be wrestled with if the institution is to maintain its reputation in research and at the same time do a creditable job in teaching returning students.

A New Look At Teaching-Learning

As pointed out earlier, returning students will not accept bad teaching. Not only will they not accept bad teaching, but also they sometimes question the assumptions that are associated with college and university teaching at many institutions. They want more out of their educational experiences than merely accumulating information that they feed back to instructors on examinations. They want the opportunity to relate the new information they are reading and receiving from their professors to their own personal experiences, and they often want the opportunity to learn from each other in a given content area.

Some returning students suggest that the definitions of *instructor* and *student* should be changed. Rather than exhibiting a superior-inferior relationship, which is the assumption of much college teaching today (the instructor knows, the student doesn't know), the learning environment should be structured in such a way that there can be a sharing, an interaction among students and teacher, with a full realization of the teacher's specific contributions but also of the students' specific contributions.

Often this approach to classroom teaching is resisted by many college and university instructors, particularly those who have enjoyed the power relationship they have had with students over the years. For some traditional instructors, teaching is a great ego trip. To suggest a sharing relationship, an interaction, suggests a different kind of relationship of instructor to student, and the instructor is often threatened.

Paul Lengrand describes the nature of this "new" relationship of instructor to student: "The only service an educator can do for anyone else, particularly an adult, is to give him the tools and put him in situations where, on the basis of his own station in society, his own daily experiences, struggles, successes and setbacks he is able to build up his own system of knowledge, to think things through on his own, by degrees, to take possession of the various elements of his personality, fill them out and give them form and expression. In other words, the ability to communicate, to stand up for oneself and to participate in the common struggles becomes, according to this view, as important as the ability to learn, whether to increase the effectiveness of one's work or trade union or political activity."[16]

Another issue within the teaching-learning area relates to self-directed learning. One of the goals that many adult educators see for education is to provide people with the tools so they can learn on their own, without dependence on institutions or teachers. As Ronald Gross has said, "Because our thinking about learning has been dominated for so long by the image of the school, we know virtually nothing about the potentialities for truly individual learning, or about how the other institutions of a society can become adjuncts to and resources for the learning process. . . . We do not know, in short, how to seize back for the individual the power over the growth of his own mind, or what to do with that power once we gain it."[17]

The issue is, Are we, as we encourage and work with returning students, perpetuating the myth that the only place where one can obtain an education is in an educational institution? To encourage lifelong learning, and lifelong *self-directed* learning, we must assist people who want to break their ties with formal education and develop their own strategies for learning.

Unfortunately, in many instances just the opposite is occurring. Some institutions see the returning older student as a means to their survival as traditional-student numbers decline. As Patricia Cross points out, "I am becoming increasingly concerned about the overeagerness of some colleges to attract adult learners into college classrooms; their goal would appear to be institutional survival rather than social good. . . . I think that the more effective colleges are in recruiting adults into traditional college programs, the more adults will be attracted away from self-directed learning projects into programs designed, directed and made legitimate by others. The point of the learning society, after all, is to develop independent, self-directed learners. It is not to create a society in which learners become increasingly dependent on an educational establishment to decide what, when, where, and how people should learn."[18]

Still another issue is the role that so-called distance education will and should play in educational programs for adults. Technology is such that we can, through the use of videotape players, bring into our homes educational packages of extremely high quality; we can, via our telephones, be a part of learning groups anyplace in the world; we can listen to lecturers via radio; we can read lectures via the newspaper; we can receive in our homes learning packages that include combinations of cassette recordings, written materials, and various types of visual material. Some educators would have us believe that the face-to-face contact of students with other students and of students with an instructor is an artifact of the past.

Although educational technology has provided us with some interesting and often useful adjuncts to the teaching-learning process, it is still clear that much education must involve the human contact of person to person. Otherwise, learning becomes a mechanical, lonely, depressing activity that lacks the joy and excitement that can and should accompany educational activity. The concept of the learning community, a group of students working together, either with or without an instructor, is not dead, although some people would have it so.

We cannot relegate teaching to a machine, no matter how sophisticated and glamorous the machine may be. The teaching-learning transaction is so much more than the mere passing of information from one place to another—from machine to student. Information is often a part of the process, to be sure. But often the gathering of information is only the beginning, as the adult student examines the information, attempts to relate the information to his or her own experience, and then works at developing a new meaning, a new insight, a new look at life. With emphasis on the accumulation of information only, we lose the adventure of thinking and the joy associated with stretching one's mind in new directions. To view learning as collecting information is to view the teaching-learning transaction in only the most superficial way. Adult learners deserve much more than that.

Participants

Who are the adults who return to school? We have answered that question previously. But are those adults who might benefit most from the experience participating? Are colleges and universities experiencing increased enrollments from minorities and from low-income persons? They are not. As we pointed out earlier, returning students tend to be those who come from middle-class homes. There is low representation among minority groups.

Patricia Cross found that, of those persons who say they would like to continue their education, two-thirds do not participate in organized learning activities. She says would-be learners lack information about learning opportunities that are available to them. They are highly interested in educational and career counseling. They are even more interested than current returning students in job-oriented education. They prefer on-the-job training, internships, and fieldwork over traditional classroom education. They are more extrinsically motivated than current returning students, preferring a certificate or degree that has credence in the marketplace, and they perceive finances as a major barrier to further learning.[19]

Although many persons within disadvantaged groups see the

value of returning to school, the lack of financial aid often blocks them completely. It was, and continues to be, an uphill battle to provide financial assistance so disadvantaged eighteen-year-olds can have the opportunity to attend postsecondary schools. The problem is worse for disadvantaged adults returning to school because of the attitude that pervades much of society—adults should pay their own way when participating in schools. Until something can be done to provide more financial aid for the disadvantaged, the number of them returning to school will remain low.

Summary

In this chapter we have explored several issues that faculty, administrators, and other higher-education decision makers face as the numbers of returning students on campuses increase. Issue areas explored include those related to the content, structure, and approaches to developing curriculum for returning students; the relationship of higher education to adult education; quality and standards; relationship of colleges and universities to business and industry; the university as a research institution; a new look at teaching-learning; and participants.

NOTES

1. Gordon C. Godbey, "Creating Diversity Through Adult Education," *Adult Leadership,* November 1974, p. 160.

2. From "Summary for Pilot Proposals," Moorhead State University, Moorhead, Minnesota, November 1979.

3. Otto Feinstein and Frank Angelo, *To Educate the People* (Detroit: Center for Urban Studies, Wayne State University, 1977), p. 4.

4. William C. Rogers, "Adult and Continuing Education: Snatching Defeat out of the Jaws of Victory," *Continuum,* The National University Extension Association Quarterly, vol. 44, no. 1, September 1979.

5. Commission on Non-Traditional Study, *Diversity by Design* (San Francisco: Jossey-Bass, 1973), pp. 28–29.

6. Peter Cowden and Frederic Jacobs, "The External Degree and the Traditions of Diversity and Completion," *Phi Delta Kappan,* vol. 60, no. 8, April 1979, p. 559.

7. Ibid., p. 560.

8. H. G. Vonk and Robert G. Brown, "A Diller, a Dollar, a Saturday Scholar," *Phi Delta Kappan,* vol. 60, no. 8, April 1979, p. 570.

9. Cyril O. Houle, *The External Degree* (San Francisco: Jossey-Bass, 1973), p. 151.

10. Ibid.

11. Ibid.

12. American Council on Education, *News* (Washington, D.C.: American Council on Education, July 30, 1979).

13. William S. Griffith, "Futures in Adult Basic and Vocational Education," *Future Encounters of a Lifelong Kind,* ed. Don Hentschel (Illinois Adult and Continuing Educators Association, Inc., 1979).

14. John T. Yantis, "The University and Industry as Partners in Education," *Phi Delta Kappan,* vol. 60, no. 8, April 1979, p. 608.

15. Fred Harvey Harrington, *The Future of Adult Education* (San Francisco: Jossey-Bass, 1977), p. 97.

16. Paul Lengrand, *An Introduction to Lifelong Education* (London: Croom Helm, Ltd., 1975), p. 14.

17. Ronald Gross, "After Deschooling, Free Learning," *After Deschooling, What?* ed. Ivan Illich et al. (New York: Perennial Library, Harper and Row, 1973), pp. 158–159.

18. K. Patricia Cross, "Our Changing Students and Their Impact on Colleges: Prospects for a True Learning Society," *Phi Delta Kappan,* vol. 61, no. 9, May 1980, p. 629.

19. Ibid., pp. 629–630.

Chapter 14

Resources for Further Study

For those who wish to pursue further, the following resources should be of value.

Characteristics of Adults Returning to College

Materials available in this area are of three types: those that describe adults returning to college, those that compare returning students with traditional college-age students, and those that specifically refer to women returning to college.

Examples of materials that describe adult learners' returning to college include a growing number of publications produced by the College Board, Future Directions for a Learning Society. These include Howard R. Bowen, *Adult Learning, Higher Education, and the Economics of Unused Capacity*, 1980; Solomon Arbeiter, Carol B. Aslanian, Frances A. Schmerbeck, and Henry M. Brickell, *40 Million Americans in Career Transition*, 1978; and Richard E. Anderson and Gordon G. Darkenwald, *Participation and Persistence in American Adult Education*, 1979.

Other references describing adults returning to college include the following:

Anderson, Richard E., and Darkenwald, Gordon G. "The Adult Part-Time Learner in Colleges and Universities: A Clientele

251

Analysis." *Research in Higher Education,* vol. 10, no. 4, June 1979, pp. 357–369.

Gallay, Ralph, and Hunter, Ronald V. "Why Adults Are Pursuing a Part-Time College Education." *Collegiate News and Views,* vol. 32, no. 2, Winter 1978/79, pp. 13–16.

Ghazzali, A. "Reasons for Adult Participation in Group Activities." *Research in Education,* no. 21, May 1979, pp. 56–70.

Kasworm, Carol E. "Old Dogs, Children, and Watermelon Wine." *Educational Horizons,* Summer 1978, pp. 200–205.

Leckie, Shirley. "The New Student on Campus." *Educational Horizons,* Summer 1978, pp. 196–199.

Nolan, Charles J., Jr. "Going Back to School." *Journal of General Education,* vol. 31, no. 2, Summer 1979, pp. 129–140. An interesting first-person account of an air force officer who returned to college for a graduate degree; includes the many problems he faced and, finally, his need to drop out.

Ray, Robert F. *Adult Part-Time Students and the C.I.C. Universities.* Iowa City: University of Iowa, Division of Continuing Education, 1977.

Stone, Gerald C. "Higher Education for the Elderly: Continuing in the Mainstream of American Life." *Research in Higher Education,* vol. 10, no. 4 (1979), pp. 317–329.

Examples of materials that report research projects in which returning and traditional students are compared include the following works:

Hameister, Dennis R., and Hickey, Tom. "Traditional and Adult Students: A Dichotomy." *Life Long Learning: The Adult Years,* December 1977, pp. 6–19.

Kuh, George D., and Ardaiolo, Frank P. "Adult Learners and Traditional Age Freshmen: Comparing the 'New' Pool with the 'Old' Pool Students." *Research in Higher Education,* vol. 10, no. 3, May 1979, pp. 208–219.

Pogrow, Stanley. "The Effect of Age on the Attitude and Performance of Doctoral Students at Stanford University." *Education,* vol. 98, no. 1, Fall 1979, pp. 78–81.

The research and writing about women returning to college is increasing rapidly. The following are examples of some of these materials:

Hooper, Judith. "Returning Women Students and Their Families: Support and Conflict." *Journal of College Student Per-*

sonnel, in press. Hooper has researched the returning woman student, particularly in terms of the conflicts that result when women return to school. See also the following two works by this author.

———— ."My Wife, the Student," in manuscript.

Hooper, Judith, and Rice, J. K. "Locus of Control and Outcomes Following Counseling of Returning Students." *Journal of College Student Personnel,* vol. 19, no. 1 (1978), pp. 42–47.

Levine, Adeline. "Between the Stages of Life: Adult Women on a College Scene." *Educational Horizons,* Summer 1976, pp. 154–161. In this report Levine discusses the following questions: (1) Why did women not complete their schooling in the first place? (2) Why did they decide to return to school now? (3) What sorts of experiences and problems are they encountering upon returning to school after a long absence? (4) How do their relationships with their families change as a consequence of their being in school? (5) What sorts of changing feelings do they have about themselves as a consequence of their ongoing school experiences?

Markus, Hazel. "The Return to School." *Educational Horizons,* Summer 1976, pp. 172–176. A number of continuing-education centers for women have sprung up around the country, designed to assist women in making the transition to campus and academic life. This is a report of one such center at the University of Michigan.

The Adult as Learner

The literature of adult education is growing rapidly, with a particular emphasis in recent years on life-span development.

Bromley, D. B. *The Psychology of Human Aging.* Baltimore: Penguin, 1966.

Erikson, Erik H. *Childhood and Society.* 2nd ed. New York: Norton, 1963.

Hall, Calvin S., and Lindzey, Gardner. *Theories of Personality.* 3rd ed. New York: Wiley, 1978.

Havighurst, Robert G. *Developmental Tasks and Education.* 3rd ed. New York: David McKay, 1972.

Knowles, Malcolm. *The Adult Learner: A Neglected Species.* 2nd ed. New York: Wiley, 1978.

Knox, Alan B. *Adult Development and Learning.* San Francisco: Jossey-Bass, 1977. An excellent summary of the literature on adult development, particularly as it relates to adult learning and adult education.

Levinson, Daniel J. *The Seasons of a Man's Life.* New York: Knopf, 1978.

Neugarten, Bernice L., and Datan, Nancy. "Sociological Perspectives on the Life Cycle." *Life-Span Developmental Psychology: Personality and Socialization.* Edited by Paul B. Baltes and K. Warner Schaie. New York: Academic Press, 1973.

Sheehy, Gail. *Passages.* New York: Dutton, 1976.

Tyler, Leona E. *Individuality.* San Francisco: Jossey-Bass, 1978.

Materials dealing with various facets of adult psychology include the following:

Baltes, P. B., and Schaie, K. W. "The Myth of the Twilight Years." *Psychology Today,* March 1974, pp. 35–40.

LaBenne, Wallace D., and Breene, Bert I. *Educational Implications of Self-Concept Theory.* Pacific Palisades, Calif.: Goodyear Publishing Company, 1969.

Moenster, P. A. "Learning and Memory in Relation to Age." *Journal of Gerontology* 27 (1972): 361–363.

Teaching Returning Students

Here are included four categories of materials: (1) broadly based materials for those who want to explore theories of teaching and learning, (2) materials from the traditional literature of college teaching, (3) materials from adult education that focus particularly on how to teach adults, and (4) materials that emphasize humanistic teaching approaches.

Three excellent books that cover various theories of teaching and learning from a broad perspective are the following:

Bigge, Morris L. *Learning Theories for Teachers.* 3rd ed. New York: Harper and Row, 1976.

Joyce, Bruce, and Weil, Marsha. *Models of Teaching.* 2nd ed. Englewood Cliffs, N.J.: Prentice-Hall, 1980.

Vandenberg, Donald, ed. *Teaching and Learning.* Urbana, Ill.: University of Illinois Press, 1969.

Materials from the literature of college teaching include the following:

Cross, K.P. *Accent on Learning.* San Francisco: Jossey-Bass, 1976.

Dubin, Robert, and Taveggia, Thomas C. *The Teaching-Learning Paradox*. Eugene, Oreg.: Center for the Advanced Study of Educational Administration, 1968.

Eble, Kenneth E. *The Craft of Teaching*. San Francisco: Jossey-Bass, 1976.

Eble, Kenneth E., ed. *Improving Teaching Styles*. San Francisco: Jossey-Bass, 1980.

Flournoy, Don M., and associates. *The New Teachers*. San Francisco: Jossey-Bass, 1972.

McKeachie, Wilbert J. *Teaching Tips*. 7th ed. Lexington, Mass.: D. C. Heath, 1978.

Milton, Ohmer, and associates. *On College Teaching*. San Francisco: Jossey-Bass, 1978. This book includes a chapter by Milton Stern on teaching returning students.

Materials that deal specifically with ways to improve adult learning include the following:

Aker, George F. *Adult Education Procedures, Methods, and Techniques*. Syracuse, N.Y.: The Library of Continuing Education, 1965.

Bergevin, Paul; Morris, Dwight; and Smith, Robert M. *Adult Education Procedures*. New York: Seabury, 1963.

Kidd, J. R. *How Adults Learn*. New York: Association Press, 1973.

Klevens, Chester, ed. *Materials and Methods in Continuing Education*. New York: Klevens Publications, 1976.

Knowles, Malcolm. *The Modern Practice of Adult Education*. 2nd. ed., rev. Chicago: Association Press/Follett Publishing Company, 1980.

Miller, Harry L. *Teaching and Learning in Adult Education*. New York: Macmillan, 1964.

Minor, Harold D., ed. *Creative Procedures for Adult Groups*. Nashville, Tenn.: Abingdon, 1968.

Robinson, Russell D. *Helping Adults Learn and Change*. Milwaukee, Wis.: Omnibook Co., 1979.

Tough, Allen. *The Adult's Learning Projects*. 2nd ed. Austin, Tex.: Learning Concepts, 1979.

Verner, Coolie, and Booth, Alan. *Adult Education*. Washington, D.C.: The Center for Applied Research in Education, 1964.

For those who wish to explore more about humanistic education approaches, refer to the following:

Combs, Arthur W., et al. *The Professional Education of Teachers: A Humanistic Approach to Teacher Preparation.* Boston: Allyn and Bacon, 1974.

Read, Donald A., and Simon, Sidney B. *Humanistic Education Sourcebook.* Englewood Cliffs, N.J.: Prentice-Hall, 1975.

Rogers, Carl R. *Freedom to Learn.* Columbus, Ohio: Charles E. Merrill, 1969.

———. *On Becoming a Person.* Boston: Houghton Mifflin, 1961.

Planning and Promoting Continuing Education

The following materials should be of particular value for those persons who are responsible for organizing and promoting higher-education programs designed particularly for adult learners:

American Council on Education. *The National Guide to Credit Recommendations for Noncollegiate Courses.* Washington, D.C.: American Council on Education, 1979. A listing of courses sponsored by noncollegiate organizations for which college credit is recommended.

Cross, K. Patricia. *Beyond the Open Door.* San Francisco: Jossey-Bass, 1971. An emphasis on the need to plan for returning students on college campuses.

Cross, K. Patricia; Valley, John R.; and associates. *Planning Non-Traditional Programs.* San Francisco: Jossey-Bass, 1974. Reports on a series of research projects sponsored by the Commission on Non-Traditional Study.

Farlow, Helen. *Publicizing and Promoting Programs.* New York: McGraw-Hill, 1979. A how-to manual for promoting continuing-education programs.

Feinstein, Otto, and Angelo, Frank. *To Educate the People.* Detroit: Wayne State University, Center for Urban Studies, 1977. This is a description of a special program organized for working adults.

Hesburgh, Theodore M.; Miller, Paul A.; and Wharton, Clifton R., Jr. *Patterns for Lifelong Learning.* San Francisco: Jossey-Bass, 1973. An exploration into changing attitudes about what education is and should be, with the increased interest on adult education.

Houle, Cyril O. *The External Degree.* San Francisco: Jossey-Bass, 1973. This book is a report of the activities of the Commission on Non-Traditional Study. It is an excellent summary of external degree programs up to the time of its publication.

Lenz, Elinor. *Creating and Marketing Programs in Continuing Education.* New York: McGraw-Hill, 1980. Approaches to curriculum development focusing on adult audiences.

Background, Issues, and Controversies

For those who want more background information on adult education and the issues related to the return of adults to college campuses, the following are suggested:

Apps, Jerold W. *Problems in Continuing Education.* New York: McGraw-Hill, 1979. An analysis of fundamental problems faced by continuing education, including an approach for the analysis of such problems.

———."Six Influences on Adult Education in the 1980's." *Lifelong Learning: The Adult Years,* vol. 3, no. 10, June 1980, pp. 4–7. An essay describing the influences of population structure, inflation, consumerism, status of women, politics, and the mood of society on adult education.

Carnegie Commission on Higher Education. *Toward a Learning Society.* New York: McGraw-Hill, 1973. The place of higher education in lifelong learning.

Freire, Paulo. *Pedagogy of the Oppressed.* New York: Herder and Herder, 1971. Freire raises questions about the present forms of adult education and the outcomes of educational activity.

Harrington, Fred Harvey. *The Future of Adult Education.* San Francisco: Jossey-Bass, 1977. An analysis of recent developments and recommendations for educational institutions regarding adult students.

Hutchins, Robert M. *The Learning Society.* New York: Praeger, 1968. An essay about higher education's fundamental problems, including a careful look at liberal education in future higher-education programs.

Illich, Ivan. *Deschooling Society.* New York: Harper and Row, 1971. Illich's recommendation is to abolish schools as we now know them and set up alternative forms of education for all ages.

Ohliger, John. "Radical Ideas in Adult Education: A Manifesto-Bibliography." *Radical Teacher,* May 1979.

Roszak, Theodore. *Person/Planet.* New York: Doubleday, 1978. Roszak's theme in this book focuses on the needs of the planet and of the person as one and on the impact of this merging of needs on institutions such as colleges and universities.

For those interested in examining philosophical questions in continuing education, the following books are suggested:

Apps, Jerold W. *Toward a Working Philosophy of Adult Education.* Syracuse, N.Y.: Syracuse University, Publications in Continuing Education, 1973.

Bergevin, Paul. *A Philosophy for Adult Education.* New York: Seabury, 1967.

Elias, John L., and Merriam, Sharan. *Philosophical Foundations of Adult Education.* Huntington, N.Y.: Krieger, 1980.

Paterson, R. W. K. *Values, Education and the Adult.* London, England: Routledge and Kegan Paul, 1979.

Resources for Returning Students

For those who want materials that can be referred to adult students, the following are suggested:

Apps, Jerold W. *Study Skills: For Those Adults Returning to School.* New York: McGraw-Hill, 1978. For those returning students who need to sharpen study skills such as reading, writing, listening, and exam taking.

Bolles, Richard Nelson. *The Three Boxes of Life.* Berkeley, Calif.: Ten Speed Press, 1978. An introduction to life-work planning with an emphasis on planning for lifelong learning.

———. *What Color Is Your Parachute?* Berkeley, Calif.: Ten Speed Press, 1980. Discusses career changing and job finding. This book is updated yearly.

Kirn, Arthur G., and Kirn, Marle O'Donahoe. *Life Work Planning.* 4th ed. New York: McGraw-Hill, 1978. Describes a process for making life-work planning choices.

Knowles, Malcolm S. *Self-Directed Learning.* Chicago: Association Press/Follett Publishing Company, 1975.

Lenz, Elinor, and Shaevitz, Marjorie Hansen. *So You Want to Go Back to School.* New York: McGraw-Hill, 1977. A guide for sorting out the problems of reentry to a college or university campus.

Index